Second Workshop on Combating Online Hostile Posts in Regional Languages during Emergency Situation (CONSTRAINT 2022)

Dublin, Ireland
27 May 2022

ISBN: 978-1-7138-6731-9

Printed from e-media with permission by:

Curran Associates, Inc.
57 Morehouse Lane
Red Hook, NY 12571

Some format issues inherent in the e-media version may also appear in this print version.

Printed with permission by Curran Associates, Inc. (2023)

For permission requests, please contact the Association for Computational Linguistics at the address below.

Association for Computational Linguistics
209 N. Eighth Street
Stroudsburg, Pennsylvania 18360

Phone: 1-570-476-8006
Fax: 1-570-476-0860

acl@aclweb.org

Additional copies of this publication are available from:

Curran Associates, Inc.
57 Morehouse Lane
Red Hook, NY 12571 USA
Phone: 845-758-0400
Fax: 845-758-2633
Email: curran@proceedings.com
Web: www.proceedings.com

CONSTRAINT 2022

Second Workshop on Combating Online Hostile Posts in Regional Languages during Emergency Situation

Proceedings of the Workshop

May 27, 2022

Preface

The advent of Web 2.0 induced the evolution of what has traditionally been described as a "participatory Web". From pop-culture music to Black Friday becoming a global phenomenon, and movements like BlackLivesMatter turning into a powerful instrument of global resistance, the Internet and social media have played a pivotal role. As much as we relish the connectedness facilitated by social media, the sentient being in all of us cannot remain obscured by the perils of the unabated misuse of the very free speech that these platforms aim to empower. Within the shadows of a transparent yet anonymous social media, lurk those disguising themselves as pseudo-flag-bearers of free speech, and pounce on every opportunity they get to spread vile content, detrimental to society. Such miscreants are desperate to misuse those 280 character sound bites to further their anti-openness agendas in the form of hate speech, disinformation, and ill-intended propaganda. Such menace experiences flare-ups during emergency situations such as the COVID-19 outbreak and geopolitically conflicting global order.

There have been numerous efforts toward addressing some of these problems computationally, but with evolving complexities of online harmful content, more robust solutions are needed. Some of these challenges stem from linguistic diversity, abstract semiotics, multimodality, anonymity of the real instigators, etc. Thus, there is a pressing need to start a discussion around such aspects, which are more inclusive than conventional efforts. With this in mind, and motivated by the success of the first edition of the CONSTRAINT Workshop on Combating Online Hostile Posts in Regional Languages during Emergency Situation, we have launched the second edition in hybrid mode, with a special focus on Multimodal Low-Resource Language Processing to Combat COVID-19 Related Online Hostile Content.

The workshop additionally highlighted three major points:

1. Regional languages: offensive posts may be written in low-resource regional languages, e.g., Tamil, Urdu, Bangali, Polish, Czech, Lithuanian, etc.

2. Emergency situations: The proposed solutions should be able to tackle misinformation during emergency situations where, due to the lack of enough historical data, machine learning models need to adopt additional intelligence to handle emerging and novel posts.

3. Early detection: Since the impact of misinformation during emergency situations can be highly detrimental to society (e.g., health-related misadvice during a pandemic may take human's life), we encourage solutions that can detect such hostile posts as early as possible after they have been posted in social media.

Our workshop also features a shared task titled: Hero, Villain and Victim: Dissecting harmful memes for Semantic role labelling of entities. The objective is to determine the role of the entities referred to within a meme: hero vs. villain vs. victim vs. other. The meme is to be analyzed from the perspective of its author. The datasets released as part of this shared task span memes from two domains: COVID-19 and US Politics. The complex and engaging nature of the shared task led to a total of 6 unique final submissions for evaluation, from amongst 105 total registered participants.

We accepted a total of ten papers: four for the regular track and six for the shared task. The workshop papers cover topics ranging from detecting multimodal/unimodal fake news (Choi et al., 2022; Lucas et al., 2022) to aggressive content (Sharif et al., 2022), with additional fine-grained analysis and sub-tasks like document retrieval towards mitigating misinformation (Sundriyal et al., 2022). On the other hand, the accepted papers for the shared task proposed various multimodal fusion strategies including state-of-the-art encoder models such as variants of ViT, BERT, and CLIP (Nandi et al., 2022; Kun et al., 2022; Montariol et al., 2022), with ensembling playing a key role in the overall performance enhancement. Consequently, diverse strategies for addressing the task along with their limitations are elucidated via the contributions made hereupon.

We are glad to have 3 eminent invited speakers: (i) Smaranda Muresan, Research Scientist at the Data Science Institute (DSI) and the Department of Computer Science at Columbia University, and Amazon, (2) Isabelle Augenstein, Associate Professor at the University of Copenhagen, Department of Computer Science, where she heads the Copenhagen Natural Language Understanding research group as well as the Natural Language Processing section, and (iii) Andreas Vlachos, Associate Professor at the Natural

Language and Information Processing group at the Department of Computer Science and Technology at the University of Cambridge and a member of the European Lab for Learning and Intelligent Systems.
We thank the authors and the task participants for their interest in the workshop. We would also like to thank the program committee for their help with reviewing the papers and with advertising the workshop.
The work was partially supported by a Wipro research grant, Ramanujan Fellowship, the Infosys Centre for AI, IIIT Delhi, India, and ihub-Anubhuti-iiitd Foundation, set up under the NM-ICPS scheme of the Department of Science and Technology, India.
It is also part of the Tanbih mega-project, which is developed at the Qatar Computing Research Institute, HBKU, and aims to limit the impact of fake news, propaganda, and media bias by making users aware of what they are reading, thus promoting media literacy and critical thinking.

The CONSTRAINT 2022 Organizers: Tanmoy Chakraborty, Md. Shad Akhtar, Kai Shu, H. Russell Bernard, Maria Liakata, and Preslav Nakov
Website: http://lcs2.iiitd.edu.in/CONSTRAINT-2022/

Organizing Committee

Program Committee Chairs

Tanmoy Chakraborty, IIIT Delhi, India
Md. Shad Akhtar, IIIT Delhi, India
Kai Shu, Illinois Institute of Technology, USA
H. Russell Bernard, Arizona State University, USA
Maria Liakata, Queen Mary, University of London, UK
Preslav Nakov, Qatar Computing Research Institute, HBKU, Qatar

Web Chair

Aseem Srivastava, IIIT Delhi, India

Invited Speakers

Isabelle Augenstein, University of Copenhagen, Denmark
Smaranda Muresan, Columbia University, USA
Andreas Vlachos, University of Cambridge, UK

Program Committee

Program Committee

Amila Silva, The University of Melbourne
Andreas Vlachos, University of Cambridge
Anoop Kunchukuttan, Microsoft
Arkaitz Zubiaga, Queen Mary University of London
Balaji Vasan Srinivasan, Adobe Research
Firoj Alam, Qatar Computing Research Institute, HBKU
Marc Spaniol, Université de Caen
Matt Lease, University of Texas at Austin
Monojit Choudhury, Microsoft Research
Tracy King, Adobe Sensei and Search
Paolo Papotti, EURECOM
Paolo Rosso, Universitat Politècnica de València
Pushpak Bhattacharya, IIT Bombay
Roy Ka-Wei Lee, Singapore University of Technology and Design
Xinyi Zhou, Syracuse University
Yingtong Dou, University of Illinois at Chicago
Reza Zafarani, Syracuse University
Nitin Agarwal, University of Arkansas at Little Rock
Victoria Rubin, Western University
Francesco Barbieri, Snap Research
Ashique KhudaBukhsh, Carnegie Mellon University
Ugur Kursuncu, Georgia State University
Vagelis Papalexakis, University of California Riverside
Sibel Adali, Rensselaer Polytechnic Institute
Shivam Sharma, IIIT Delhi, Wipro AI Research
Chhavi Sharma, Wipro AI Research
Shivani Kumar, IIIT Delhi
Yash Kumar Atri, IIIT Delhi
Sarah Masud, IIIT Delhi
Sunil Saumya, IIIT Dharwad
Megha Sundriyal, IIIT Delhi
Karan Goyal, IIIT Delhi
Anam Fatima, IIIT Delhi

Table of Contents

Program

Friday, May 27, 2022

09:00 - 09:10 *Opening Remarks*

09:10 - 10:10 *Keynote 1: Isabelle Augenstein — Automatically Detecting Scientific Misinformation*

10:10 - 10:30 *Regular Paper Session - I*

M-BAD: A Multilabel Dataset for Detecting Aggressive Texts and Their Targets
Omar Sharif, Eftekhar Hossain and Mohammed Moshiul Hoque

10:30 - 11:00 *Coffee break*

11:00 - 12:00 *Keynote 2: Andreas Vlachos — Fact-Checking Using Structured and Unstructured Information*

13:00 - 12:00 *Regular Paper Session - II*

How does fake news use a thumbnail? CLIP-based Multimodal Detection on the Unrepresentative News Image
Hyewon Choi, Yejun Yoon, Seunghyun Yoon and Kunwoo Park

Detecting False Claims in Low-Resource Regions: A Case Study of Caribbean Islands
Jason Lucas, Limeng Cui, Thai Le and Dongwon Lee

Document Retrieval and Claim Verification to Mitigate COVID-19 Misinformation
Megha Sundriyal, Ganeshan Malhotra, Md Shad Akhtar, Shubhashis Sengupta, Andrew Fano and Tanmoy Chakraborty

13:00 - 14:00 *Lunch Break*

14:00 - 15:00 *Keynote 3: Smaranda Muresan — The Role of Text Generation in Fighting Hostile Posts*

15:00 - 15:30 *Coffee Break*

15:30 - 17:15 *Shared Task Session*

Findings of the CONSTRAINT 2022 Shared Task on Detecting the Hero, the Villain, and the Victim in Memes
Shivam Sharma, Tharun Suresh, Atharva Kulkarni, Himanshi Mathur, Preslav Nakov, Md. Shad Akhtar and Tanmoy Chakraborty

DD-TIG at Constraint@ACL2022: Multimodal Understanding and Reasoning for Role Labeling of Entities in Hateful Memes
Ziming Zhou, Han Zhao, Jingjing Dong, Jun Gao and Xiaolong Liu

Are you a hero or a villain? A semantic role labelling approach for detecting harmful memes.
Shaik Fharook, Syed Sufyan Ahmed, Gurram Rithika, Sumith Sai Budde, Sunil Saumya and Shankar Biradar

Logically at the Constraint 2022: Multimodal role labelling
Ludovic Kun, Jayesh Bankoti and David Kiskovski

Combining Language Models and Linguistic Information to Label Entities in Memes
Pranaydeep Singh, Aaron Maladry and Els Lefever

Detecting the Role of an Entity in Harmful Memes: Techniques and their Limitations
Rabindra Nath Nandi, Firoj Alam and Preslav Nakov

Fine-tuning and Sampling Strategies for Multimodal Role Labeling of Entities under Class Imbalance
Syrielle Montariol, Étienne Simon, Arij Riabi and Djamé Seddah

16:50 - 17:15 *Closing*

Findings of the CONSTRAINT 2022 Shared Task on Detecting the Hero, the Villain, and the Victim in Memes

Shivam Sharma[1,3], **Tharun Suresh**[1], **Atharva Kulkarni**[1], **Himanshi Mathur**[1], **Preslav Nakov**[2], **Md. Shad Akhtar**[1], **Tanmoy Chakraborty**[1]

[1]Indraprastha Institute of Information Technology - Delhi, India

[2]Qatar Computing Research Institute, HBKU, Doha, Qatar

[3]Wipro AI Labs, India

{shivams, tharun20119, atharvak, himanshi18037, shad.akhtar, tanmoy}@iiitd.ac.in

pnakov@hbku.edu.qa

Abstract

We present the findings of the shared task at the CONSTRAINT 2022 workshop on "*Hero, Villain, and Victim: Dissecting Harmful Memes for Semantic Role Labeling of Entities*." The task aims to delve deeper into meme comprehension by deciphering the connotations behind the entities present in a meme. In more nuanced terms, the shared task focuses on determining the victimizing, glorifying, and vilifying intentions embedded in meme entities to explicate their connotations. To this end, we curate `HVVMemes`, a novel meme dataset of about 7,000 memes spanning the domains of COVID-19 and US Politics, each containing entities and their associated roles: *hero*, *villain*, *victim*, or *other*. The shared task attracted 105 registered participants, but eventually only nine of them made official submissions. The most successful systems used ensembles combining textual and multimodal models, with the best system achieving an F1-score of 58.67.

1 Introduction

The unwarranted spread of misinformation (Wu et al., 2019; Hardalov et al., 2022), propaganda (Da San Martino et al., 2020a,b), fake news (Lazer et al., 2018; Vosoughi et al., 2018), COVID-19 infodemic (Alam et al., 2021b; Nakov et al., 2022), hate speech (MacAvaney et al., 2019; Zampieri et al., 2019a), and other harmful content (Nakov et al., 2021) has plagued social media. Lately, *memes* have emerged as a powerful multimodal means to disseminate malicious content due to their ability to circumvent censorship norms (Mina, 2014) and to their fast-spreading nature. With an aptly crafted combination of images and text, a seemingly naïve meme can easily become a source of harmful information diffusion. As a result, exploring the noxious side of memes has become a pressing research topic; see also recent surveys on harmful memes (Sharma et al., 2022b) and on multimodal disinformation detection (Alam et al., 2021a).

While meme analysis has been studied in a variety of contexts, such as hate speech (Zhou et al., 2021; Kiela et al., 2020) harmfulness (Pramanick et al., 2021a,b), emotions (Sharma et al., 2020), misinformation (Zidani and Moran, 2021), sarcasm (Kumar and Garg, 2019), offensiveness (Suryawanshi et al., 2020), and propaganda (Dimitrov et al., 2021a,b), limited forays have been made on comprehending the role of the entities that make up a meme. This is our main focus here: on identifying the *hero*, the *villain*, and the *victim* entities present in a meme. Given a meme and a list of the entities it involves, the task is to identify which entity plays what role. Such categorization of the entities in the meme can help understand the entity-specific connotation and their nature, attitudes, decisions, and demeanour. For instance, when the meme creators intend to spread misinformation and hatred towards minority communities or to defame certain individuals, politicians, or organizations, they would depict the target entities as *villains*. Similarly, when the intent is to shed light on the deplorable state of certain entities or to glorify them, these entities would be portrayed as *victims* or as *heroes*, respectively.

Fig. 1 depicts apt examples for *hero*, *villain*, and *victim* categorization of the entities in a meme. The meme in Fig. 1a draws a comparison between Abraham Lincoln, John F. Kennedy, Barack Obama, and Donald Trump, where the former three are portrayed as *heroes*, while Donald Trump is shown in negative light, as a *villain*. Similarly, Fig. 1b mocks Jill Stein and the Green Party as *villains* for allegedly getting bribed by the rich. Fig. 1c on the other hand, frames the Republican Party as a *villain*, for their inconsiderate views on the poor, the minorities, and women, thus making them the *victims*. In conclusion, through depictions of heroism, villainy, and victimization, memes act as an appealing means to propagate certain views about the targeted entities.

Proceedings of the Workshop on Combating Online Hostile Posts in Regional Languages during Emergency Situations, pages 1 - 11

(a) (b) (c)

Figure 1: Examples of heroes, villains and victims, as portrayed within memes.

While some previous meme studies have sought to identify harmfulness and the entities (Sharma et al., 2022a) or the categories that are being targeted, e.g., a person, a group, an organization, or society (Pramanick et al., 2021a,b), none of them has scrutinized the entity's connotation. Our shared task aims to bridge this gap. We release HVVMemes, a meme dataset with about 7,000 memes on COVID-19 and US Politics, where each meme is annotated with a list of entities, each labeled with its role: *hero*, *villain*, *victim*, or *other*. The shared task attracted 105 teams, and nine of them made official submissions. Most teams fine-tuned pre-trained language and multimodal models or used ensembles, with the best system achieving an F1-score of 58.67. We discuss the submissions and their approaches in more detail in Section 5.

Despite the growing body of research on meme analysis, understanding the connotation underlying the individual entities in the meme remains a challenging endeavour. Their camouflaged semantics, satirical outlook, and cryptic nature make their analysis a daunting task (Sabat et al., 2019). Moreover, categorizing the entities as *heroes*, *villains*, or *victims* requires real-world and commonsense knowledge, which often are not present in popular pre-trained language models. Thus, it should not be surprising that, as the shared task's results show, off-the-shelf multimodal models, as well as various ensembles thereof, struggle with this task (Kiela et al., 2020). This highlights that the current state-of-the-art visual-linguistic models are unable to grasp the veiled information present in the memes. Thus, we hope that the dataset and task will foster further research in this interesting direction.

More details about the shared task is available at http://constraint-lcs2.github.io/

2 Related Work

Studies on Online Targeting. Previous work studied affective content in the context of harmful discourse in social media (Zainuddin et al., 2017, 2018; Gautam et al., 2020; Ousidhoum et al., 2019). Sarcastic content was detected by leveraging data sparseness (Zainuddin et al., 2019) towards studying aspect-based sentiment analysis. Shvets et al. (2021) established enhancements in target detection by examining generic concept extraction for hate speech detection. Targeted protected categories were characterised by harmful online engagements whilst addressing societal bias along with explainability (Sap et al., 2020; Mathew et al., 2021). For affective target characterisation, sequence modeling was explored in a hierarchical formulation of stacked BiGRUs (Ma et al., 2018) as well as in low-resource scenarios (Mitchell et al., 2013). Most approaches did not consider the variability in target referencing and the associated affective spectrum (Shvets et al., 2021). Finally, (Gomez-Zara et al., 2018) discussed hero/villain/victim analysis of news text; unlike their work, here we focus on multi-modality and memes.

Studies on Detecting Harmful Memes. The constant transitioning of harmful memes from unfiltered and largely anonymous communities and platforms such as 4chan, Reddit, and Gab to more mainstream social media has made the entire social media ecosystem both sensitive and vulnerable to extremism (Zannettou et al., 2018). Research on offense (Suryawanshi et al., 2020), hate speech (Kiela et al., 2020; Gomez et al., 2020), and online harm detection (Pramanick et al., 2021b) has found the availability of large datasets and the use of multi-modal frameworks crucial for these tasks.

Additional contextual cues involving commonsense knowledge (Shang et al., 2021), semantic entities, cues about the protected categories (Pramanick et al., 2021b; Karkkainen and Joo, 2021), along with other meta information, have also been explored for characterising various aspects of the online harm conveyed by memes. Most such tasks address *affect* detection at various levels of granularity, sometimes organised in a taxonomy. Still, none of these tasks has focused on explicitly modeling the complex narrative framework of the memetic discourse surrounding the specific entities referred to in the meme. With this in mind, here we attempt to alleviate a few associated challenges by exploring the feasibility of entity-specific visual-semantic role labelling for memes.

Other Related Shared Tasks. Several shared tasks have targeted the broad field of harmful social media content. Some tasks investigated the characterisation of *offensive language, hate speech, profanity,* and associated fine-grained attributes such as *implicit* and *explicit* implications in binary, multi-class, multi-label, and hierarchical settings (Struß et al., 2019; Zampieri et al., 2019b, 2020). Their coverage has been fairly comprehensive in terms of the languages covered including *Arabic, Danish, Greek, English, Turkish,* and *Dravidian Languages* like *Tamil, Malayalam, Kannada* as well as *German and English/Indo-Aryan code-mixing* (Zampieri et al., 2019b; Mubarak et al., 2020; Zampieri et al., 2020; Chakravarthi et al., 2021; Modha et al., 2021). They also address harmful content dissemination, targeting various protected categories such as *religious affiliation, national origin, sex,* etc. (Zhang et al., 2019). Other efforts have targeted misinformation, propaganda, and persuasiveness detection (Aly et al., 2021; Shaar et al., 2021; Da San Martino et al., 2020a), where the goal is to detect verifiable claims, their veracity, span, and check-worthiness. Persuasive technique detection has also been explored for images besides text-based content, e.g., Dimitrov et al. (2021b) introduced the task of propaganda in *memes*.

Some tasks have attempted to address affect concerning various targets. Xu et al. (2016) focused on stance prediction for given targets, i.e., whether the comment is in favour or against the target, both in supervised and in unsupervised scenarios. Molla and Joshi (2019) modeled sarcastic targeting of specific entities. Rosenthal et al. (2017) focused on sentiment analysis in Twitter.

Domain	Splits	# Memes	# Referenced Entities				
			Hero	*Villain*	*Victim*	*Other*	**Total**
COVID-19	Train	2,700	163	576	317	2,438	3,494
	Val	300	19	65	40	268	392
	Test	381	18	106	50	359	533
	Total	3,381	200	747	407	3,065	4,419
Politics	Train	2,852	230	1,308	441	2,617	4,596
	Val	350	27	166	58	317	568
	Test	350	31	167	45	308	551
	Total	3,552	288	1,641	544	3,242	5,715

Table 1: Statistics about our `HVVMemes` dataset.

In contrast, here we focus not only on the polarity of the target entity, but also on understanding complex connotations such as *glorification, vilification,* and *victimisation* in memes. This is both challenging and important, as memetic discourse has taken over a sizable portion of online engagement and as it requires specialised moderation given its multimodal nature.

3 Dataset Curation

Towards curating a dataset that would enable the identification of *hero*, *villain*, and *victim* as roles in memes, we leveraged and reannotated the `HarMeme` dataset released in (Pramanick et al., 2021b), and we call this new dataset `HVVMemes`. `HarMeme` includes 3,544 memes about COVID-19 and 3,552 memes about US Politics, which are annotated for *harmfulness* as well as for *target type*, in case the meme is harmful, with four categories for the latter: *individual*, *organisation*, *community*, and *society*. Table 1 gives some statistics about `HVVMemes` (note that for COVID-19, we filtered out some of the memes in `HarMeme`, keeping 3,381 of the original 3,554 memes). As a general trend for both domains, we observe a neutral reference for most of the entities mentioned in the memes (3,065 for COVID-19, and 3,242 for US Politics); for such cases, we assign a fourth category: *other*. We further see that *villain* is the second most frequent role (747 memes for COVID-19, and 1,641 for US Politics), followed by *victim* (407 memes for COVID-19, and 544 for US Politics), and then *hero* (200 memes for COVID-19, and 288 for US Politics). We believe that this is a realistic representation of social media engagement involving memes, which are mostly humorous with neutral connotations, and less frequently harmful by indulging in vilification. Victimisation can also be interpreted as a countering resistance to incessant vilification. Finally, glorification is generally the weakest voice in memetic discourse.

S. No.	Annotation Guidelines
1	Meme author's perspective needs to be considered as the frame of reference, while assigning roles.
2	Towards complete assimilation, both visual and textual cues should be factored in.
3	Relevant background context should be acquired before assigning roles.
4	Ambiguous memes can be categorised as *other*.
5	A 3-point Likert scale based mental frame of reference, implying *negative*, *neutral* and *positive* sentiments involved, should steer the connotation adjudication.
6	All reasonably *intelligible* (without ambiguity) entities that are referred to in the meme must be considered as valid targets.
7	Entities with multiple interpretations should be categorised as *other*.
8	The role of the original speaker of a quote, as expressed within a meme, must not be presumed.

Table 2: Key considerations in our annotation guidelines.

Entity	Resolution Remark
`Corona`	resolved to `Corona Beer` (whenever valid).
`Govt.`	resolved to `Government`.
`Putin`	resolved to `Vladimir Putin`.
`CDC`	standardised as `Centre of Disease Control (CDC)`.

Table 3: Examples of *resolution remarks* that we provided to the annotators towards entity identification.

(a) COVID-19

(b) US Politics

Figure 2: Word clouds for (a) COVID-19 and (b) US Politics domains in `HVVMemes`.

3.1 Annotation Setup

Since entity role labelling is complex and subjective, we formulated clear annotation guidelines, which are summarized in Table 2. Each meme was annotated by three annotators, and the disagreements were resolved with the help of a consolidator. We asked the annotators (*i*) to identify the entities, and (*ii*) to assign roles to these entities.

3.1.1 Identifying the Entities

This step requires the annotators to elicit all entities that the meme refers to. This includes *persons*, *norp* (nationalities, religious, or political groups), *facilities, organizations, geopolitical entities, locations*, *products*, and other, as defined by spaCy's label scheme for named entity recognition.[1]

[1] `spacy.io/models/en#en_core_web_sm`

To assist the annotators, we provided them an exhaustive list of all automatically identified entities along with *resolution remarks* whenever needed as shown in Table 3. Note that the annotators were not restricted to select entities from our provided list, which can be error-prone as automatic named entity recognition is not perfect; in fact, they were encouraged to add additional entities as needed, e.g., such shown in the image, but not mentioned in the textual part of the meme.

Fig. 2a shows a word cloud visualization of the entities referenced in COVID-19 memes: we can see social, global, political, and economic entities such as *coronavirus, China, home, Wuhan, mask, work*, etc. Similarly, in Fig. 2b shows a word cloud for US Politics memes, where we see entities like *Biden, party, Donald, Democratic, Obama*, etc.

To assess the general agreement between the annotators, we considered an agreement towards entity identification if at least two annotators agreed on an entity in the meme. The number of memes with agreed entities was normalised by the total number of memes with at least one valid entity assignment by the annotators. This was done independently of the implied role category, as the emphasis in this first step is on entity identification. The highest agreement towards this was 0.98, which suggests the reliability associated with the annotator's collective understanding of the task. We followed a similar approach for the overall role-wise inter-annotator agreement; see below.

3.1.2 Role Assignment

The annotation was done in three stages: (*i*) dry-run, (*ii*) complete annotation, and (*iii*) consolidation. As part of the dry-run, the annotators and the consolidator annotated a random subset of 250 memes, assigning the entities the roles of *hero*, *villain*, *victim*, and *other*. Then, we gave them feedback and we trained them carefully by issuing detailed guidelines that included the formal definitions of the role categories and the instructions exemplifying the edge scenarios identified as part of the dry-run disagreements. In the second stage, the annotators performed a complete annotation. This was followed by a third consolidation stage with the help of a consolidator.

Due to the varying annotation responses and co-referencing for each role, conventional annotation agreement measures are not suitable for our setup. We consider an agreement when at least two annotators agree on one of the candidate entities for a particular role, which we formalize as the following role-wise agreement score a:

$$a = \frac{v_{agr}}{v_{tot}} \quad (1)$$

We define v_{agr}, which refers to the total number of valid agreements, and v_{tot}, which is the total number of valid responses, as follows:

$$v_{agr} = \sum_{i=1}^{N} I_i;\ v_{tot} = \sum_{i=1}^{N} Z_i \quad (2)$$

where I_i is a valid agreement (1, iff two or more annotators agree on an entity in example i), Z_i is a valid response (1, iff at least one annotator provides a valid entity as a response in example i), and N is the total number of examples in the dataset.

Roles	Covid-19 (a)		US Politics (a)		Stage-3
	Stage-2	Stage-3	Stage-2	Stage-3	Avg. (a)
Hero	0.30	0.54	0.36	0.51	0.53
Villain	0.31	0.55	0.55	0.73	0.64
Victim	0.21	0.55	0.24	0.43	0.49
Other	0.58	0.68	0.76	0.88	0.78
Avg.	0.35	**0.58**	0.48	**0.64**	**0.61**

Table 4: Inter-annotator agreement (IAA) summary for *completed* (Stage-2) and *consolidated* (Stage-3) stages of the annotation process. Note that the average IAA for the dry-run (Stage-1), for COVID-19 and US Politics combined, was 0.50 (hero), 0.35 (villain), 0.14 (victim), and 0.55 (other).

In the *first* dry-run stage of the annotation process, the annotators worked on 250 memes, and then we examined their agreement, which was 0.50, 0.35, 0.14, and 0.55, for the roles of *hero*, *villain*, *victim*, and *other*, respectively, for COVID-19 and US Politics combined. The inter-annotator agreement for stages 2 and 3 is shown in Table 4. We can see that the average agreement scores after the *completion* stage (stage-2) are 0.35 and 0.48 for COVID-19 and US Politics, respectively. After the consolidation stage (stage-3), these numbers increased to 0.58 and 0.64, respectively.

3.2 Role-wise Analysis of `HVVMemes`

The distribution of the referencing entities within our `HVVMemes` dataset is somewhat skewed towards specific entities as well as towards specific predominant roles for these specific entities. The entities fairly emulate the prevalent trends and discourse topics that social media engagement around the period of the dataset collection reflected, which was at the onset of the COVID-19 pandemic and the surrounding political outlook within the United States of America. We observed that entities like *Donald Trump* and *China* were referenced almost equally in *COVID-19* memes as a *villain* and *other*, while other entities are invariably referenced as *other* using humor, sarcasm, limerick, etc. For the domain of *US Politics*, on one hand, entities like *Donald Trump*, the *Democratic Party*, the *Republican Party*, and the *Democrats* are observed to have similar trend of pre-dominantly being referenced as a *villain* and *other*, and on the other hand, as a general trend, most of the memes have at least one vilified reference.

Rank	System	Precision	Recall	F1
1	shiroe	55.76	62.73	58.67
2	jayeshbankoti	53.58	59.45	56.01
3	c1pher	53.91	57.25	55.24
4	zhouziming	54.19	55.36	54.71
5	smontariol	57.96	44.97	48.48
6	zjl123001	47.98	44.97	46.18
7	amanpriyanshu	30.98	34.35	31.94
8	IIITDWD	25.57	23.79	23.86
9	rabindra.nath	25.30	25.30	23.72

Table 5: Leaderboard summary for the shared task.

4 Shared Task Details

The CONSTRAINT 22 Shared Task on Detecting the Hero, Villain, and the Victim in Memes asked to predict which entities are glorified, vilified, and victimised in a given meme. We gave the participants the above-described labeled training and validation datasets, where for each meme, we had the list of corresponding entities and their labeled role. The task was, given a meme and a list of entities, to predict the role of each of these entities in the meme. We provided the data split by topic (COVID-19 and US Politics), as discussed in Section 3. For the test set, we combined and shuffled the memes from the two topics, and we provided the memes with a list of corresponding entities, but no labels.

The task was organized on CodaLab, an open-source platform widely used to host machine learning and data science competitions. Our competition link[2] provided all the necessary resources for the participants including archived news, notifications, and forum posts communicated during the running of the competition. We allowed the participants a maximum of 25 submissions, and the best submission was considered for the leaderboard.

The official evaluation measure was macro-F1 score, as we have an imbalanced multi-class problem. We further report precision and recall.

5 Participation and Results

The total of 105 teams registered for the competition, and nine of them made submissions to the leaderboard, making a total of 71 attempts to improve their scores. The teams tried a variety of approaches, and below we discuss the approaches by the six teams who also submitted a system description paper with information about their runs.

- **shiroe/jayeshbankoti** (Kun et al., 2022) achieved the best results overall. One of the distinctive approaches that the authors followed was to make use of Celebrity face detection from the input meme images using Giphy's Github.[3] In addition, a sub-image detector using YoloV5[4] leveraged the bounding boxes for memes with multiple images. This was input into an ensemble model of DeBERTa (He et al., 2021) + RoBERTa (Liu et al., 2019) + ViLT (Kim et al., 2021) + EfficientNetB7 (Tan and Le, 2019) with averaging of the predictions in the final layer. Though they incorporated a celebrity detector, the lack of other external knowledge limited their system performance. Their source code is available at `https://bitbucket.org/logicallydevs/constraint_2022/src/master/`

- **c1pher** (Singh et al., 2022) were ranked third. It is remarkable that they achieved this result using just the text input. They formulated the problem as a Multiple Choice Question Answering Task (MCQA), and they used an ensemble of three modules: twitter-xlm-roberta + COVID-BERT (Müller et al., 2020) + BERT-tweet (Nguyen et al., 2020). They further added a sentiment module trained using RoBERTa, with the final classification layer comprising Support Vector Machine (SVM). A major drawback of this approach is that they ignored the image as an input altogether.

- **zhouziming/zjl123001** (Zhou et al., 2022) leveraged the Visual Commonsense Reasoning (VCR) framework in a multimodal model. They built an ensemble of VisualBERT (Li et al., 2019) + UNITER (Chen et al., 2020) + OSCAR (Li et al., 2020) + ERNIE-Vil (Yu et al., 2021), combined using an SVM. To handle the disproportionately large number of *Other* examples, they introduced loss-reweighting. The lack of sufficient external knowledge and position information about the OCR text with the image restricted their system performance. Their source code is available at `https://github.com/zjl123001/DD-TIG-Constraint`

[2]`https://codalab.lisn.upsaclay.fr/competitions/906`

[3]`http://github.com/Giphy/celeb-detection-oss`

[4]`https://github.com/ultralytics/yolov5`

System	BERT	R-BERT	D-BERT	*CLIP*	EB7	OFA	ViLT	ViT	VB	U	O	E-V	SVM	XGB	BF	VADER	W-P
shiroe		✓	✓		✓		✓										
c1pher	✓	✓											✓				
zhouziming									✓	✓	✓	✓	✓				
smontariol				✓		✓			✓					✓			
IIITDWD																✓	✓
rabindra.nath	✓							✓					✓		✓		

Table 6: Models used by the participants as part of their system submissions. **R-BERT:** RoBERTa, **D-BERT:** DeBERTa, **EB7:** EfficientNetB7, **OFA:** Once-for-All, **ViLT:** Visual and Language Transformer, **ViT:** Visual Transformer, **VB:** Visual BERT, **U:** UNITER, **O:** OSCAR, **E-V:** ERNIE-Vil, **SVM:** Support Vector Machines, **XGB:** XGBoost, **BF:** Block Fusion and **W-P:** Wu-Palmer.

- **smontariol** (Montariol et al., 2022) experimented with sampling to handle data imbalance, trying six strategies. On top of that, they used an ensemble of CLIP (Radford et al., 2021) + VisualBERT + OFA (Cai et al., 2020) with XGBoost as the final layer for classification. The potential limitations of this approach include OCR errors and issues with image–text correspondence. Their source code is available at `https://github.com/smontariol/mmsrl_constraint`

- **IIITDWD** (Fharook, 2022) combined sentiment- and lexicon-based approaches to associate sentiment polarity and roles with each entity. For sentiment classification, they used VADER[5]. Moreover, to associate commonly used words for *hero*, *villain*, and *victim*, they developed a corpus and used Wu-Palmer similarity.[6] The way was done and its impact are described in insufficient detail. Their source code is available at `https://github.com/fharookshaik/shared-task_constraint-2022`

- **rabindra.nath** (Nandi et al., 2022) proposed an approach using BLOCK fusion (Ben-younes et al., 2019) for combining the image with text embeddings. They used a combination of ViT (Bobicev and Sokolova, 2017) and BERT (Devlin et al., 2019) for the image and for the text, respectively, followed by SVM as the final layer for classification. The empirical approach limits their system performance despite adding several data augmentation techniques. Their source code is available at `https://github.com/robi56/harmful_memes_block_fusion`

[5] `https://pypi.org/project/vaderSentiment/`

[6] `https://arxiv.org/ftp/arxiv/papers/1310/1310.8059.pdf`

The evaluation results for the above systems are shown in Table 5. We can see that the macro-F1 scores range between 58.67 and 23.72, with a mean of 44.31 and a median of 48.48.

Table 6 further gives a summary of the most important components of the participating systems. We can see that one commonly used architecture is BERT and its variants, including multi-modal variants, whereas SVM is the preferred way to combine the components of ensemble systems.

6 Conclusion

Understanding and interpreting the connotations behind the entities in a meme is a difficult problem, which we pioneered in this shared task. Given a meme and a list of entities, the task asks to detect the role of each entity as a *hero*, a *villain*, a *victim*, or *other*. We curated `HVVMemes`, a large-scale meme dataset of 7,000 memes spanning the domains of COVID-19 and US Politics, annotated with the entities they refer to as well as with their role. The shared task attracted 105 registered participants, out of which nine made official submissions, and six submitted papers describing their systems. We hope that our dataset and task setup will enable further research towards understanding how entities are portrayed in memes.

Acknowledgments

The work was partially supported by a Wipro research grant, Ramanujan Fellowship, the Infosys Centre for AI, IIIT Delhi, and ihub-Anubhuti-iiitd Foundation, set up under the NM-ICPS scheme of the Department of Science and Technology, India. It is also part of the Tanbih mega-project, which is developed at the Qatar Computing Research Institute, HBKU, and aims to limit the impact of "fake news," propaganda, and media bias by making users aware of what they are reading, thus promoting media literacy and critical thinking.

References

Firoj Alam, Stefano Cresci, Tanmoy Chakraborty, Fabrizio Silvestri, Dimiter Dimitrov, Giovanni Da San Martino, Shaden Shaar, Hamed Firooz, and Preslav Nakov. 2021a. A survey on multimodal disinformation detection. *CoRR*, abs/2103.12541.

Firoj Alam, Shaden Shaar, Fahim Dalvi, Hassan Sajjad, Alex Nikolov, Hamdy Mubarak, Giovanni Da San Martino, Ahmed Abdelali, Nadir Durrani, Kareem Darwish, Abdulaziz Al-Homaid, Wajdi Zaghouani, Tommaso Caselli, Gijs Danoe, Friso Stolk, Britt Bruntink, and Preslav Nakov. 2021b. Fighting the COVID-19 infodemic: Modeling the perspective of journalists, fact-checkers, social media platforms, policy makers, and the society. In *Findings of EMNLP*, pages 611–649, Punta Cana, Dominican Republic.

Rami Aly, Zhijiang Guo, Michael Sejr Schlichtkrull, James Thorne, Andreas Vlachos, Christos Christodoulopoulos, Oana Cocarascu, and Arpit Mittal. 2021. The fact extraction and VERification over unstructured and structured information (FEVEROUS) shared task. In *Proceedings of the Fourth Workshop on Fact Extraction and VERification (FEVER)*, pages 1–13, Punta Cana, Dominican Republic.

Hedi Ben-younes, Remi Cadene, Nicolas Thome, and Matthieu Cord. 2019. BLOCK: Bilinear superdiagonal fusion for visual question answering and visual relationship detection. In *Proceedings of the Thirty-Third AAAI Conference on Artificial Intelligence*, AAAI '19, Honolulu, Hawaii, USA.

Victoria Bobicev and Marina Sokolova. 2017. Inter-annotator agreement in sentiment analysis: Machine learning perspective. In *Proceedings of the International Conference Recent Advances in Natural Language Processing*, RANLP '17, pages 97–102, Varna, Bulgaria.

Han Cai, Chuang Gan, Tianzhe Wang, Zhekai Zhang, and Song Han. 2020. Once-for-All: Train One Network and Specialize it for Efficient Deployment. *arXiv:1908.09791 [cs, stat]*.

Bharathi Raja Chakravarthi, Ruba Priyadharshini, Navya Jose, Anand Kumar M, Thomas Mandl, Prasanna Kumar Kumaresan, Rahul Ponnusamy, Hariharan R L, John P. McCrae, and Elizabeth Sherly. 2021. Findings of the shared task on offensive language identification in Tamil, Malayalam, and Kannada. In *Proceedings of the First Workshop on Speech and Language Technologies for Dravidian Languages*, pages 133–145, Kyiv.

Yen-Chun Chen, Linjie Li, Licheng Yu, Ahmed El Kholy, Faisal Ahmed, Zhe Gan, Yu Cheng, and Jingjing Liu. 2020. UNITER: UNiversal Image-TExt Representation Learning. *arXiv:1909.11740 [cs]*.

Giovanni Da San Martino, Alberto Barrón-Cedeño, Henning Wachsmuth, Rostislav Petrov, and Preslav Nakov. 2020a. SemEval-2020 task 11: Detection of propaganda techniques in news articles. In *Proceedings of the Fourteenth Workshop on Semantic Evaluation*, pages 1377–1414, Barcelona (online).

Giovanni Da San Martino, Stefano Cresci, Alberto Barrón-Cedeño, Seunghak Yu, Roberto Di Pietro, and Preslav Nakov. 2020b. A survey on computational propaganda detection. In *Proceedings of the 29th International Joint Conference on Artificial Intelligence and the 17th Pacific Rim International Conference on Artificial Intelligence*, IJCAI-PRICAI '20, pages 4826–4832, Yokohama, Japan.

Jacob Devlin, Ming-Wei Chang, Kenton Lee, and Kristina Toutanova. 2019. BERT: Pre-training of deep bidirectional transformers for language understanding. In *Proceedings of the 2019 Conf. of the North American Chapter of the Association for Comp. Linguistics: Human Language Technologies*, pages 4171–4186, Minneapolis, Minnesota.

Dimitar Dimitrov, Bishr Bin Ali, Shaden Shaar, Firoj Alam, Fabrizio Silvestri, Hamed Firooz, Preslav Nakov, and Giovanni Da San Martino. 2021a. Detecting propaganda techniques in memes. In *Proceedings of the Joint Conference of the 59th Annual Meeting of the Association for Computational Linguistics and the 11th International Joint Conference on Natural Language Processing*, ACL-IJCNLP '21, pages 6603–6617.

Dimitar Dimitrov, Bishr Bin Ali, Shaden Shaar, Firoj Alam, Fabrizio Silvestri, Hamed Firooz, Preslav Nakov, and Giovanni Da San Martino. 2021b. SemEval-2021 task 6: Detection of persuasion techniques in texts and images. In *Proceedings of the 15th International Workshop on Semantic Evaluation (SemEval-2021)*, pages 70–98, Online.

Shaik Fharook. 2022. Are you a hero or a villain? a semantic role labelling approach for detecting harmful memes. In *Proceedings of the Workshop on Combating Online Hostile Posts in Regional Languages during Emergency Situations*, CONSTRAINT '22, Dublin, Ireland.

Akash Gautam, Puneet Mathur, Rakesh Gosangi, Debanjan Mahata, Ramit Sawhney, and Rajiv Ratn Shah. 2020. #MeTooMA: Multi-aspect annotations of tweets related to the MeToo movement. *Proceedings of the International AAAI Conference on Web and Social Media*, 14(1):209–216.

Raul Gomez, Jaume Gibert, Lluis Gomez, and Dimosthenis Karatzas. 2020. Exploring hate speech detection in multimodal publications. In *Proceedings of the 2020 IEEE Winter Conference on Applications of Computer Vision*, WACV '20, pages 1459–1467.

Diego Gomez-Zara, Miriam Boon, and Larry Birnbaum. 2018. Who is the hero, the villain, and the victim? Detection of roles in news articles using natural language techniques. In *23rd International Conference on Intelligent User Interfaces*, IUI '18, page 311315, Tokyo, Japan.

Momchil Hardalov, Arnav Arora, Preslav Nakov, and Isabelle Augenstein. 2022. A survey on stance detection for mis- and disinformation identification. In *Findings of NAACL*, Seattle, Washington, USA.

Pengcheng He, Xiaodong Liu, Jianfeng Gao, and Weizhu Chen. 2021. DeBERTa: Decoding-enhanced BERT with Disentangled Attention. *arXiv:2006.03654 [cs]*.

Kimmo Karkkainen and Jungseock Joo. 2021. Fairface: Face attribute dataset for balanced race, gender, and age for bias measurement and mitigation. In *Proceedings of the IEEE/CVF Winter Conference on Applications of Computer Vision*, WACV '21, pages 1548–1558.

Douwe Kiela, Hamed Firooz, Aravind Mohan, Vedanuj Goswami, Amanpreet Singh, Pratik Ringshia, and Davide Testuggine. 2020. The hateful memes challenge: Detecting hate speech in multimodal memes. In *Proceedings of the 34th International Conference on Neural Information Processing Systems*, volume 33 of *NeurIPS '20*.

Wonjae Kim, Bokyung Son, and Ildoo Kim. 2021. ViLT: Vision-and-language transformer without convolution or region supervision. In *Proceedings of the 38th International Conference on Machine Learning*, volume 139 of *ICML '21*, pages 5583–5594.

Akshi Kumar and Geetanjali Garg. 2019. Sarc-M: Sarcasm detection in typo-graphic memes. In *Proceedings of the International Conference on Advances in Engineering Science Management & Technology*, ICAESMT '19, Dehradun, India.

Ludovic Kun, Jayesh Bankoti, and David Kiskovski. 2022. Logically at the CONSTRAINT 2022: Multimodal role labelling. In *Proceedings of the Workshop on Combating Online Hostile Posts in Regional Languages during Emergency Situations*, CONSTRAINT '22, Dublin, Ireland.

David M.J. Lazer, Matthew A. Baum, Yochai Benkler, Adam J. Berinsky, Kelly M. Greenhill, Filippo Menczer, Miriam J. Metzger, Brendan Nyhan, Gordon Pennycook, David Rothschild, Michael Schudson, Steven A. Sloman, Cass R. Sunstein, Emily A. Thorson, Duncan J. Watts, and Jonathan L. Zittrain. 2018. The science of fake news. *Science*, 359(6380):1094–1096.

Liunian Harold Li, Mark Yatskar, Da Yin, Cho-Jui Hsieh, and Kai-Wei Chang. 2019. VisualBERT: A Simple and Performant Baseline for Vision and Language. *arXiv:1908.03557 [cs]*.

Xiujun Li, Xi Yin, Chunyuan Li, Pengchuan Zhang, Xiaowei Hu, Lei Zhang, Lijuan Wang, Houdong Hu, Li Dong, Furu Wei, Yejin Choi, and Jianfeng Gao. 2020. Oscar: Object-semantics aligned pre-training for vision-language tasks. In *Proceedings of the 16th European Conference in Computer Vision*, volume 12375 of *ECCV '20*, pages 121–137, Glasgow, UK.

Yinhan Liu, Myle Ott, Naman Goyal, Jingfei Du, Mandar Joshi, Danqi Chen, Omer Levy, Mike Lewis, Luke Zettlemoyer, and Veselin Stoyanov. 2019. RoBERTa: A Robustly Optimized BERT Pretraining Approach. *arXiv:1907.11692 [cs]*.

Dehong Ma, Sujian Li, and Houfeng Wang. 2018. Joint learning for targeted sentiment analysis. In *Proceedings of the 2018 Conference on Empirical Methods in Natural Language Processing*, pages 4737–4742, Brussels, Belgium.

Sean MacAvaney, Hao-Ren Yao, Eugene Yang, Katina Russell, Nazli Goharian, and Ophir Frieder. 2019. Hate speech detection: Challenges and solutions. *PLOS ONE*, 14(8):1–16.

Binny Mathew, Punyajoy Saha, Seid Muhie Yimam, Chris Biemann, Pawan Goyal, and Animesh Mukherjee. 2021. Hatexplain: A benchmark dataset for explainable hate speech detection. *Proceedings of the AAAI Conference on Artificial Intelligence*, 35(17):14867–14875.

An Xiao Mina. 2014. Batman, Pandaman and the Blind Man: A case study in social change memes and internet censorship in China. *Journal of Visual Culture*, 13(3):359–375.

Margaret Mitchell, Jacqui Aguilar, Theresa Wilson, and Benjamin Van Durme. 2013. Open domain targeted sentiment. In *Proceedings of the 2013 Conference on Empirical Methods in Natural Language Processing*, pages 1643–1654, Seattle, Washington, USA.

Sandip Modha, Thomas Mandl, Gautam Kishore Shahi, Hiren Madhu, Shrey Satapara, Tharindu Ranasinghe, and Marcos Zampieri. 2021. Overview of the HASOC subtrack at FIRE 2021: Hate speech and offensive content identification in english and indo-aryan languages and conversational hate speech. In *Proceedings of the Forum for Information Retrieval Evaluation*, FIRE '21, pages 1–3.

Diego Molla and Aditya Joshi. 2019. Overview of the 2019 ALTA shared task: Sarcasm target identification. In *Proceedings of the 17th Annual Workshop of the Australasian Language Technology Association*, ALTA '19, pages 192–196, Sydney, Australia.

Syrielle Montariol, Étienne Simon, Arij Riabi, and Djamé Seddah. 2022. Fine-tuning and sampling strategies for multimodal role labeling of entities under class imbalance. In *Proceedings of the Workshop on Combating Online Hostile Posts in Regional Languages during Emergency Situations*, CONSTRAINT '22, Dublin, Ireland.

Hamdy Mubarak, Kareem Darwish, Walid Magdy, Tamer Elsayed, and Hend Al-Khalifa. 2020. Overview of OSACT4 Arabic offensive language detection shared task. In *Proceedings of the 4th Workshop on Open-Source Arabic Corpora and Processing Tools, with a Shared Task on Offensive Language Detection*, pages 48–52, Marseille, France.

Martin Müller, Marcel Salathé, and Per E. Kummervold. 2020. COVID-Twitter-BERT: A Natural Language Processing Model to Analyse COVID-19 Content on Twitter. *arXiv:2005.07503 [cs]*.

Preslav Nakov, Alberto Barrón-Cedeño, Giovanni Da San Martino, Firoj Alam, Julia Maria Struß, Thomas Mandl, Rubén Míguez, Tommaso Caselli, Mucahid Kutlu, Wajdi Zaghouani, Chengkai Li, Shaden Shaar, Gautam Kishore Shahi, Hamdy Mubarak, Alex Nikolov, Nikolay Babulkov, Yavuz Selim Kartal, and Javier Beltrán. 2022. The CLEF-2022 CheckThat! lab on fighting the COVID-19 infodemic and fake news detection. In *Proceedings of the 44th European Conference on IR Research: Advances in Information Retrieval*, ECIR '22, pages 416–428, Berlin, Heidelberg.

Preslav Nakov, Vibha Nayak, Kyle Dent, Ameya Bhatawdekar, Sheikh Muhammad Sarwar, Momchil Hardalov, Yoan Dinkov, Dimitrina Zlatkova, Guillaume Bouchard, and Isabelle Augenstein. 2021. Detecting abusive language on online platforms: A critical analysis. *arXiv/2103.00153*.

Rabindra Nath Nandi, Firoj Alam, and Preslav Nakov. 2022. Detecting the role of an entity in harmful memes: Techniques and their limitations. In *Proceedings of the Workshop on Combating Online Hostile Posts in Regional Languages during Emergency Situations*, CONSTRAINT '22, Dublin, Ireland.

Dat Quoc Nguyen, Thanh Vu, and Anh Tuan Nguyen. 2020. BERTweet: A pre-trained language model for English tweets. In *Proceedings of the 2020 Conference on Empirical Methods in Natural Language Processing: System Demonstrations*, EMNLP '20, pages 9–14, Online.

Nedjma Ousidhoum, Zizheng Lin, Hongming Zhang, Yangqiu Song, and Dit-Yan Yeung. 2019. Multilingual and multi-aspect hate speech analysis. In *Proceedings of the 2019 Conference on Empirical Methods in Natural Language Processing and the 9th International Joint Conference on Natural Language Processing (EMNLP-IJCNLP)*, pages 4675–4684, Hong Kong, China.

Shraman Pramanick, Dimitar Dimitrov, Rituparna Mukherjee, Shivam Sharma, Md. Shad Akhtar, Preslav Nakov, and Tanmoy Chakraborty. 2021a. Detecting harmful memes and their targets. In *Findings of ACL*, ACL-IJCNLP '21, pages 2783–2796.

Shraman Pramanick, Shivam Sharma, Dimitar Dimitrov, Md. Shad Akhtar, Preslav Nakov, and Tanmoy Chakraborty. 2021b. MOMENTA: A multimodal framework for detecting harmful memes and their targets. In *Findings of EMNLP 2021*, pages 4439–4455, Punta Cana, Dominican Republic.

Alec Radford, Jong Wook Kim, Chris Hallacy, Aditya Ramesh, Gabriel Goh, Sandhini Agarwal, Girish Sastry, Amanda Askell, Pamela Mishkin, Jack Clark, Gretchen Krueger, and Ilya Sutskever. 2021. Learning transferable visual models from natural language supervision. In *Proceedings of the 38th International Conference on Machine Learning*, volume 139 of *Proceedings of Machine Learning Research*, pages 8748–8763.

Sara Rosenthal, Noura Farra, and Preslav Nakov. 2017. SemEval-2017 task 4: Sentiment analysis in Twitter. In *Proceedings of the 11th International Workshop on Semantic Evaluation*, SemEval '17, pages 502–518, Vancouver, Canada.

Benet Oriol Sabat, Cristian Canton Ferrer, and Xavier Giro-i Nieto. 2019. Hate speech in pixels: Detection of offensive memes towards automatic moderation. *arXiv:1910.02334*.

Maarten Sap, Saadia Gabriel, Lianhui Qin, Dan Jurafsky, Noah A. Smith, and Yejin Choi. 2020. Social bias frames: Reasoning about social and power implications of language. In *Proceedings of the 58th Annual Meeting of the Association for Computational Linguistics*, ACL '20, pages 5477–5490, Online.

Shaden Shaar, Firoj Alam, Giovanni Da San Martino, Alex Nikolov, Wajdi Zaghouani, Preslav Nakov, and Anna Feldman. 2021. Findings of the NLP4IF-2021 shared tasks on fighting the COVID-19 infodemic and censorship detection. In *Proceedings of the Fourth Workshop on NLP for Internet Freedom: Censorship, Disinformation, and Propaganda*, pages 82–92, Online.

Lanyu Shang, Christina Youn, Yuheng Zha, Yang Zhang, and Dong Wang. 2021. KnowMeme: A knowledge-enriched graph neural network solution to offensive meme detection. In *Proceedings of the 2021 IEEE 17th International Conference on eScience*, eScience '21, pages 186–195.

Chhavi Sharma, Deepesh Bhageria, William Scott, Srinivas PYKL, Amitava Das, Tanmoy Chakraborty, Viswanath Pulabaigari, and Björn Gambäck. 2020. SemEval-2020 task 8: Memotion analysis- the visuo-lingual metaphor! In *Proceedings of the Fourteenth Workshop on Semantic Evaluation*, SemEval '20, pages 759–773.

Shivam Sharma, Md Shad Akhtar, Preslav Nakov, and Tanmoy Chakraborty. 2022a. DISARM: Detecting the victims targeted by harmful memes. In *Findings of NAACL*, Seattle, Washington, USA.

Shivam Sharma, Firoj Alam, Md. Shad Akhtar, Dimitar Dimitrov, Giovanni Da San Martino, Hamed Firooz, Alon Halevy, Fabrizio Silvestri, Preslav Nakov, and Tanmoy Chakraborty. 2022b. Detecting and understanding harmful memes: A survey. In *Proceedings of the 31st International Joint Conference on Artificial Intelligence*, IJCAI-ECAI '22, Vienna, Austria.

Alexander Shvets, Paula Fortuna, Juan Soler, and Leo Wanner. 2021. Targets and aspects in social media hate speech. In *Proceedings of the 5th Workshop on Online Abuse and Harms (WOAH 2021)*, pages 179–190, Online.

Pranaydeep Singh, Aaron Maladry, and Els Lefever. 2022. Combining language models and linguistic information to label entities in memes. In *Proceedings of the Workshop on Combating Online Hostile Posts in Regional Languages during Emergency Situations*, CONSTRAINT '22, Dublin, Ireland.

Julia Maria Struß, Melanie Siegel, Josef Ruppenhofer, Michael Wiegand, and Manfred Klenner. 2019. Overview of GermEval task 2, 2019 shared task on the identification of offensive language. Proceedings of the 15th Conference on Natural Language Processing, pages 352 – 363, München [u.a.].

Shardul Suryawanshi, Bharathi Raja Chakravarthi, Mihael Arcan, and Paul Buitelaar. 2020. Multimodal meme dataset (MultiOFF) for identifying offensive content in image and text. In *Proceedings of the Second Workshop on Trolling, Aggression and Cyberbullying*, pages 32–41, Marseille, France.

Mingxing Tan and Quoc V. Le. 2019. EfficientNet: Rethinking model scaling for convolutional neural networks. In *Proceedings of the 36th International Conference on Machine Learning*, volume 97 of *ICML '19*, pages 6105–6114, Long Beach, California, USA.

Soroush Vosoughi, Deb Roy, and Sinan Aral. 2018. The spread of true and false news online. *Science*, 359(6380):1146–1151.

Liang Wu, Fred Morstatter, Kathleen M. Carley, and Huan Liu. 2019. Misinformation in social media: Definition, manipulation, and detection. *SIGKDD Explor. Newsl.*, 21(2):8090.

Ruifeng Xu, Yu Zhou, Dongyin Wu, Lin Gui, Jiachen Du, and Yun Xue. 2016. Overview of NLPCC shared task 4: Stance detection in Chinese microblogs. In *Natural Language Understanding and Intelligent Applications*, pages 907–916, Cham.

Fei Yu, Jiji Tang, Weichong Yin, Yu Sun, Hao Tian, Hua Wu, and Haifeng Wang. 2021. ERNIE-ViL: Knowledge enhanced vision-language representations through scene graphs. *Proceedings of the AAAI Conference on Artificial Intelligence*, 35(4):3208–3216.

Nurulhuda Zainuddin, Ali Selamat, and Roliana Ibrahim. 2017. Twitter hate aspect extraction using association analysis and dictionary-based approach. In *New Trends in Intelligent Software Methodologies, Tools and Techniques - Proceedings of the 16th International Conference (SoMeT'17)*, volume 297 of *Frontiers in Artificial Intelligence and Applications*, pages 641–651, Kitakyushu City, Japan.

Nurulhuda Zainuddin, Ali Selamat, and Roliana Ibrahim. 2018. Evaluating aspect-based sentiment classification on Twitter hate speech using neural networks and word embedding features. In *New Trends in Intelligent Software Methodologies, Tools and Techniques*, pages 723–734.

Nurulhuda Zainuddin, Ali Selamat, and Roliana Ibrahim. 2019. Hate crime on Twitter: Aspect-based sentiment analysis approach. In *Advancing Technology Industrialization Through Intelligent Software Methodologies, Tools and Techniques*, pages 284–297.

Marcos Zampieri, Shervin Malmasi, Preslav Nakov, Sara Rosenthal, Noura Farra, and Ritesh Kumar. 2019a. Predicting the type and target of offensive posts in social media. In *Proceedings of the 17th Annual Conference of the North American Chapter of the Association for Computational Linguistics: Human Language Technologies*, NAACL-HLT '19, pages 1415–1420, Minneapolis, MN, USA.

Marcos Zampieri, Shervin Malmasi, Preslav Nakov, Sara Rosenthal, Noura Farra, and Ritesh Kumar. 2019b. SemEval-2019 task 6: Identifying and categorizing offensive language in social media (OffensEval). In *Proceedings of the International Workshop on Semantic Evaluation*, SemEval '19, pages 75–86, Minneapolis, MN, USA.

Marcos Zampieri, Preslav Nakov, Sara Rosenthal, Pepa Atanasova, Georgi Karadzhov, Hamdy Mubarak, Leon Derczynski, Zeses Pitenis, and Çağrı Çöltekin. 2020. SemEval-2020 task 12: Multilingual offensive language identification in social media (OffensEval 2020). In *Proceedings of the Fourteenth Workshop on Semantic Evaluation*, pages 1425–1447.

Savvas Zannettou, Tristan Caulfield, Jeremy Blackburn, Emiliano De Cristofaro, Michael Sirivianos, Gianluca Stringhini, and Guillermo Suarez-Tangil. 2018. On the origins of memes by means of fringe web communities. In *Proceedings of the Internet Measurement Conference 2018*, IMC '18, page 188202, New York, NY, USA.

Mike Zhang, Roy David, Leon Graumans, and Gerben Timmerman. 2019. Grunn2019 at SemEval-2019 task 5: Shared task on multilingual detection of hate. In *Proceedings of the 13th International Workshop on Semantic Evaluation*, pages 391–395, Minneapolis, Minnesota, USA.

Yi Zhou, Zhenhao Chen, and Huiyuan Yang. 2021. Multimodal learning for hateful memes detection. In *Proceedings of the International Conference on Multimedia Expo Workshops*, ICMEW '21, pages 1–6.

Ziming Zhou, Han Zhao, Jingjing Dong, Jun Gao, and Xiaolong Liu. 2022. DD-TIG at Constraint@ACL2022: Multimodal understanding and reasoning for role labeling of entities in hateful memes. In *Proceedings of the Workshop on Combating Online Hostile Posts in Regional Languages during Emergency Situations*, CONSTRAINT '22, Dublin, Ireland.

Sulafa Zidani and Rachel Moran. 2021. Memes and the spread of misinformation: Establishing the importance of media literacy in the era of information disorder. *Teaching Media Quarterly*, 9(1).

DD-TIG at Constraint@ACL2022: Multimodal Understanding and Reasoning for Role Labeling of Entities in Hateful Memes

Ziming Zhou[2], Han Zhao[1], Jingjing Dong[2], Jun Gao[1], Xiaolong Liu[1]
[1]DD-TIG
[2]Peking University
{zhaohan,gaojun_i,xlongliu}@didiglobal.com
{zhouziming,djj}@stu.pku.edu.cn

Abstract

The memes serve as an important tool in online communication, whereas some hateful memes endanger cyberspace by attacking certain people or subjects. Recent studies address hateful memes detection while further understanding of relationships of entities in memes remains unexplored. This paper presents our work at the Constraint@ACL2022 Shared Task: Hero, Villain and Victim: Dissecting harmful memes for semantic role labelling of entities. In particular, we propose our approach utilizing transformer-based multimodal models through a visual commonsense reasoning (VCR) method with data augmentation, continual pretraining, loss re-weighting, and ensemble learning. We describe the models used, the ways of preprocessing and experiments implementation. As a result, our best model achieves the Macro F1-score of 54.707 on the test set of this shared task[1].

1 Introduction

Memes are getting popular as a communication tool on social media platforms for expressions of opinions and emotions, conveying a subtle message through multimodal information from both images and texts. However, memes are increasingly abused to spread hate instigate social unrest and therefore seem to be a new form of expression of hate speech on online platforms (Bhattacharya, 2019).

Automatic hateful memes detection is difficult since it primarily requires context and external knowledge to understand online speech, which sometimes can be very short and contains nuanced meaning (Pramanick et al., 2021). A new type of challenging task has been introduced by The Hateful Memes Challenge (Kiela et al., 2020) proposed by Facebook AI to leverage machine learning models to address hateful memes detection problems, which can only be solved by joint reasoning and understanding of visual and textual information (Zhu, 2020).

In previous studies, researchers focus on binary classification problems, labelling a meme as hateful or non-hateful based on image and text features (Afridi et al., 2020). Moreover, the relationships of entities in memes remain unexplored, and the task of role labelling of entities in hateful memes can be more sophisticated.

The Constraint@ACL2022 Shared Task: Hero, Villain and Victim: Dissecting harmful memes for semantic role labelling of entities offers us a perspective on this issue (Sharma et al., 2022). This task aims to promote the detection and classification of glorified, vilified or victimized entities within a meme. The shared dataset concerns memes from US Politics domains and Covid-19. Covid-19-related online hostile content especially demands to be detected as early as possible after their appearance on social media.

In this paper, we present our work on this task. Specifically, mainstream multimodal models of transformer-based architecture are applied through a visual commonsense reasoning (VCR) method, with the leverage of continual pretraining to fit models with our dataset. Then, data augmentation and loss re-weighting are implemented to improve the performance of models. The predictions from variant models are combined in a machine learning method to produce final results.

2 Related Work

Hateful memes understanding and reasoning is a vision and language task. Current state-of-the-art Vision-Language machine learning models are based on the transformer architecture (Vaswani et al., 2017). Multimodal models learn the joint visual and textual representations through self-supervised learning that utilize large-scale unlabelled data to conduct auxiliary tasks (Chen et al., 2022), including masked language modelling based

[1]https://github.com/zjl123001/DD-TIG-Constraint

Proceedings of the Workshop on Combating Online Hostile Posts in Regional Languages during Emergency Situations, pages 12 - 18
May 27, 2022 ©2022 Association for Computational Linguistics

on randomly-masked sub-words, masked region prediction and image-text matching. Among these models, there are two prevalent approaches: single-stream and dual-stream (Du et al., 2022).

In single-stream architecture, the representations of two modalities are learned by a single transformer encoder. Particularly, the text embeddings $L = \{w_1, w_2, w_3, \cdots, w_l\}$ and image features $V = \{o_1, o_2, o_3, \cdots, o_k\}$ are concatenated together as $X = \{L \parallel V\}$, added some special embeddings to indicate position and modalities, and fed into a transformer-based encoder.

There are many implementations in single-stream models, such as VisualBERT (Li et al., 2019), UNITER (Chen et al., 2020), OSCAR (Li et al., 2020).

In dual-stream models, the image and text features are first sent to two independent encoders. Then two features are separately fed into cross-modal transformer layers, where the query vectors are from one modality while the key and value vectors are from another. They are responsible for exchanging the information and aligning the semantics between the two modalities L and V. The formula of cross-modal transformer layers is represented as follows.

$$L_i^m = CrossAtt_{L-V}(L_i^{m-1}, \{V_1^{m-1}, \cdots, V_k^{m-1}\}) \quad (1)$$

$$V_i^m = CrossAtt_{V-L}(V_i^{m-1}, \{L_1^{m-1}, \cdots, L_l^{m-1}\}) \quad (2)$$

where m is the mth cross-attention layer, k is the number of visual tokens, and l is the length of text tokens.

Following each cross-attention layer, there is also a layer computing the self-attention of each modality independently. Features are combined at the end of the model.

Several dual-stream models have been proposed in former studies, such as LXMERT (Tan and Bansal, 2019), ERNIE-Vil (Yu et al., 2020), DeVLBERT (Zhang et al., 2020), VilBERT (Lu et al., 2019),

3 Task Definition

Given the image and transcribed text of a meme, the role of a certain entity in this meme will be determined as hero, villain, victim or other, which can be interpreted as a multi-class classification task.

- **Input:** a meme image V, text transcriptions L, a entity E
- **Output:** $y \in \{hero, villain, victim, other\}$

The official evaluation measure for the shared task is the macro-F1 score for the multi-class classification.

4 Data Composition

The dataset provided in this task is a combination of memes from Covid-19 and US Politics domain. Every sample in the train and validation set contains an image, a transcription of texts and a list of entities with annotated labels. The shared task organizers provide the definitions for each class [2]:

- **Hero:** the entity is presented in a positive light, glorified for its actions.
- **Villain:** the entity is portrayed negatively, e.g., in an association with adverse traits like wickedness, cruelty, hypocrisy, etc.
- **Victim:** the entity is portrayed as suffering the negative impact of someone else's actions or conveyed implicitly within the meme.
- **Other:** the entity is not a hero, a villain, or a victim.

We present the distribution of entities' roles in Table 1.

	Covid-19			
	Hero	**Villain**	**Victim**	**Other**
Train	190	662	360	6022
Val	20	81	48	674
Test	21	124	58	1087
	US Politics			
	Hero	**Villain**	**Victim**	**Other**
Train	285	1765	550	7680
Val	34	224	73	915
Test	31	226	56	830

Table 1: Numbers of sample for each role label in Covid-19 and US Politics domain

There is a considerable imbalance in the distribution of entities' roles where the "other" class accounts for more than 80 percent of the whole

[2] https://codalab.lisn.upsaclay.fr/competitions/906

dataset. Meanwhile, the distribution of entities' frequency also shows a disparity. We present some most frequent entities with their roles distribution in Figure 1.

	Hero	Villiain	Victim	Other
donald trump	47	560	68	708
coronavirus	3	68	12	661
joe biden	22	183	17	587
barack obama	39	90	28	438
mask	-	-	-	326
work from home	-	-	-	272
2020	-	35	-	167
democratic party	-	161	24	115

Figure 1: Roles distribution of most frequent entities

5 System Descriptions

5.1 Preparation

For visual feature preprocessing, we use the pretrained Mask-RCNN model provided in the detectron2 framework[3] to obtain the object detection based region feature embedding $V = [o_1, o_2, \cdots, o_k]$ of images. Detectron2 is proposed by Facebook AI with state-of-the-art detection and segmentation algorithms. Specifically, 50 boxes of 2048 dimensions region-based image features are extracted for every meme. For the text transcriptions, we make the content lower-case and remove punctuation and stopwords with NLTK library (Loper and Bird, 2002).

5.2 Vision and Language Models

Four mainstream multimodal models of VL transformer architectures are applied in this work, namely: VisualBERT, UNITER, OSCAR, and ERNIE-Vil.

VisualBERT (Li et al., 2019), known as the first image-text pre-training model, uses the visual features extracted by Faster R-CNN, concatenates the visual features and textual embeddings, and then feeds the concatenated features to a single transformer initialled by BERT.

UNITER (Chen et al., 2020) learns contextualized joint representation of both visual and textual modalities through local alignment in the reconstruction of masked tokens/regions across modalities, powering heterogeneous downstream V+L tasks with joint multimodal embeddings.

OSCAR (Li et al., 2020), instead of simply using image-text pair, adds object tags detected from the image and represent the image-text pair as a <Word, Tag, Image> triple to help the fusion encoder better align different modalities.

ERNIE-Vil (Yu et al., 2020), as a typical dual-stream model, enhances the model with the application of scene utilizing scene graphs of visual scenes, which can learn the joint representations characterizing the alignments of the detailed semantics across vision and language.

For domain adaptation, we carry out continual pretraining on our dataset to reduce the distribution gap between the pretraining dataset and our memes dataset. Masked Language Modeling (MLM) pretraining task is taken on pretraining VisualBERT-large, UNITER-large, and OSCAR-large model.

5.3 VCR Implementation

Visual Commonsense Reasoning (VCR) focuses on a higher-order cognitive and commonsense understanding of relationships of the visual components in the image (Zellers et al., 2019). Former studies take a question, answer choices and an image into models to predict the right answer as a multi-class classification problem (Su et al., 2019). We modify this method's input and output format to conduct our experiments.

As can be seen in Figure 2, we concatenate the given entity and text tokens as the textual input with a separate token $[SEP]$, while different segment embedding will be added respectively to indicate their states. Then, textual input and visual will be concatenated in the single-stream model like VisualBERT. They would be separately sent into encoders in the dual-stream model like ERNIE-Vil. In the single-stream model, the final output feature of $[CLS]$ element is taken. In the dual-stream model, textual and visual features are fused through sum or multiplication. Then, features are fed to a linear layer with softmax to predict the role of the given entity.

The final objective is to minimize the cross-entropy (CE) loss between the predicted distribution and the targeted role category, which can be formally defined as:

[3]https://github.com/facebookresearch/detectron2

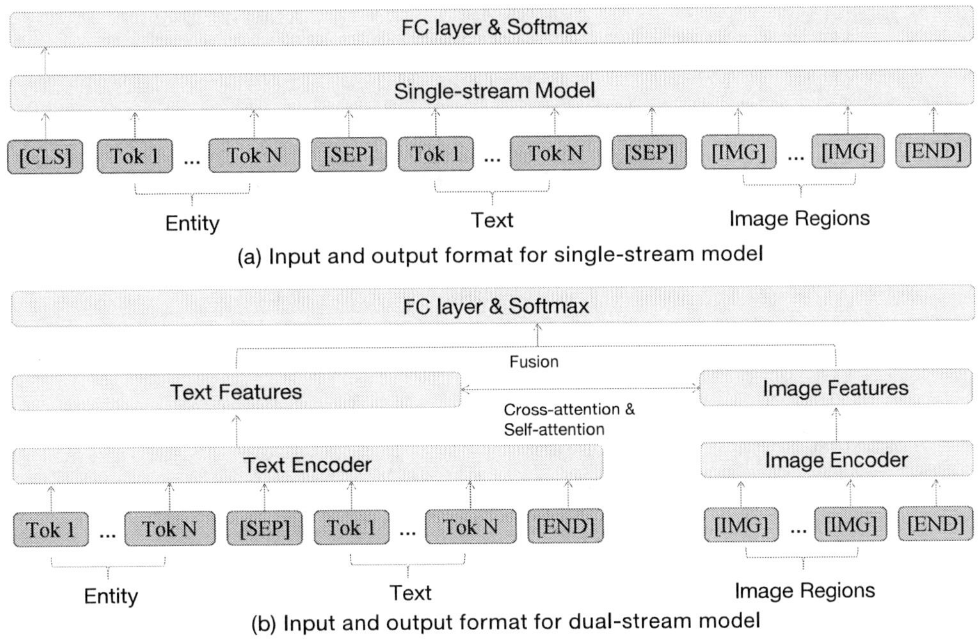

Figure 2: The input and output format of our system

$$p(x) = \frac{exp(g(x)_i)}{\sum_{j=1}^{N} exp(g(x)_j)} \quad (3)$$

$$L = -\sum logp(x) \cdot y \quad (4)$$

where $g(x)$ is the output of the FC layer and N is the number of labels.

5.4 Loss Re-weighting

A loss re-weighting strategy has been applied in our experiment since the "other" class accounts for the overwhelming majority of entries in samples, while hero, villain, and victim roles shall be stressed. Thus, our new loss function is defined as follows:

$$L = -\sum \alpha \cdot \log p(x) \quad (5)$$

$$\alpha = \begin{cases} \alpha_{neg} & y = other \\ \alpha_{pos} & else \end{cases} \quad (6)$$

where α_{neg} and α_{pos} are the weights for the "other" role and "non-other" role respectively as $\alpha_{neg} < \alpha_{pos}$ and $\alpha_{neg} + \alpha_{pos} = 1$.

5.5 Data Augmentation

We adopt the data augmentation with the back-translation strategy. Specifically, the provided text of each meme is paraphrased with Baidu translation API: English-Chinese-English and English-French-English. Diverse sentences are produced for each meme to enrich our dataset.

5.6 Ensemble Learning

We train these four base models with different seeds to produce a total of 16 models. The predicted scores on validation set are generated by all models. Then, a SVM model is trained with the predictions and true labels. In the testing phase, the predictions on the test set are fed into the trained SVM model to make final ensemble predictions.

5.7 Experimental Setting

For continual pretraining on VisualBERT, OSCAR, and UNITER, each word in the text transcriptions is randomly masked at a probability of 15 percent. The final output feature corresponding to the masked word is fed into a classifier over the whole vocabulary, driven by softmax cross-entropy loss.

We finetune all models with a focal loss (Lin et al., 2017) and a batch size of 16. The max sequence length is set at 256. The Adam optimizer is used with a learning rate of 1e-5 and 10 percent linear warm-up steps. VisualBERT, OSCAR, and UNITER are trained for 10 epochs and ERNIE-Vil models are trained for 10000 steps. The weights with the best scores on the validation set are saved and used for inference on the test set.

Source	Model	Macro F1-score
Original model	VisualBERT-large	47.8
	UNITER-large	48.8
	OSCAR-large	48.5
	ERNIE-Vil-large	50.9
Continual pretrained model	VisualBERT-large	48.2
	UNITER-large	49.9
	OSCAR-large	49.2
	Ensemble	**54.7**

Table 2: Results of models in our systems

6 Results and Discussion

In Table 2, we present the results of our experiments in a step by step manner. We started with finetuning base models provided by original authors. Then, VisualBERT-large, UNITER-large, and OSCAR-large models are pretrained on our dataset with MLM task and finetuned on our task. After that, ensemble learning is implemented to combine results of various models. We evaluate our models using official metrics Macro F1-score on test set.

ERNIE-Vil has been the SoTA model on the multimodal task leaderboard and in this task it also achieves competitive performance at 50.9 on the test set without further continual pretraining, which outperforms all the single-stream models by over 2 in Macro F1-score. We consider that through incorporating structured knowledge obtained from scene graphs during cross-modal pretraining, ERNIE-Vil learns more knowledge which benefits the downstream task.

Meanwhile, VisualBERT-large, UNITER-large, and OSCAR-large models shows improvements in performance through continual pretraining, which can be interpreted as domain adaptation on our dataset.

Ensemble learning remarkably raises our score by 3.5 than the best single model, which achieves the best score for our submission in this task.

6.1 Error Analysis

A classification report is presented in table 3, which allows us to do further assessments on our system.

Our system has a relatively poor performance on the class Hero. On the one hand, we interpret it as a lack of sample of this class in the training set. It is insufficient for our model to learn the features of this class. On the other hand, through observing bad cases, we find some memes need considerable external knowledge about history and politics, which can even be challenging for human beings to comprehend and do classification.

	precision	recall	f1-score	support
Hero	0.31	0.33	0.32	52
Villain	0.55	0.50	0.52	350
Victim	0.44	0.41	0.43	114
Other	0.88	0.89	0.89	1917
Macro-avg	0.54	0.53	0.54	2433

Table 3: An classification report for our final submission

6.2 Future Directions

In our experiment, we use an End2End solution to do roles classification, concatenating the entity with input sequence as a <entity, text, image> triplet. However, we do not directly point out the entity's corresponding region in the image. Some other researchers (Li et al., 2020) have discussed this problem: it is naturally weakly-supervised learning since there are no explicitly labelled alignments between regions or objects in an image and words or phrases in the text. We hypothesize that our model can not align some unusual entities correctly with its image and text. Moreover, comprehending a meme in the political domain heavily relies on knowledge, while the size of the whole dataset is relatively small, so our continual pretraining on a task-specific dataset is far from sufficient. There are two directions for further development of our system on this issue. On the one hand, more in-domain data can be incorporated to enlarge the dataset. On the other hand, knowledge-based models or external knowledge sources can be introduced to help the model understand the background and reason the relations of entities.

7 Conclusion

In this paper, we have exploited a VCR approach to tackle the role labelling of entities in hateful memes, which is a novel task in multimodal understanding and reasoning. Four popular transformer-based multimodal models, VisualBERT, UNITER, OSCAR, and ERNIE-Vil are applied as base models while strategies like loss re-weighting and data augmentation are implemented during the training of models. Then, continual pretraining is taken for domain adaptation and achieves better performance. Ensemble learning of variant models achieves the impressive Macro F1-score of 0.5470 on the final (unseen) test set.

References

Tariq Habib Afridi, Aftab Alam, Muhammad Numan Khan, Jawad Khan, and Young-Koo Lee. 2020. A multimodal memes classification: A survey and open research issues. In *The Proceedings of the Third International Conference on Smart City Applications*, pages 1451–1466. Springer.

Prithvi Bhattacharya. 2019. Social degeneration through social media: A study of the adverse impact of 'memes'. In *2019 Sixth HCT Information Technology Trends (ITT)*, pages 44–46. IEEE.

Feilong Chen, Duzhen Zhang, Minglun Han, Xiuyi Chen, Jing Shi, Shuang Xu, and Bo Xu. 2022. Vlp: A survey on vision-language pre-training. *arXiv preprint arXiv:2202.09061*.

Yen-Chun Chen, Linjie Li, Licheng Yu, Ahmed El Kholy, Faisal Ahmed, Zhe Gan, Yu Cheng, and Jingjing Liu. 2020. Uniter: Universal image-text representation learning. In *European conference on computer vision*, pages 104–120. Springer.

Yifan Du, Zikang Liu, Junyi Li, and Wayne Xin Zhao. 2022. A survey of vision-language pre-trained models. *arXiv preprint arXiv:2202.10936*.

Douwe Kiela, Hamed Firooz, Aravind Mohan, Vedanuj Goswami, Amanpreet Singh, Pratik Ringshia, and Davide Testuggine. 2020. The hateful memes challenge: Detecting hate speech in multimodal memes. *Advances in Neural Information Processing Systems*, 33:2611–2624.

Liunian Harold Li, Mark Yatskar, Da Yin, Cho-Jui Hsieh, and Kai-Wei Chang. 2019. Visualbert: A simple and performant baseline for vision and language. *arXiv preprint arXiv:1908.03557*.

Xiujun Li, Xi Yin, Chunyuan Li, Pengchuan Zhang, Xiaowei Hu, Lei Zhang, Lijuan Wang, Houdong Hu, Li Dong, Furu Wei, et al. 2020. Oscar: Object-semantics aligned pre-training for vision-language tasks. In *European Conference on Computer Vision*, pages 121–137. Springer.

Tsung-Yi Lin, Priya Goyal, Ross Girshick, Kaiming He, and Piotr Dollár. 2017. Focal loss for dense object detection. In *Proceedings of the IEEE international conference on computer vision*, pages 2980–2988.

Edward Loper and Steven Bird. 2002. Nltk: The natural language toolkit. *arXiv preprint cs/0205028*.

Jiasen Lu, Dhruv Batra, Devi Parikh, and Stefan Lee. 2019. Vilbert: Pretraining task-agnostic visiolinguistic representations for vision-and-language tasks. *Advances in neural information processing systems*, 32.

Shraman Pramanick, Dimitar Dimitrov, Rituparna Mukherjee, Shivam Sharma, Md Akhtar, Preslav Nakov, Tanmoy Chakraborty, et al. 2021. Detecting harmful memes and their targets. *arXiv preprint arXiv:2110.00413*.

Shivam Sharma, Tharun Suresh, Atharva Jitendra, Himanshi Mathur, Preslav Nakov, Md. Shad Akhtar, and Tanmoy Chakraborty. 2022. Findings of the constraint 2022 shared task on detecting the hero, the villain, and the victim in memes. In *Proceedings of the Workshop on Combating Online Hostile Posts in Regional Languages during Emergency Situations - CONSTRAINT 2022, Collocated with ACL 2022*.

Weijie Su, Xizhou Zhu, Yue Cao, Bin Li, Lewei Lu, Furu Wei, and Jifeng Dai. 2019. Vl-bert: Pre-training of generic visual-linguistic representations. *arXiv preprint arXiv:1908.08530*.

Hao Tan and Mohit Bansal. 2019. Lxmert: Learning cross-modality encoder representations from transformers. *arXiv preprint arXiv:1908.07490*.

Ashish Vaswani, Noam Shazeer, Niki Parmar, Jakob Uszkoreit, Llion Jones, Aidan N Gomez, Łukasz Kaiser, and Illia Polosukhin. 2017. Attention is all you need. *Advances in neural information processing systems*, 30.

Fei Yu, Jiji Tang, Weichong Yin, Yu Sun, Hao Tian, Hua Wu, and Haifeng Wang. 2020. Ernie-vil: Knowledge enhanced vision-language representations through scene graph. *arXiv preprint arXiv:2006.16934*.

Rowan Zellers, Yonatan Bisk, Ali Farhadi, and Yejin Choi. 2019. From recognition to cognition: Visual commonsense reasoning. In *Proceedings of the IEEE/CVF conference on computer vision and pattern recognition*, pages 6720–6731.

Shengyu Zhang, Tan Jiang, Tan Wang, Kun Kuang, Zhou Zhao, Jianke Zhu, Jin Yu, Hongxia Yang, and Fei Wu. 2020. Devlbert: Learning deconfounded visio-linguistic representations. In *Proceedings of the 28th ACM International Conference on Multimedia*, pages 4373–4382.

Ron Zhu. 2020. Enhance multimodal transformer with external label and in-domain pretrain: Hateful meme challenge winning solution. *arXiv preprint arXiv:2012.08290.*

Are you a hero or a villain? A semantic role labelling approach for detecting harmful memes

Shaik Fharook and **Syed Sufyan Ahmed** and **Gurram Rithika**
Sumith Sai Budde and **Sunil Saumya** and **Shankar Biradar**
Department of Computer Science and Engineering
Indian Institute of Information Technology
Dharwad, Karnatka, India
(fharookshaik.5@gmail.com)@iiitdwd.ac.in

Abstract

Identifying good and evil through representations of victimhood, heroism, and villainy (i.e., role labeling of entities) has recently caught the research community's interest. Because of the growing popularity of memes, the amount of offensive information published on the internet is expanding at an alarming rate. It generated a larger need to address this issue and analyze the memes for content moderation. Framing is used to show the entities engaged as heroes, villains, victims, or others so that readers may better anticipate and understand their attitudes and behaviors as characters. Positive phrases are used to characterize heroes, whereas negative terms depict victims and villains, and terms that tend to be neutral are mapped to others. In this paper, we propose two approaches to role label the entities of the meme as hero, villain, victim, or other through Named-Entity Recognition(NER), Sentiment Analysis, etc. With an F1-score of **23.855**, our team secured **eighth** position in the **Shared Task @ Constraint 2022**.

1 Introduction

The availability of smartphones and the internet has caught the interest of today's youth in social media. These applications provide a large platform for users to communicate with the outside world and share their thoughts and opinions. With these advantages comes a disadvantage: many people exploit the platform to spread offensive content on social media under the guise of freedom of expression (Boon, 2017). This incendiary material is usually directed towards a single person, a small group of people, a religious group, or a community. People create offensive content and aggressively spread it over social media (P. Fortuna, 2018; T. Davidson, 2017). For many purposes, including commercial and political benefit, this type of information is created (Jeff Goodwin and Polletta, 2009; Biradar et al., 2022). This type of communication can disturb societal harmony and spark riots. It also has the ability to have a negative psychological impact on readers. It has the potential to harm people's emotions and behavior (Stieglitz and Dang-Xuan, 2013; Biradar et al., 2021). As a result, identifying such content is crucial. Further, researchers, politicians, and investors are working to build a reliable method for dissecting the dangerous memes present over the internet.

Framing allows a communication source to portray and describe a problem within a "field of meaning" by employing conventional narrative patterns and cultural references (Scheufele, 1999). By connecting with readers' existing knowledge, cultural narratives, and moral standards, framing helps to construct events (Green). It can portray the characters in a story as heroes, villains, or victims, making it easier for the audience to anticipate and comprehend their attitudes, beliefs, decisions, and actions. Narrative frames can be found in various media, including memes, films, literature, and the news. Narrators use emotionality to plainly distinguish between good and evil through vivid descriptions of victimization, heroism, and villainy, which is a major feature of the popular storytelling culture (Diego Gomez-Zara, 2018). Positive adjectives are used to portray heroes, whereas negative terms depict victims and villains. In popular culture, heroes represent bravery, great accomplishments, or other noble attributes, whereas villains represent malicious intents, conspiring, and other undesirable characteristics (Diego Gomez-Zara, 2018). To summarise, narrative frames are essential for understanding new situations in terms of prior ones and therefore making sense of the causes, events, and consequences.

The standard method for detecting frames of the narrative is by examining the semantic relationships between the various elements in the meme about the events it portrays. Understanding the events in a narrative and the roles that the entities

Proceedings of the Workshop on Combating Online Hostile Posts in Regional Languages during Emergency Situations, pages 19 - 23
May 27, 2022 ©2022 Association for Computational Linguistics

in that meme play in those events, on the other hand, is a complex, tough, and computationally expensive task.

Thus, rather than determining all of the specific events and event types described in the meme, as well as the semantic relationships among the entities involved in those events in great detail, we propose methodologies in which the entities are analyzed at a much higher level of abstraction, specifically in terms of whether they hold the qualities of heroes, victims, villains, or none as conveyed by the terms used to characterize them. As a result, we arrive at a rather basic realization. The terms nearest to each entity are evaluated for their sentiment polarity or closeness to associated terms with heroes, villains, or victims.

2 Literature review

The topic of entity role detection from narrative has recently piqued the interest of several corporate and academic researchers in recent times. However, there were just a few efforts to extract knowledge and present it from newspaper articles that especially utilized the newspaper article bodies to derive meaning, focusing on the headline (Boon, 2017; Dor, 2003; Diego Gomez-Zara, 2018). But there have been hardly any attempts to identify the entities that had been exalted, demonized, or victimized (Melodrama and of Communication, 2005). Instead, studies were conducted to see how satire delivered through the means of internet memes affects brand image (Christopher Kontio). However, no existing approach has been able to handle harmful content identification in multimodal data employing the role labeling notion. In this paper, the emphasis is on detecting which entities are vilified, glorified or victimized in a meme by assuming the frame of reference from the meme author's perspective (Sharma et al., 2022).

3 Task and Dataset description

3.1 Task

As noted in the competition's problem statement, the focus is on recognizing whether entities are glorified, condemned, or victimized within a meme by assuming the meme author's frame of reference[1].

Given a meme and an entity, the task is to determine the role of each entity detected in the meme as hero or villain or victim or other. The constraint here is that the meme has to be analyzed from the perspective of the author of the meme (Sharma et al., 2022).

3.2 Dataset description

The dataset for this task was provided by the organizers of the competition Shared Task @ Constraint 2022. This dataset is a collection of memes and their associated entities from two domains: Covid-19 and US Politics. It is organized into three parts: train, validation, and test set, respectively. Each item of the dataset from train and validation contains an image of the meme and its pre-extracted OCR with its entities mapped to Hero, Villain, Victim, and Other Categories. A sample item of the dataset can be seen in Figure 1.

Corresponding JSONL Text input

{
"OCR": "Bernie or Elizabeth? \n Be informed. Compare them on the issues that matter.\n Issue: Who makes the dankest memes?\n",
"image": "covid_memes_18.png",
"hero": [],
"villain": [],
"victim": [],
"other": ["bernie sanders", "elizabeth warren"]
}

Figure 1: Train/Validation Dataset sample

Each item of the test dataset contains an image of meme and its corresponding pre-extracted OCR and its entities. The total dataset contains 6920 items, and a detailed domain-wise distribution of train, validation, and test sets can be seen in Table 1.

4 Methodology

This study has proposed two submissions based on two different methods. In the first method, we perform entity recognition then sentiment analysis.

[1]`https://constraint-lcs2.github.io/`

	Train	Valid -ation	Test
Covid-19	2700	300	718 (Combined)
US Politics	2852	350	
Total	5552	650	718

Table 1: Data set Distribution

In the second method, we perform entity recognition and then use Wu-Palmer similarity (S. Bird, 2009) to calculate similarity scores of entities with each of the roles, i.e., hero, villain, victim, and other.

4.1 Data Processing

The following data processing steps were performed while creating an end-to-end system, i.e., given a meme image, the OCR text recognizes the entities present in that meme by performing entity recognition on the text. However, in the competition, as the entities are already recognized and given as an entity list, we can skip the entity recognition step here for the competition.

Then each entity is linked to its corresponding parts of the sentence (words surrounding the entity) present in the OCR text of that respective meme. Here a fair assumption was made that the words nearer to the entities weigh more than those farther from the entity in its role assignment. So first, we search for entity occurrence in the OCR sentences. Then using a window approach(i.e., selecting the n-words occurring before that entity and the n-words occurring after the entity), we create a sub-part of that sentence. By doing this on the whole OCR of that respective meme, we create a list of sub-sentences, one for each entity present in that particular meme as shown in Figure 2.

```
"memes_4576.png": {
    "nation": [
        "this great nation must bear the"
    ],
    "thomas paine": []
},
```

Figure 2: Entity sentence linking example

4.2 Methods and models

In this study, two different frameworks have been experimented for role detection. The description of the frameworks are discussed in the following subsections.

4.2.1 Framework-I

1. For each entity given in a particular meme, identify the words close(i.e., surrounding words) to these entities by linking the entity sentence.

2. Perform sentiment analysis to determine the polarity of these words, thus making out the sentiment attributed to the entity.

3. Use sentiment polarity to role label the entities, according to the proposed semantic classes.

After performing entity sentence linking, we determine the sentiment score of the words(sub-sentences) linked with an entity; we do this for all the entities mentioned in that particular meme. To do this, we calculate the sentiment(i.e., word polarity) for each word using a standard toolkit like VADER-Sentiment[2](as it has a huge vocabulary of the word polarities), thus getting a polarity for each word, which ranges between [-1, 1] (i.e., very-negative to very-positive). These sentiment-polarities are then summed up for each sentence. Finally, the sentiment-polarities for each sentence are normalized and then averaged to get an overall sentiment ascribed for the entity.

As we know, that hero is linked with positive words with positive sentiment. Similarly, victims and villains are linked with negative words with negative sentiments. If the words(sub-sentences) have no polarity, they don't glorify or vilify or victimize any entity thus semantically similar to the class "other" as described in Figure 3.

4.2.2 Framework-II

1. For each entity given in a particular meme, identify the words close(i.e., surrounding words) to these entities by linking the entity sentence.

2. Determine the resemblance of these words with the words used to describe heroes, villains, and victims by curating word sets or dictionaries for each role.

3. Role label the entities by analyzing their similarity scores with those of hero, villain, and victim. If the scores are zero or almost the same, role label it to "other" class.

[2]https://pypi.org/project/vaderSentiment/

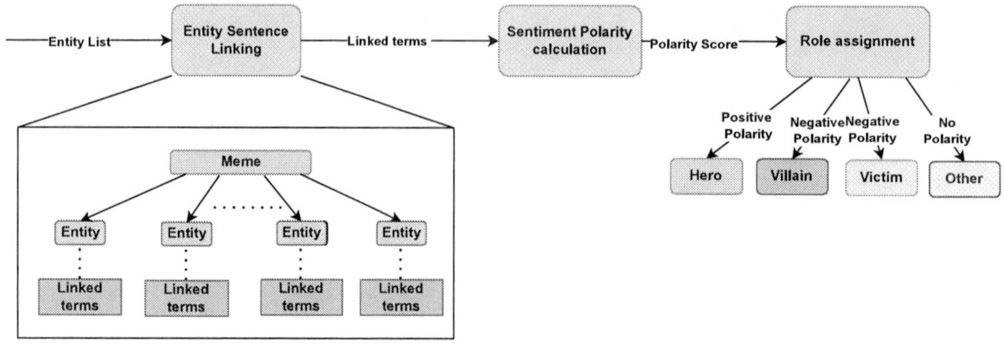

Figure 3: Framework-I architecture

After performing entity sentence linking, We create three dictionaries, one for each hero, villain, and victim containing the words or terms similar to them, respectively. Then by using a method like Wu-Palmer similarity[3] we calculate the similarity score of each word from the entity-sentence linking step with hero dictionary, villain dictionary, victim dictionary to create the similarity dictionary Figure 5. Then the similarity score for each entity is determined by summing the similarity scores of all the words found in the sub-sentences. Then it is normalized to get an overall similarity of a particular entity with the roles of hero, villain, victim, and others. We assign an entity to the role whose similarity score is the highest using these similarity scores. If the similarity scores with each of the roles are almost similar or zero, we assign it to the class "other" in the proposed role assignment approach as described in Figure 4. Implementation details of the proposed model are made publicly available [4]

5 Results

In the competition, teams were ranked based on macro F1-Score across all the classes. The suggested method and model secured the eighth position in the competition for the task of dissecting harmful memes for Semantic role-labeling of entities. Table 2 shows the rankings of various teams, and the performance of the proposed system is indicated in bold letters.

The model performs well in the role labeling task. However, in some cases, the model under performs in identifying the categories due to the difficulty in capturing some of the attributes or traits related to the roles. As a result, the overall systems' macro F1-score has been low at 23.855. In addition, the ensembling of multiple NLP sub-tasks also have contributed to the decrease of the F1-score of the system. The systems' performance can be further improved by modeling those NLP sub-tasks in the proposed methods using better parameters which could potentially increase the score.

SL. no	Username / Team Name	F1 Score
1	Shiroe	58.671
2	jayeshbanukoti	56.005
3	c1pher	55.240
4	zhouziming	54.707
5	smontariol	48.483
6	zjl123001	46.177
7	amanpriyanshu	31.943
8	**Team IIITDWD (fharookshaik)**	**23.855**
9	rabindra.nath	23.717

Table 2: Top performing teams in the Competition

6 Conclusion and future enhancement

The current system implementations use NLP techniques such as entity recognition, sentiment analysis, and word sets and dictionaries, all of which have shown promising results in the role labeling task. Across all classes, the existing system implementation produced a good F1 score. However, as the model is based on simple proximity measures, it has issues when dealing with OCR text that contains composite grammatical structures such as indirect speech, passive voice etc. In this experiment, the n-words window size used for data processing is n=3. As a result, there is potential

[3]https://arxiv.org/ftp/arxiv/papers/1310/1310.8059.pdf

[4]The source code for reproducing our work can be found at https://github.com/fharookshaik/shared-task_constraint-2022

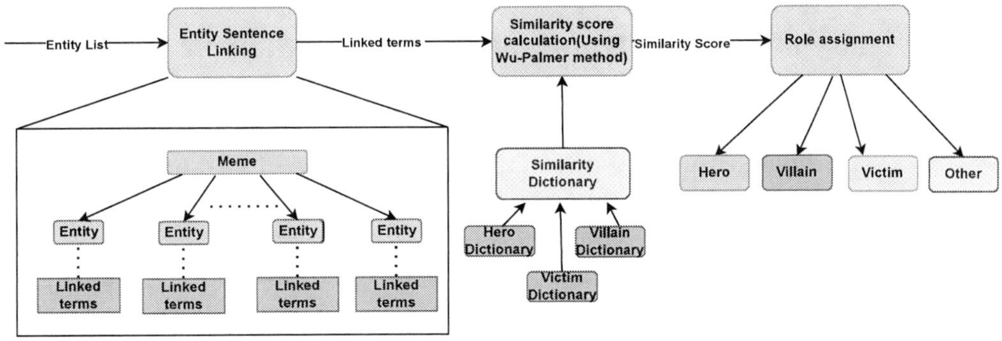

Figure 4: Framework-II architecture

```
"sentaient": [
    0,
    0,
    0
],
"inquire": [
    0.25236209659286585,
    0.2891268554312031,
    0.2690599133637109
],
```

Figure 5: Similarity Dictionary

for various future changes to increase the system's performance.

Further, in future experiments and add-ons, we plan to leverage some of the SOTA(State Of The Art) machine learning models such as SVM to discover distinct sentiment polarity boundaries for various sub-tasks to enhance the working of sub-tasks and thereby improving the system's role labeling performance.

References

Shankar Biradar, Sunil Saumya, and Arun Chauhan. 2021. Hate or non-hate: Translation based hate speech identification in code-mixed hinglish data set. In *2021 IEEE International Conference on Big Data (Big Data)*, pages 2470–2475. IEEE.

Shankar Biradar, Sunil Saumya, and Arun Chauhan. 2022. Combating the infodemic: Covid-19 induced fake news recognition in social media networks. *Complex & Intelligent Systems*, pages 1–13.

Miriam L. Boon. 2017. Augmenting media literacy with automatic characterization of news along pragmatic dimensions. *ACM Conference on Computer Supported Cooperative Work and Social Computing*.

Melker Pripp Viktor Magnusson Christopher Kontio, Klara Gradin. An exploration of satirical internet memes effect on brand image. *Linnaeus University*.

Larry Birnbaum Diego Gomez-Zara, Miriam Boon. 2018. Detection of roles in news articles using natural language techniques. *23rd International Conference on Intelligent User Interfaces*.

Daniel Dor. 2003. On newspaper headlines as relevance optimizers. *Journal of Pragmatics*.

Melanie C. Green. Transportation into narrative worlds: The role of prior knowledge and perceived realism. *Discourse processes*.

James M. Jasper Jeff Goodwin and Francesca Polletta. 2009. Passionate politics: Emotions and social movements. *University of Chicago Press*.

Melodrama and September 11. Journal of Communication. 2005. *Villains, victims and heroes: Melodrama, media, and September 11. Journal of Communication 55*.

S. Nunes P. Fortuna. 2018. A survey on automatic detection of hate speech in text. *ACM Computing Surveys (CSUR)*.

E. Loper S. Bird, E. Klein. 2009. Natural language processing with python: analyzing text with the natural language toolkit. *O'Reilly Media, Inc.*

Dietram A. Scheufele. 1999. Framing as a theory of media effects. *Journal of communication*.

Shivam Sharma, Tharun Suresh, Atharva Kulkarni, Himanshi Mathur, Preslav Nakov, Md. Shad Akhtar, and Tanmoy Chakraborty. 2022. Findings of the constraint 2022 shared task on detecting the hero, the villain, and the victim in memes. In *Proceedings of the Workshop on Combating Online Hostile Posts in Regional Languages during Emergency Situations - CONSTRAINT 2022, Collocated with ACL 2022*.

Stefan Stieglitz and Linh Dang-Xuan. 2013. Emotions and information diffusion in social media—sentiment of microblogs and sharing behavior. *Journal of management information systems*.

M. Macy I. Weber T. Davidson, D. Warmsley. 2017. Automated hate speech detection and the problem of offensive language. *Proceedings of the International AAAI Conference on Web and Social Media*.

Logically at the Constraint 2022: Multimodal role labelling

Ludovic Kun * , Jayesh Bankoti * , and **David Kiskovski**
Logically, London, UK

Abstract

This paper describes our system for the Constraint 2022 challenge at ACL 2022, whose goal is to detect which entities are glorified, vilified or victimised, within a meme . The task should be done considering the perspective of the meme's author. In our work, the challenge is treated as a multi-class classification task. For a given pair of a meme and an entity, we need to classify whether the entity is being referenced as Hero, a Villain, a Victim or Other. Our solution combines (ensembling) different models based on Unimodal (Text only) model and Multimodal model (Text + Images). We conduct several experiments and benchmarks different competitive pre-trained transformers and vision models in this work. Our solution, based on an ensembling method, is ranked first on the leaderboard and obtains a macro F1-score of 0.58 on test set. The code for the experiments and results are available at here .

1 Introduction

The rapid rise in the amount of harmful content being spread online is becoming a major societal challenge, with still unknown negative consequences. Large resources have been invested by many actors in the field of social media to shield users from harmful content. It is imperative to understand in a systematic way how information is spread, and be able to scalably monitor existing narratives and flag hateful ones circulating using technology. One way this is done is using entity recognition coupled with entity sentiment (Kiritchenko et al., 2021). The former technique is to support OSINT(open source intelligence) analysts in understanding who or what are the subjects of discussion, and the latter automates the process of analysing if they are coupled with positive or negative feelings, in order to assist with understanding the stance of online users on specific topics. Efforts to tackle this challenge were mainly focused on English-language text-based data formats such as articles (Wankhade et al., 2022). However, the complexity of content being posted online has drastically increased over time, and the challenge of harmful content detection now extends to multimedia, including memes (Alam et al., 2021). The emergence and proliferation of memes on social media have made their analysis a crucial challenge to understand online interactions. A point can also be made about the study of entities sentiment online, as the polarising portrayal of famous (or infamous) personalities or institutions often give rise to inflammatory views and content.

Extracting insights from memes is a novel field and still has a lot of opportunities for growth. The multimodality of text and image adds a layer of complexity which contains more information, but is also harder to extract. Indeed each modality needs to understand their intrinsic properties but also capture cross-modal semantic understanding (Müller-Budack et al., 2021). This paper delves into the field of multimodal semantic role labelling, a new task with particular challenges.

Examples of the multimodal dataset (Sharma et al., 2022) used to tackle this problem and provided as part of the CONSTRAINT competition are presented in Figure 1. The first sample shows a meme image displaying two politicians from opposite parties separated on two sides of the image, with text around them, as well as the associated JSON line input with the extracted text from the image (also known as Optical Character Recognition or OCR), as well as the entities' mentioned labelled roles. In this case, all entities are referenced in the text of the image. In the second sample, however, we notice that not all are mentioned in the text, and visual information is needed to classify all entities.

Depending on the textual information in the image, textual role classification is insufficient as some memes' underlying message requires under-

Proceedings of the Workshop on Combating Online Hostile Posts in Regional Languages during Emergency Situations, pages 24 - 34
May 27, 2022 ©2022 Association for Computational Linguistics

```
{
'image' : memes_1486.png',
'OCR': "AAE RNC\nCONVENTION 2020:\nHOPE AND\nPOSITIVITY\nDNC CONVENTION 2020:\nDOOM
AND GLOOM\n",
'hero' : ['Donald Trump'],
'villain' : ['Joe Biden'],
'victim' : [],
'other' : ['Democratic National Convention (DNC)', 'Republican National Convention
(RNC)']
}
```


Figure 1: CONSTRAINT dataset example

standing of the visual information it contains, especially with the use of humour and sarcasm often associated with the format.
The work done in this competition aims at finding unique and effective ways of tackling harmful meme classification as seen in the current social media space. An algorithm is designed for the task of role labelling for memes using a twin model (and ensemble) method. This Siamese network is constructed by combining the output of pre-trained State-of-the-Art (SoTA) models for both the visual components in the form of a CNN (Efficientnet-B7 (Tan and Le, 2019)) and for textual components using a transformer (DeBERTa (He et al., 2020)). The feature outputs obtained from both branches are then combined to obtain a final solution. Data analysis and investigation into potential bias in the dataset are also conducted to contextualise the task and present the difficulties of curating accurate multimodal datasets aimed at tackling the task for data in the wild (Gao et al., 2021). In this paper, an overview of past work in the field is presented (section 2), followed by a deep dive into the problem statement as well as the method followed to respond to it (section 3), then data analysis (section 4). Experiments ran are presented in section 5, with results and discussion in section 6, and finally conclusion (section 7).

2 Related Work

There have been some work done with respect to semantic role labelling in text. The idea of ABSA(Aspect Based Sentiment Analysis) works along the same line. Hence, utilisation of DeBERTa has provided the SoTA results (Silva and Marcacini) due to the disentangled attention improving the focus more on the positional embeddings rather than just based on the word embeddings. Hence, improved results were also obtained in various SNLI task for this algorithm(He et al., 2020).They are nowadays very popular in Natural Language Processing (NLP) as they usually get SoTA for a variety of NLP tasks such as classification, sentiment analysis, Named Entity Recognition, Translation, Question Answering, etc.

Classifying memes into relevant classes is a field that has got much more interest over the past few years. The Facebook Hateful meme competition(Kiela et al., 2020) was a very publicised initiative to try and augment the field's capabilities. The task was a binary classification of hateful/not hateful meme based on a dataset curated by META. The winning solutions all comprised of ensembles of multimodal models. The Memotion competitions(Sharma et al., 2020) are another example of work done in the meme space. This time, the classification was based on sentiment (positive, negative, neutral), as well as the strength of the sentiment and the underlying aim of the meme (satirical, humour or harmful). Multimodal models here also obtained the top scores.

Multimodal models have seen a change over the past few years from twin networks like Siamese (Gu et al., 2018) to models pretrained on multiple multimodal tasks such as image captioning and visual question answering using transformers (Devlin et al., 2018). Object detection is used in these models to extract image features thanks to pre-trained two-staged detectors Faster R-CNN model (Ren et al., 2015)), or single-stage detectors (YOLO V3 (Adarsh et al., 2020)). Inspired by BERT (Devlin et al., 2018), models such as Uniter (Chen et al., 2019) and VisualBERT (Li et al., 2019b) use a transformer architecture to jointly encode text and images, while LXMERT (Tan and Bansal, 2019) and ViLBERT (Lu et al., 2019) innovated by splitting their architectures in two, where a different transformer is applied to images and text individually before the features are combined by a third transformer. OSCAR (Object-Semantics Aligned

Pre-training)((Li et al., 2020)) add in the text input the class objects detected from the images by a Faster R-CNN detector called object tags. The use of object tags in images as anchor points, significantly ease the learning of alignments during the pretraining. These models' effectiveness are demonstrated through their SoTA results on different multimodal dataset tasks such as NLVR2. This can be attributed to the models' increased capability to understand cross-modal correlations. However, these models are only as good as the data they've been pretrained on, which will present a challenge for the use case of the competition tackled in this paper. Another point is that the architectures of the textual streams of these models are a few years old (such as BERT) and inferior to the current SoTA (DeBERTa).

3 Methodology

3.1 Problem Statement

The CONSTRAINT competition is a multimodal semantic role labelling multi-class classification problem. The aim is to classify the role of entities present in a meme using the image, its textual information and the entities it contains. The different classes are ("Hero", "Villain", "Victim", "Other"). The label applied for each entity depends on how the entity is presented in the meme:

Hero: The entity is glorified

Villain: the entity is vilified

Victim: the entity is victimised,

Other: none of the above.

3.2 Ensembling :

Our final model is an ensemble of 5 classifiers based on existing pretrained Unimodal (text) and Multimodal (text + images) architectures. (see figure 3) An ensemble combine several models to obtain a better generalised one. It usually gives a boost of performance in exchange for a more time-consuming model compared to more shallow model. Different methods of ensembling exist such as bagging, boosting, stacking, etc. We consider that this strategy will be very helpful to reduce the overfitting given the small number of instances we have, and how imbalanced the dataset is. To combine our models, we average the predictions of our individual models.

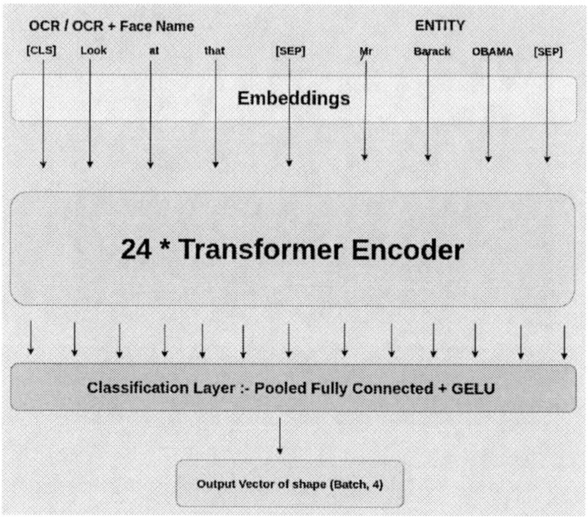

Figure 2: UniModal Model

3.2.1 Unimodal :

We experimented a few unimodal architectures based on transformers (Vaswani et al., 2017) such as DeBERTa and RoBerta (Liu et al., 2019) using only texts (OCR) and entities provided. The idea here was to see how much performance could be obtained just by textual information. These models are based on self-attention layers and an improved version of the BERT method pretrained on millions of sentences (Devlin et al., 2018) for language modelling. We fine-tuned on these models and found DeBERTa to be performing the best among the pretrained BERT models. For the fine-tuning, the last FC layer added over pooler layer of DeBERTa. The last layer was a FC layer of size 4 to provide us with the respective role label. The architecture for this structure is given (see figure 2) .

3.2.2 Multi-Modal :

We also experimented Multi Modal models which include as input data : images and texts (OCR + entity). We tried different approaches:
(1) The "Naive" approach consisted in extracting text features with a strong Language model - DeBERTa - and concatenating it with visual features with Convolutional Neural Network - EfficientNet-B7. We added on top of these concatenated features a Linear Layer to predict the class.
(2) The second approach was based on fine-tuning the whole image-text multimodal model. We experimented with two models: MMBT transformers (Multimodal Bitransformers) (Kiela et al., 2019) and VisualBERT (Li et al., 2019b) which has been pre-trained on classifying multimodal experiments.

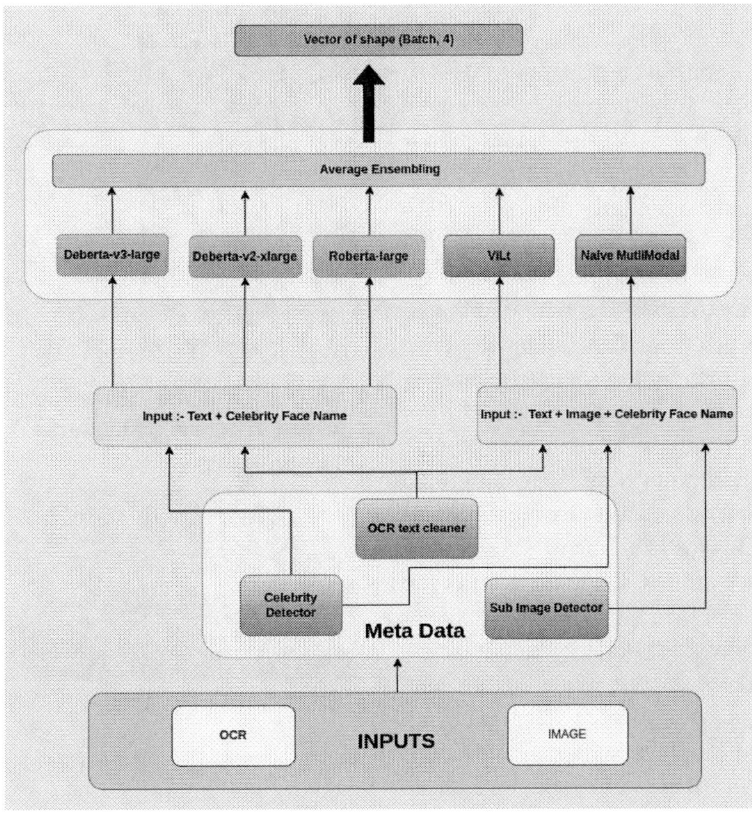

Figure 3: Final model used for the Constraint22 competition.

(i) The MMBT transformer model utilise bert-base-uncased model as text encoder and the CLIP model (Radford et al., 2021) as image encoder. The main idea was to reuse the BERT text model we had fine-tuned for the task and freeze the 12 encoder layers. Further we fine-tuned the MMBT multimodal model by projecting the image embeddings to text token space. (ii) The VisualBERT was pretrained model (Li et al., 2019b) for image-and-language tasks like VQA, VCR, NLVR2, and Flickr30Ks. We used the detectron2 embeddings (Ren et al., 2015) as image encodings with bert-base-uncased as text encoder to finetune the model.
(3) The last architecture used was ViLT (Kim et al., 2021) (Vision and Language Transformers) which is one of the simplest architectures for a vision and language model. ViLT is composed of a transformer module which extracts and processes textual and visual features without using separate embedder as it can be the case for MMBT for instance. That method gave a significant runtime and parameter optimisation. (see figure 5)

3.3 Meta Data extractions :

We attempted to extract meta data information from images in order to improve the insight from those. Indeed, using only the OCR was sometimes insufficient because the entities were not always present in the text. Multiple strategies were investigated for gathering insights from images.

3.3.1 Celebrity Detector :

The first observation made was in the image below (see figure 4) , the MEME is talking about Donald Trump (who is considered as a villain in the author's view). However he is not mentioned explicitly. His face is visible in the MEME though. That is why we decided to use a celebrities face detector which detects if a select famous face is visible in the MEME. The model is composed of two main steps : (i) a face detector based on the popular MTCNN face detector ((Zhang et al., 2016)) (ii) the face recognition part is based on a ResNet Architecture. We consider adding the face in the jsonl provided by the host when the confidence score of the face celebrities was above 0.95. The celebrity detector comes from Giphy's github.

3.3.2 Sub Image Detector

The second observation made was that a MEME can contain multiples "sub images". In fact, as in the figure 4, the MEME contains two images in it. A "sub images" detector was implemented based on YoloV5 (https://github.com/ultralytics/yolov5). We generated an artificial dataset, based on the Hateful MEME competition (Kiela et al., 2020), where we filtered and kept only the MEMEs with one image. Different single images were then combined to create one artificial MEME, with associated bounding boxes of the multiple subimages it contained. For the evaluation, 100 manually labelled images were used. The YOLO checkpoint is shared in our github solution. Our original idea was to extract with our detector each sub images from the MEME and associate each sentence of the OCR to the correct sub image with the name of the famous face if it existed. However, the OCR provided did not contain the coordinate of the sentence. We attempted to make the OCRed text match an open source OCR framework containing word coordinates, which yielded poor results. Therefore, the final multimodal model used the sub image as well as the face name into the text processing. The input of the transformer for text data was then as follows : "[CLS] Sentence OCR [SEP] entity to classify [SEP] face names [SEP]"

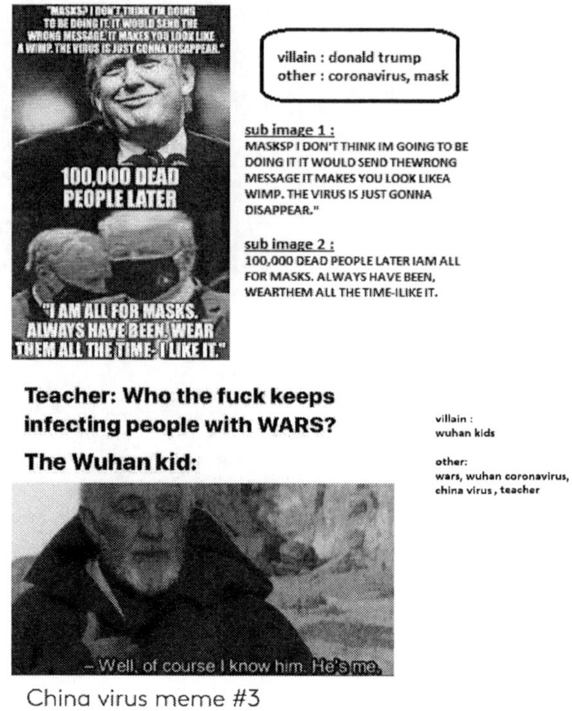

Figure 4: Constraint dataset example : The first MEME contains two sub images whereas the second MEME don't have the entity we are looking for.

split	other	villain	hero	victim
train	13702	2427	475	910
train (ratio)	0.782	0.139	0.027	0.052
val	1589	305	54	121
val (ratio)	0.768	0.147	0.026	0.058

Table 1: distribution class of Constraint22 dataset

4 Dataset

The competition dataset consists of 2 memes subsets, one about US politics, and the other about Covid-19, totalling 5552 images with associated OCR and entity annotation in the training set, and 650 in the validation set. This size is very small to expect to build any robust SoTA vision or multimodal capabilities, training from scratch.

The distributions of the 4 labels are heavily imbalanced (see table 1). Over three quarters of the entities belong to the "other" class, and of the remaining classes, "villain" appears around twice as much as both the "hero" and "victim" class combined. An analysis of the entities in the dataset was undertaken and they were observed to be well balanced amongst the 4 classes. Indeed, as can be expected of using data from the political domain over the past few years, examples of common mentions were of "Donald Trump", "Barrack Obama", "The Republicans", "The Democrats". The fact that they were all amongst the most cited entities in each label indicates the sources used to curate the dataset was unbiased politically. Table 2 shows the top 5 most common entity per class.

The OCRed text was obtained by running the Google OCR API on the images, which in some examples leads to imperfect text detection or extraction. These two issues materialise in the form of either poorly clustered text paragraphs into the appropriate text boxes, meaning sentences from two separate paragraphs would be concatenated together midway through, but also through more basic spelling mistakes.

Another point relevant to meme analysis is the presence of sub images inside each image. An image might itself contain two separate images which tell a different story, often contrasting between sentiments of entities in each, such as in figure 4.

A big challenge with this task of entity classification is detecting where the entity is mentioned whether in the OCR or in the image. Table 3 shows

top-n entity	other	villain	hero	victim
1	donald trump	donald trump	donald trump	donald trump
2	coronavirus	joe biden	barack obama	america
3	joe biden	democratic party	green party	people
4	barack obama	republican party	joe biden	barack obama
5	mask	barack obama	libertarian party	democratic party

Table 2: Top 5 most common entities per class in training dataset

split	ratio matching
multimodal heighttrain	0.572
val	0.602

Table 3: Ratio of entities which are present in OCR provided

the percentage of entities present in the OCR of the image in the dataset. Some examples, such as in figure 4, have one of the entities to classify not present in neither the OCR nor the image, and must be classified from understanding of context, which makes the task more difficult.

5 Experiments

5.1 Experimental Setting :

To train and evaluate our different models, we used the Google Cloud Service with VM using the V100 GPU (16GB) and A100(40GB). We use the famous Pytorch framework with the Huggingface library in python. All our training used mixed precision and gradient accumulation in order to speed up some training time and allow larger model training.

5.2 Data Analysis :

Data Analysis was performed in order to understand the underlying problem better and find potential imbalances that could be leveraged for higher performances. The distribution of the number of entities per class, as well as each individual entity for each class was computed. Based on an a given entity, the aim was to try and predict which class it would most likely belong. An issue we came across was that some entities were mentioned in different ways: "americans" vs "american people". A rule-based approach was incorporated in an attempt to group these similar terms together.

Analysis was running on the OCR as well as the output of the celebrity detection model to determine if the entity was mentioned inside the text, in the image, both or neither. References to single entities in the textual format would vary, one example being for the entity "Donald Trump", which would be referenced as "Trump", "donald", "Donald Trump" to name a few. A rule based classifier was implemented to group these terms together for the entities that showed up most frequently.

A prediction was made based on the heuristics of the imbalances found to establish a baseline model, by classifying all the entities as "other", which is the class which contains over 75% of entities. Learning models would have to beat the accuracy of this rule based baseline to add value.

5.3 Augmentations :

Only one augmentation was used during the training. The augmentation was applied to the entity which needed to be classified. In fact, the entities provided were all without any punctuation and in lowercase format. We created a simple script which found the entity in the original text. The original text could contain punctuation and/or uppercase letter. We used this augmentation for the training, not the inference of the test set.

5.4 Unimodal NLP :

We trained a few competitive transformer architectures on text-only data, DeBERTa-v3 and RoBERTa.

5.4.1 DeBERTa

Two experiements were conducted for DeBERTa (1) The first was a direct approach where we found the role for the entity based on the OCR extracted by the google model. The input of the transformer was as follows : "[CLS] Sentence OCR [SEP] entity to classify [SEP]"

(2) The second approach consisted of incorporating image signals in the unimodal training. We ran the celebrity face detection algorithm and further added these faces names text with the extracted OCR. The input of the transformer was as follow : "[CLS] Sentence OCR "\n" face name [SEP] entity to classify [SEP]"

We utilized both DeBERTa-small and DeBERTa-large for these experiments. During the training, a batch size of 16 was used, with a sequence length of 128 and a linear scheduler where the learning rate was reduced linearly during the training. The initial learning rate was $1e-5$, gradient accumulation is set at 3 epochs, and the optimizer used was AdamW. We trained these models for 6-7 epochs.

5.4.2 RoBERTa large

A batch size of 8 was used, with a sequence length of 275 and a linear scheduler where the learning rate was reduced linearly during the training. The initial learning rate was $5e-6$, and the optimizer used was AdamW. We trained these models for 6-7 epochs.

5.5 MultiModal

5.5.1 Naive Merging:

We used a batch size of 4 (A100 GPU), with a sequence length of 275. As a unimodal model, we use the face name in the text input processing. We use 4 sub images when they exist and the MEME image. We use an attention system inspired by the Word Attention in (Li et al., 2019a) , before concatenating the image features with the text features. We use a linear scheduler where the learning rate is reduced linearly during the training. The initial learning rate is $5e-6$, gradient accumulation is set at 3 epochs, and the optimizer used is AdamW. We trained these models for 7-8 epochs with early stopping of 2 epoch.

5.5.2 ViLT:

We use a batch size of 4, with a sequence length of 275. As unimodal model, we use the face name in the text input processing. We don't use here a linear scheduler, but ReduceLROnPlateau where the learning rate is reduced by a factor of 0.5 when there is no improvement during 5 epochs. The initial learning rate is $2e-5$, and the optimizer used is Adam. We trained these models for 7-8 epochs with early stopping of 2 epoch.

5.5.3 MultiModal : MMBT and VisualBERT

We use a batch size of 16, with a sequence length of 128. As for multimodal model, we use the image embeddings obtained from CLIP(Radford et al., 2021) and detectron2 (Ren et al., 2015) model individually for MMBT and VisualBERT. The text model used in both the architecture is bert. We use a linear scheduler where the learning rate is reduced linearly during the training. The initial learning rate is $1e-5$, gradient accumulation is set at 3 epochs, and the optimizer used is AdamW. We trained these models for 7-8 epochs with early stopping of 2 epoch.

5.6 Ensembling :

To improve the robustness of our solution we decide to combine 5 of our models (table 4). We chose the models to combine based on the results of the validation score and also the diversity they could bring. For instance, we did not select DeBERTa-v3-small because it is just a smaller version of DeBERTa-v3-large. We select only two multimodal models, as most of them perform quite badly compared to the unimodal. Otherwise they would just harm the ensemble.

6 Results and discussion

Just the simple experiment classifying all entities as "other" yielded 0.21 f1 score. We experimented with various models starting with just the text-based model, further adding image signals to using the image embeddings and finally a fully image-and-language based multimodal model to evaluate the model architecture efficiency in predicting a low resource multimodal problem. Here are some observations :-
(1) Unimodal - We can see the difference in results moving from "DeBERTa-v3-small" to "DeBERTa-v3-large" in Table 4. We can also see 2% improvement in the model when we tried to add image signal naively by adding the celebrity face name in text.
(2) Multi-Modal - We can see that multimodal model under performed a lot as seen in Table 4. We tried to fine-tune the Visual-BERT model and the mmbt model i.e. pre-trained vision-and-language model but they seem to under perform due to the lack of pre-training data. As they had been pre-trained on much less data and very different problem like VQA , it failed to capture the model understanding required for the transfer learning. So as to solve this issue we went ahead and utilised trained "DeBERTa-v3-large" model final output layer embeddings and concatenated them with pooled sub-image embedding with EfficientNetB7. Thus we utilised the transfer learning from both the models to give us the optimum results.
(3) Ensemble - The ensemble approach was our final approach where we combined all the different

Model	F1-score val (macro)	F1-score test (macro)
(a) DeBERTa-v2-xlarge w/o face's name	0.54	0.53
(b) DeBERTa-v3-small w/o face's name	0.46	0.46
(c) DeBERTa-v3-small w face's name	0.48	0.47
(e) DeBERTa-v3-large w/o face's name	0.55	0.55
(f) DeBERTa-v3-large w/ face's name	0.56	0.57
(g) RoBERTa-large w/ face's name	0.53	0.51
(h) ViLT w face's name	0.42	0.42
(i) Naive Multi Modal (DeBERTa-v3-large + EfficientNetB7) w/ face's name	0.525	0.55
(j) MMBT (BERT + CLIP) w/ face's name	0.48	0.46
(k) VisualBERT w/ face's name	0.43	0.44
Ensembling Mean(a, f, g, h, i)	**0.578**	**0.583**

Table 4: Experiments Results

Rank	Team	Final accuracy
1	Logically	**58.671%**
2	c1pher	55.240%
3	zhouziming	54.707%
4	smontariol	48.483%
5	zjl123001	46.177%
6	amanpriyanshu	31.943%
7	fharookshaik	23.855%
8	rabindra.nath	23.717%

Table 5: Constraint22 Leaderboard

model outputs . We tried various ensembles and blending techniques but we got the best LB score with averaging of ViLT, RoBERTa large, DeBERTa large, naive multimodal and DeBERTa-xlarge models. Final test set results and competition leaderboard are presented in Table 5. Our best model ("Ensemble") outperforms all competition systems and best baseline models. Test result of $Ensemble$ model achieved 0.58 avg. F1.

7 Conclusion

We described our participation in the CONSTRAINT 2022 Shared Task on "Detecting the Hero, the Villain, and the Victim in Memes" with the implementation of various models. Ensemble model based system outperforms all the models on val set and test set. A challenge in this task is the low resource of data available for training models. Hence, transfer learning provides the best results.
The best performing model in this competition combines the simple averaging of ViLT, RoBERTa large, DeBERTa large, naive multimodal and DeBERTa xlarge models. The ensemble seems to perform the best as the data size is small and we use a large model to allow for better transfer learning, This ultimately leads to some overfit of models but applying the averaging improves the results, like the boosted trees systems.

We found that there were two major challenges with the problem :- (i) The entities were sometimes not present in the image or the text. (ii) The size of data required to learn this implicit learning was not sufficient. This ultimately undermines the performance of our deep learning architecture.
Creating a dataset for real-word multimodal problems, particularly the natural language inference problem of role labelling is challenging (Le Bras et al., 2020). We appreciate the work by the CONSTRAINT 2022 organizers, yet, a more elaborate and extensive data would make this dataset more suitable for benchmarking. As an emergent research field, we hope our extensive model analysis and proposed solutions can act as baseline and inspire further work.

References

Pranav Adarsh, Pratibha Rathi, and Manoj Kumar. 2020. Yolo v3-tiny: Object detection and recognition using one stage improved model. In *2020 6th International Conference on Advanced Computing and Communication Systems (ICACCS)*, pages 687–694. IEEE.

Firoj Alam, Stefano Cresci, Tanmoy Chakraborty, Fabrizio Silvestri, Dimiter Dimitrov, Giovanni Da San Martino, Shaden Shaar, Hamed Firooz, and Preslav Nakov. 2021. A survey on multimodal disinformation detection. *arXiv preprint arXiv:2103.12541*.

Yen-Chun Chen, Linjie Li, Licheng Yu, Ahmed El Kholy, Faisal Ahmed, Zhe Gan, Yu Cheng, and Jingjing Liu. 2019. Uniter: Learning universal image-text representations.

Jacob Devlin, Ming-Wei Chang, Kenton Lee, and Kristina Toutanova. 2018. Bert: Pre-training of deep bidirectional transformers for language understanding. *arXiv preprint arXiv:1810.04805*.

Jie Gao, Hella-Franziska Hoffmann, Stylianos Oikonomou, David Kiskovski, and Anil Bandhakavi. 2021. Logically at the factify 2022: Multimodal fact verification. *arXiv preprint arXiv:2112.09253*.

Jiuxiang Gu, Jianfei Cai, Shafiq R Joty, Li Niu, and Gang Wang. 2018. Look, imagine and match: Improving textual-visual cross-modal retrieval with generative models. In *Proceedings of the IEEE Conference on Computer Vision and Pattern Recognition*, pages 7181–7189.

Pengcheng He, Xiaodong Liu, Jianfeng Gao, and Weizhu Chen. 2020. Deberta: Decoding-enhanced bert with disentangled attention. *arXiv preprint arXiv:2006.03654*.

Douwe Kiela, Suvrat Bhooshan, Hamed Firooz, and Davide Testuggine. 2019. Supervised multimodal bitransformers for classifying images and text. *arXiv preprint arXiv:1909.02950*.

Douwe Kiela, Hamed Firooz, Aravind Mohan, Vedanuj Goswami, Amanpreet Singh, Pratik Ringshia, and Davide Testuggine. 2020. The hateful memes challenge: Detecting hate speech in multimodal memes. *Advances in Neural Information Processing Systems*, 33:2611–2624.

Wonjae Kim, Bokyung Son, and Ildoo Kim. 2021. Vilt: Vision-and-language transformer without convolution or region supervision. In *International Conference on Machine Learning*, pages 5583–5594. PMLR.

Svetlana Kiritchenko, Isar Nejadgholi, and Kathleen C Fraser. 2021. Confronting abusive language online: A survey from the ethical and human rights perspective. *Journal of Artificial Intelligence Research*, 71:431–478.

Ronan Le Bras, Swabha Swayamdipta, Chandra Bhagavatula, Rowan Zellers, Matthew Peters, Ashish Sabharwal, and Yejin Choi. 2020. Adversarial filters of dataset biases. In *International Conference on Machine Learning*, pages 1078–1088. PMLR.

Jianping Li, Yimou Xu, and Huaye Shi. 2019a. Bidirectional lstm with hierarchical attention for text classification. In *2019 IEEE 4th Advanced Information Technology, Electronic and Automation Control Conference (IAEAC)*, volume 1, pages 456–459. IEEE.

Liunian Harold Li, Mark Yatskar, Da Yin, Cho-Jui Hsieh, and Kai-Wei Chang. 2019b. Visualbert: A simple and performant baseline for vision and language. *arXiv preprint arXiv:1908.03557*.

Xiujun Li, Xi Yin, Chunyuan Li, Xiaowei Hu, Pengchuan Zhang, Lei Zhang, Lijuan Wang, Houdong Hu, Li Dong, Furu Wei, Yejin Choi, and Jianfeng Gao. 2020. Oscar: Object-semantics aligned pre-training for vision-language tasks. In *ECCV*.

Yinhan Liu, Myle Ott, Naman Goyal, Jingfei Du, Mandar Joshi, Danqi Chen, Omer Levy, Mike Lewis, Luke Zettlemoyer, and Veselin Stoyanov. 2019. Roberta: A robustly optimized bert pretraining approach. *arXiv preprint arXiv:1907.11692*.

Jiasen Lu, Dhruv Batra, Devi Parikh, and Stefan Lee. 2019. Vilbert: Pretraining task-agnostic visiolinguistic representations for vision-and-language tasks. *arXiv preprint arXiv:1908.02265*.

Eric Müller-Budack, Jonas Theiner, Sebastian Diering, Maximilian Idahl, Sherzod Hakimov, and Ralph Ewerth. 2021. Multimodal news analytics using measures of cross-modal entity and context consistency. *International Journal of Multimedia Information Retrieval*, 10(2):111–125.

Alec Radford, Jong Wook Kim, Chris Hallacy, Aditya Ramesh, Gabriel Goh, Sandhini Agarwal, Girish Sastry, Amanda Askell, Pamela Mishkin, Jack Clark, et al. 2021. Learning transferable visual models from natural language supervision. In *International Conference on Machine Learning*, pages 8748–8763. PMLR.

Shaoqing Ren, Kaiming He, Ross Girshick, and Jian Sun. 2015. Faster r-cnn: Towards real-time object detection with region proposal networks. *Advances in neural information processing systems*, 28:91–99.

Chhavi Sharma, Deepesh Bhageria, William Scott, Srinivas Pykl, Amitava Das, Tanmoy Chakraborty, Viswanath Pulabaigari, and Bjorn Gamback. 2020. Semeval-2020 task 8: Memotion analysis–the visuolingual metaphor! *arXiv preprint arXiv:2008.03781*.

Shivam Sharma, Tharun Suresh, Atharva Kulkarni, Himanshi Mathur, Preslav Nakov, Md. Shad Akhtar, and Tanmoy Chakraborty. 2022. Findings of the constraint 2022 shared task on detecting the hero, the villain, and the victim in memes. In *Proceedings of the Workshop on Combating Online Hostile Posts in Regional Languages during Emergency Situations - CONSTRAINT 2022, Collocated with ACL 2022*.

Emanuel H Silva and Ricardo M Marcacini. Aspect-based sentiment analysis using bert with disentangled attention.

Hao Tan and Mohit Bansal. 2019. Lxmert: Learning cross-modality encoder representations from transformers. *arXiv preprint arXiv:1908.07490*.

Mingxing Tan and Quoc Le. 2019. Efficientnet: Rethinking model scaling for convolutional neural networks. In *International conference on machine learning*, pages 6105–6114. PMLR.

Ashish Vaswani, Noam Shazeer, Niki Parmar, Jakob Uszkoreit, Llion Jones, Aidan N Gomez, Łukasz Kaiser, and Illia Polosukhin. 2017. Attention is all you need. *Advances in neural information processing systems*, 30.

Mayur Wankhade, Annavarapu Chandra Sekhara Rao, and Chaitanya Kulkarni. 2022. A survey on sentiment analysis methods, applications, and challenges. *Artificial Intelligence Review*, pages 1–50.

Kaipeng Zhang, Zhanpeng Zhang, Zhifeng Li, and Yu Qiao. 2016. Joint face detection and alignment using multitask cascaded convolutional networks. *IEEE signal processing letters*, 23(10):1499–1503.

A Appendix I

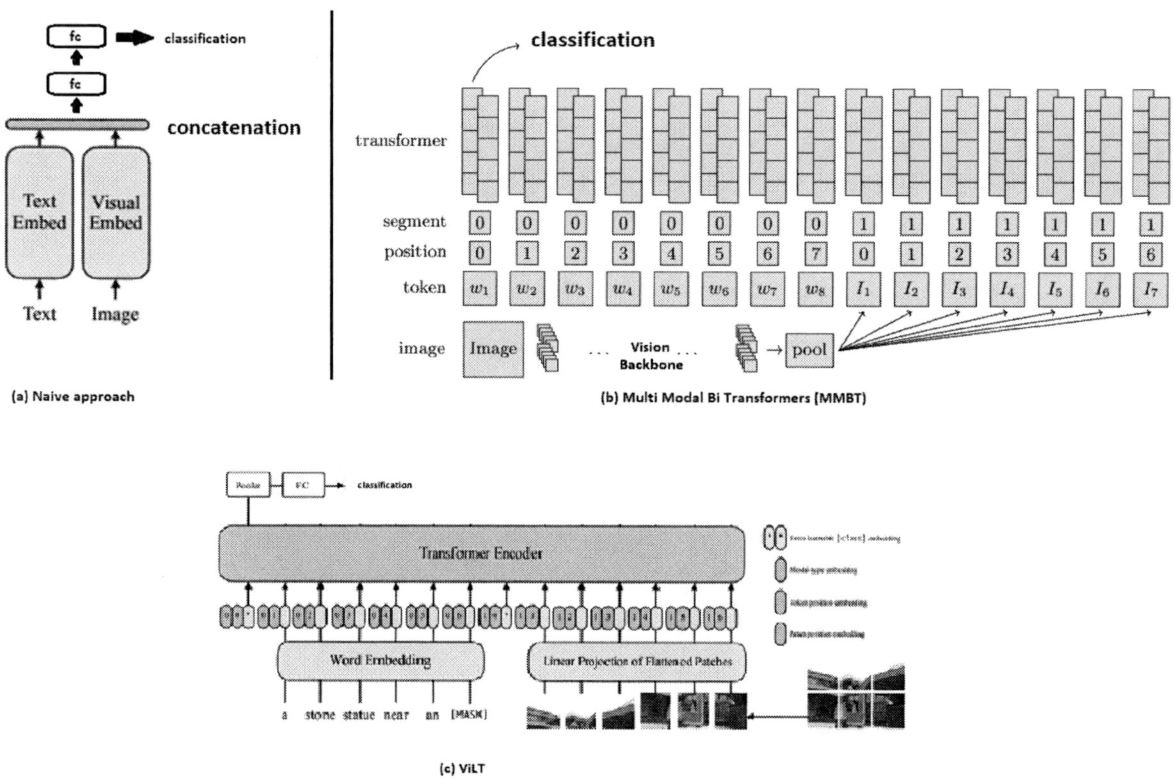

Figure 5: Example of Multimodal Architecture used

Combining Language Models and Linguistic Information to Label Entities in Memes

Pranaydeep Singh, Aaron Maladry, Els Lefever
LT3, Language and Translation Technology Team, Ghent University, Belgium
Groot-Brittanniëlaan 45, 9000 Ghent, Belgium
firstname.lastname@ugent.be

Abstract

This paper describes the system we developed for the shared task "Hero, Villain and Victim: Dissecting harmful memes for Semantic role labeling of entities" organized in the framework of the Second Workshop on Combating Online Hostile Posts in Regional Languages during Emergency Situation (Constraint 2022). We present an ensemble approach combining transformer-based models and linguistic information, such as the presence of irony and implicit sentiment associated to the target named entities. The ensemble system obtains promising classification scores, with a macro F-score of 55%, resulting in a third place finish in the competition.

1 Introduction

The exponential growth of social media such as Twitter, Facebook or Youtube has created a variety of novel ways to communicate. This daily exposure to other users' opinions and comments has become a constant in many people's lives. Unfortunately, this new way of freely communicating online has also given a forum to people who want to denigrate others because of their race, color, gender, sexual orientation, religion, etc., or to spread fake news and disinformation. The automatic processing of this user generated text by means of Natural Language Processing (NLP) techniques may contribute to an effective analysis of public opinion, but also to the automatic detection of this harmful online content.

One very popular mode of expression on social media today are internet memes. Memes are often used for entertainment purposes, but they are also used for online trolling, because of their potential for spreading provocative and attention-grabbing humor (Leaver, 2013). They have been described both as speech acts (Grundlingh, 2018) and performative acts, involving a conscious decision to either support or reject an ongoing social discourse (Gal et al., 2016). Their multi-modal nature, composed of a mixture of text and image, makes them a very challenging research object for automatic analysis. Research has already been proposed to automatically process harmful memes in various downstream tasks. A related shared task was proposed by Kiela et al. (2020), who organized the hateful memes challenge, where systems were developed to detect hate speech in multimodal memes. Most systems participating to the task applied fine-tuning of state-of-the-art transformer methods, such as supervised multimodal bitransformers (Kiela et al., 2022), ViLBERT (Lu et al., 2019) and VisualBERT (Li et al.) to classify memes as being hateful or not.

This paper presents our system developed to classify entities as *hero*, *villain*, *victim* or *other*, in memes about two controversial topics provoking a lot of hate speech and disinformation, namely the presidential election in the US and the COVID-19 pandemic spreading. To tackle the task, we incorporated both transformer-based embeddings as well as linguistic information (implicit entity connotations and irony detection labels) into our classifier.

The remainder of this paper is organized as follows. Section 2 introduces the shared task and data sets, whereas Section 3 describes the information sources and ensemble system we developed to label named entities in memes. Section 4 lists the experimental results and provides a detailed analysis and discussion. Section 5 ends with concluding remarks and indications for future research.

2 Shared Task and Data

The research described in this paper was carried out in the framework of the Constraint 2020 shared task: *Hero, Villain and Victim: Dissecting harmful memes for Semantic role labeling of entities* (Sharma et al., 2022). Given a meme and an entity, systems have to determine the role of the

Proceedings of the Workshop on Combating Online Hostile Posts in Regional Languages during Emergency Situations, pages 35 - 42
May 27, 2022

	Villain	Hero	Victim	Other	Total nr of entities
COVID-19 train memes					
2700 memes	662	190	360	6022	7234 (1927 unique)
Politics train memes					
2852 memes	1765	285	550	7680	10280 (2798 unique)
Total train memes					
5552 memes	2427 (14%)	475 (3%)	910 (5%)	13702 (78%)	17514 (4398 unique)
Held-out test memes					
718 memes	350 (14%)	52 (2%)	114 (5%)	1917 (79%)	2433 (1103 unique)

Table 1: Statistics of the training and test data set, showing the number of entities per class, and the unique number of entities per data partition.

entity in the meme, namely:

- *hero*: "The entity is presented in a positive light. Glorified for their actions conveyed via the meme or gathered from background context"
- *villain*: "The entity is portrayed negatively, e.g., in an association with adverse traits like wickedness, cruelty, hypocrisy, etc."
- *victim*: "The entity is portrayed as suffering the negative impact of someone else's actions or conveyed implicitly within the meme."
- *other*: "The entity is not a hero, a villain, or a victim."

The task is conceived as a multi-class classification task, which has to be analyzed from the meme author's perspective.

2.1 Training and Test Data

The task organizers provided training data for two controversial topics triggering a lot of hostile social media posts, and memes in particular, viz. the presidential election and COVID-19 pandemic. Table 1 shows the statistics of the training and held-out test data. As can be noticed, the data set is very skewed towards the "other" category (78% of the training and 79% of the test entities). It is also interesting to mention that out of the 1103 unique test entities, only 542 entities also appeared in the training data.

The data was provided in the following json format, containing the OCR'ed text from the meme, the file name of the corresponding meme, and a list of gold entities per category:

{"OCR": "IF PROPERLY FITTED, ONE MASK CAN\n SAVE MANY THOUSANDS OF LIVES\n Dr. Fauci\nXESH\nHE WH\nWASE\n", "image": "covid_memes_1797.png", "hero": ["dr. anthony fauci"], "villain": ["donald trump"], "victim": [], "other": ["mask"] }

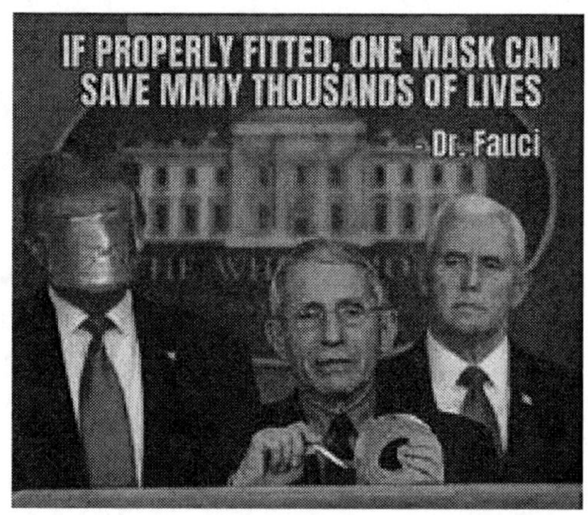

Figure 1: covid_memes_1797.png

3 System Description

We approached the meme entity labeling task as a multi-class classification task, where a category is predicted for all entities occurring in the meme. To this end, an ensemble classifier is built combining probability scores output by various transformer-based language models and linguistic information assigning implicit sentiment to the entities and detecting irony in the meme text. We first give an overview of all different information sources in-

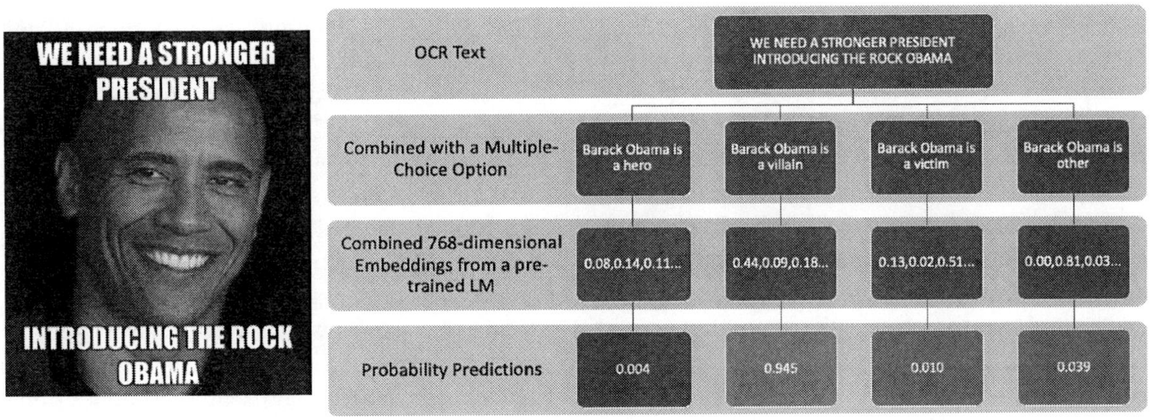

Figure 2: Illustration of the MCQA setup and features obtained for the transformer-based language models.

corporated in the feature vector (Section 3.1), and then describe the ensemble method combining the various information sources into a feature vector for classification (Section 3.2).

3.1 Information Sources

3.1.1 Transformer-based Language Models

The information used for our first feature group are similarity probabilities per class output by state-of-the-art transformer-based language models. As the target entities do not (always) occur in the OCR'ed meme text (for example, "Donald Trump" is an entity not present in the text in Figure 1), we had to find a different way to fine-tune the pre-trained language models for labeling the entities. To tackle this issue, we recast the labeling task as a multiple choice QA task (MCQA), where the various questions are formulated as "<entity> is a hero", "<entity> is a vilain", etc. The model then appends the question (OCR'ed meme text) to each option individually, and computes a probability output for the similarity.

Three different transformer-based pre-trained language models were fine-tuned for the task, applying different transformer architectures, namely BERT (Devlin et al., 2019) and RoBERTa (Liu et al., 2019) and pre-trained on different types of data: (1) twitter-base-roberta, (2) bert-tweet, and (3) COVID-bert.

twitter-base-roberta (Barbieri et al., 2020) is trained on 58M tweets and is a language model applying a RoBERTa architecture. While Twitter data is already closer to meme text than the standard Wikipedia and Common Crawl text, the tweets collected for training this language model are quite a bit older than our shared task data set.

COVID-bert (Müller et al., 2020) is trained on a corpus of 160M more recent tweets (spanning the first half of 2019) about the corona virus. The content of the tweets is, however, very related to the content of the shared task data, as they contain covid-related key words.

bert-tweet (Nguyen et al., 2020) uses similar pre-training data to twitter-base-roberta but is a larger architecture with significantly increased and recent pre-training data. The large RoBERTa architecture was trained on 850M English Tweets, containing 845M Tweets streamed from 01/2012 to 08/2019 and 5M Tweets related to the COVID-19 pandemic.

Each pre-trained language model was optimized using cross-entropy for the task of multiple-choice QA as illustrated in Figure 2. Each entity along with it's possible class, is treated as a separate multiple-choice option. The Language models were fine-tuned for 5 epochs with an LR of 1e-5, batch size of 4 per device, on 2 Tesla V100 GPUs.

3.1.2 Implicit Sentiment

The creation of the implicit sentiment feature was motivated by the assumption that entities might have a predominant connotation on Twitter. To determine the implicit sentiment of the entities, we collected 400 to 800 tweets containing each entity and combined them into a large background corpus of three million tweets. As memes and tweets both originate from social media platforms, we considered this the most reliable source for the implicit sentiment from the perspective of most users, although we recognize that meme-makers might have very different opinions about certain politicians. We analyzed the sentiment of the collected tweets with a pre-trained RoBERTa model (Heitmann et al., 2020)[1] that was pre-trained using 15 data sets across different text types, including tweets. We grouped the tweets per entity and considered the implicit sentiment of an entity to be determined by the percentages of positive, negative and neutral tweets for that entity in our background corpus. Additionally, we constructed another categorical feature reflecting the dominant implicit sentiment (positive, neutral or negative). This way, we ended up with four *implicit sentiment* features: the distribution values for positive, negative and neutral tweets in the background corpus and the dominant sentiment for that target entity based on those values. These features were finally combined with the output of the BERT question-answering systems into the ensemble model.

3.1.3 Irony Detection

As we assume that a lot of memes contain figurative language, and irony in particular, we modeled a second linguistic feature by performing irony detection on the OCR text. To detect irony, we used a pre-trained RoBERTa model (Barbieri et al., 2020)[2], which contains the RobBERTa-base model and was fine-tuned using the SemEval 2018 data set for Irony Detection in English tweets (Van Hee et al., 2018). The value of the resulting feature is the probability score for the irony label (between 0 and 1).

In hindsight, we think most of the irony did not occur inside the OCR text but is expressed in a multi-modal way between the image and the text. This was confirmed by the experimental results, as the feature for irony detection inside the OCR text did not increase the accuracy of our system for entity classification.

3.1.4 FastText Embeddings

The final feature group we modeled is based on FastText embeddings (Bojanowski et al., 2017). As we scraped a relevant background corpus containing all target entities, we hypothesized this would also be an interesting corpus for training embeddings. Although FastText outputs static, and not contextualized embeddings, it was very popular before the transformer-based revolution in NLP, and is computationally cheap to train word vectors. First, the background corpus was tokenised using NLTK's tokenizer for tweets[3], which for instance keeps hashtags intact. FastText embedddings were then trained using the continuous-bag-of-words (cbow) model, which predicts the target word according to its context. The context here is represented as a bag of all words contained in a fixed size window around the target word. This resulted in a vocabulary of 61,871 words and 100-dimensional word vectors for the Twitter background corpus. The FastText embeddings of the entities were integrated in the feature vector as 100 separate features.

3.2 Ensemble System

We trained an ensemble system combining the results from each of the information sources listed above as features. We use the probability predictions for each class from the fine-tuned language model, an average score for each implicit sentiment (positive, negative, neutral) present in the background corpus for the respective entity, the probability score for the irony associated with the OCR text, and the 100-dimensional pre-trained FastText embeddings for the entity text (averaged for multiple tokens in an entity), resulting in a feature vector containing 108 features. We explain the construction of the feature vector with the 4 sets of features in Figure 3.

We experimented with 3 classifiers, Gradient Boosted Trees (XGB**dd**oost), Random Forest and Support Vector Machines as implemented in sklearn (Pedregosa et al., 2011). We used grid searching with 5-fold cross-validation to find the optimal hyperparameters for each classifier, and our final classifier in all cases is an SVM with an RBF Kernel, a C value of 0.1 and a gamma value of 0.01.

While experimenting with the different classifiers and features, we calculated feature importance according to the linear kernel SVM classsifier. The respective scores reflecting the contribution of the various features to solve the task are listed in Figure 4.

[1]https://huggingface.co/siebert/sentiment-roberta-large-english

[2]https://huggingface.co/cardiffnlp/twitter-roberta-base-irony

[3]https://www.nltk.org/api/nltk.tokenize.html

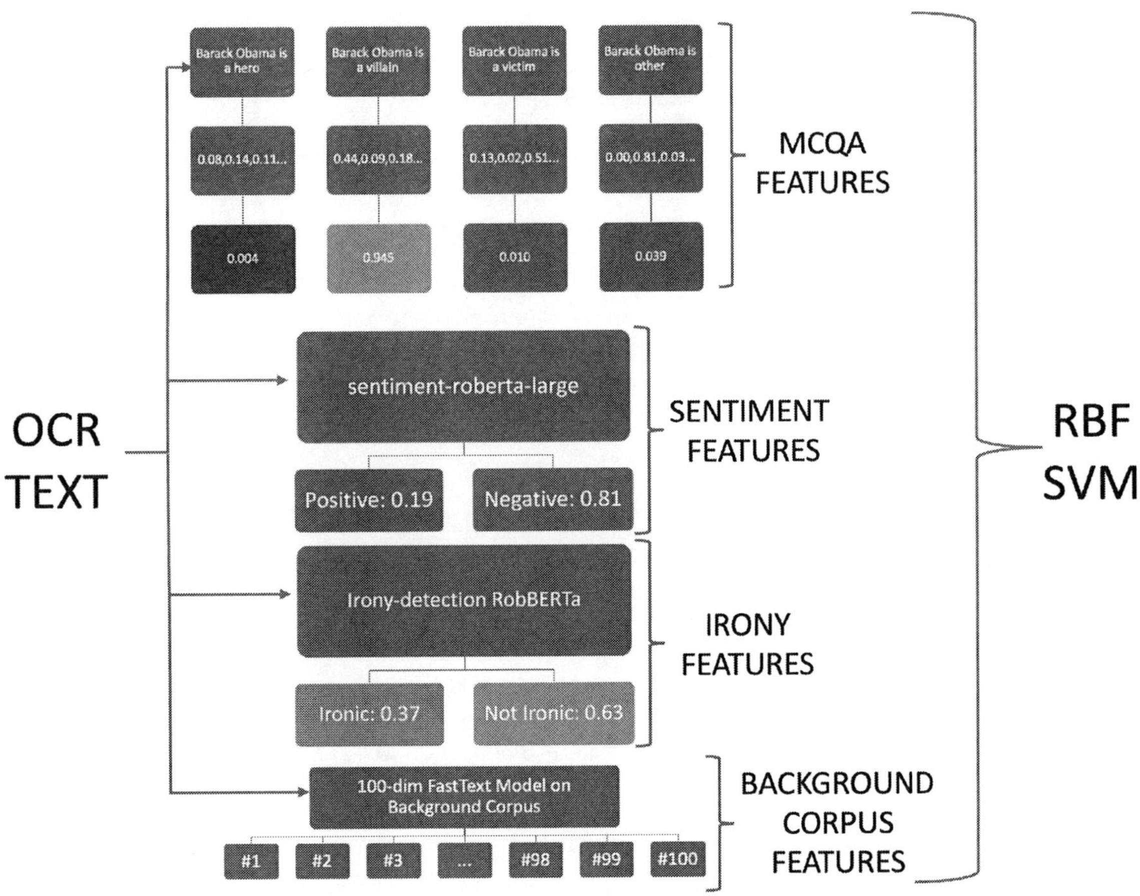

Figure 3: A visual summary of the ensemble setup and the features involved.

4 Experimental Results

A first set of experiments was carried out to assess the classification performance of the different language models. In this case, the classifier is trained and evaluated on feature vectors containing similarity scores for the four different labels. The first three lines of Table 2 show the classification scores for this multiple choice QA language model systems. It is clear from the results that the bert-tweet model performs best, resulting in a Macro F1-score of 0.5467. When adding implicit sentiment for the target entities, the score only slightly improves.

For a second set of experiments, we created an ensemble system containing various combinations of the MCQA language model probability scores per label, together with the implicit sentiment feature for the target entity. The best performing ensemble appeared to be a combination of the twitter-xlm-roberta, COVID-bert and bert-tweet similarity scores per label, together with the implicit sentiment features, resulting in the best performance scores on the held-out test set, viz. a macro F1-score of 0.5514. Combining this ensemble system with the irony detection and FastText word vector features resulted in a lower F-score (0.5495) and precision (0.5201), but in a higher recall score (0.6045).

Table 3 lists the precision, recall and F-scores per entity label for the best performing system, being the ensemble system containing the best three language model predictions together with the implicit sentiment feature. As expected, the *Other* category, which represents 78% of the training targets, performs best and the *Hero* category performs worst (only 3% of training entities), especially obtaining a very low recall of 0.27. For the other two labels, *Villain* and *Victim*, precision and recall are better balanced.

To gain more insights into the performance of the best classifier, we constructed a confusion matrix for all labels and performed an error analysis. Completely in line with the classification scores per label, we can notice in the confusion matrix (Fig-

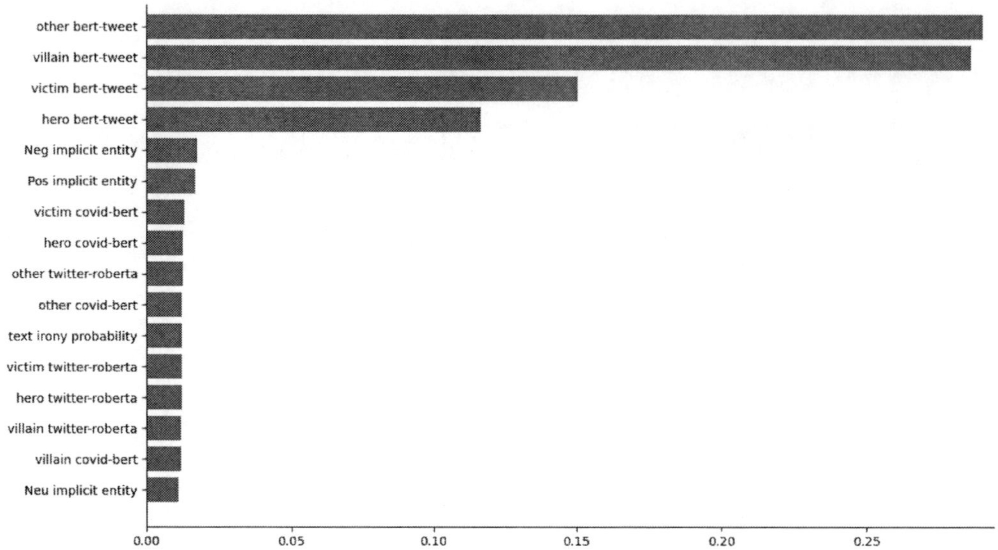

Figure 4: Feature importances of the classifier we used for our ensemble model. The features include the MCQA values per label for each of our language models, the percentages of positive, negative and neutral tweets found for the entity and the probability of the text being ironic.

Model	Macro-F1	Precision	Recall
MCQA twitter-xlm-roberta	0.3433	0.4211	0.2898
MCQA COVID-bert	0.5083	0.5188	0.4997
MCQA bert-tweet	0.5467	0.524	0.5812
MCQA bert-tweet + Sentiment	0.5471	0.5274	0.5814
MCQA ensemble + Sentiment	**0.5524**	**0.5391**	0.5725
MCQA ensemble + Sentiment + + FastText + Irony	0.5495	0.5201	**0.6045**

Table 2: Macro-averaged F1-scores, precision and recall for the various classification systems.

Label	F1-score	Precision	Recall
Hero	0.33	0.41	0.27
Villain	0.55	0.55	0.54
Victim	0.45	0.44	0.46
Other	0.89	0.88	0.89

Table 3: Classification scores (F1-score, precision, recall) for the different named entity labels.

ure 5) that most of the missed labels are wrongly predicted as "Other" (even up to 60% for the *hero* label). Another remarkable fact is that 12% of the *victim* labels are predicted as *villain*.

Apart from challenges posed by the data set itself, such as noise in the OCR text, very skewed class distribution, or spelling mistakes in the target entities [4], our error analysis revealed some other trends in wrongly predicted named entity labels.

First, it is clear that labeling entities in memes is a very hard task. Systems have to both understand the OCR text, but also correctly process the picture that sometimes contains crucial information. As we only incorporate text processing features in our ensemble system, a lot of the erroneous predictions are caused because of lacking visual information to correctly interpret the picture of the meme, as illustrated by Figure 6.

In addition, some memes require a lot of common sense or factual/news knowledge. As an example, we can refer to Figure 7, where the entity *Melania Trump* had to be labeled as "Villain", but was predicted by the system as "Other". It is impossible, however, to interpret this meme correctly without knowing that Donald Trump's wife, Melania, took center stage on the first day of the Republican National Convention, and was accused of the fact that a portion of her speech plagiarized Michelle Obama.

[4]Mistakes like "dr. dr. anthony fauci" and "valdimir puitin".

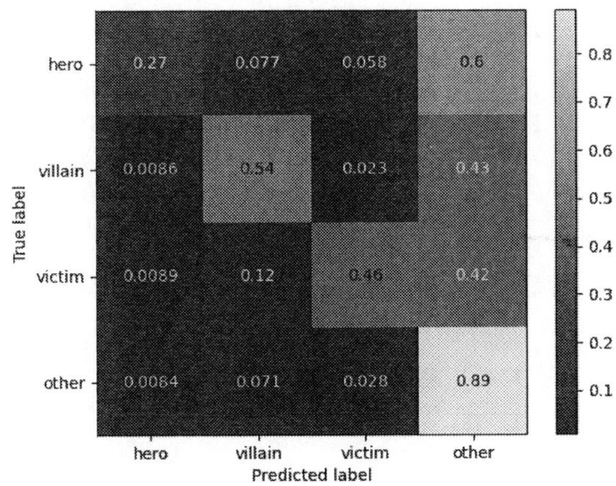

Figure 5: confusion matrix of the prediction results on the held-out test set.

Figure 6: Meme requiring visual information features.

Figure 7: Meme requiring common sense/factual knowledge.

5 Conclusion

In this paper, we describe the system proposed for the Constraint 2022 shared task on labeling entities in memes as *Hero*, *Villain*, *Victim* or *Other*. To tackle the task, we built an ensemble classifier combining the output predictions of various transformer-based language models with implicit sentiment features for the target entities, irony predictions on the OCR text and FastText word vectors. The best performing system combines the predictions of three different language models with the implicit sentiment feature, obtaining a Macro F1-score of 55%. As the data set was very skewed, we obtained much better results for the "Other" class than for the other three labels. Especially for the *Hero* class, only represented by 3% of the training entities, classification appeared to be challenging (F1-score of 33%).

The analysis of the results showed there is still a lot of room for improvement. In future research, we plan to integrate visual information into our ensemble system, as it is clear that we lacked this information to properly address this multimodal task. In addition, we will investigate other ways to set up the multiple choice QA system, in order to construct better sentences containing the target entities. Finally, the system would also benefit from more semantic information, in order to model entities that are now not explicitly mentioned in the OCR text. It would, for instance, be interesting to semantically link an OCR text line talking about *Brexit* with the entity *UK Government*. This would allow to inject some common sense into the meme classification system.

References

Francesco Barbieri, Jose Camacho-Collados, Luis Espinosa-Anke, and Leonardo Neves. 2020. TweetEval:Unified Benchmark and Comparative Evaluation for Tweet Classification. In *Proceedings of Findings of EMNLP*.

P. Bojanowski, E. Grave, A. Joulin, and T. Mikolov. 2017. Enriching Word Vectors with Subword Information. *Transactions of the Association for Computational Linguistics*, 5:135–146.

J. Devlin, M.-W. Chang, K. Lee, and K. Toutanova. 2019. BERT: Pre-training of deep bidirectional transformers for language understanding. In *Proceedings of the 2019 Conference of the North American Chapter of the Association for Computational Linguistics: Human Language Technologies, Volume 1 (Long and Short Papers)*, pages 4171–4186, Minneapolis, Minnesota. Association for Computational Linguistics.

Noam Gal, Limor Shifman, and Zohar Kampf. 2016. "it gets better": Internet memes and the construction of collective identity. *New media & society*, 18(8):1698–1714.

Lezandra Grundlingh. 2018. Memes as speech acts. *Social Semiotics*, 28(2):147–168.

Mark Heitmann, Christian Siebert, Jochen Hartmann, and Christina Schamp. 2020. More than a feeling: Benchmarks for sentiment analysis accuracy. *Available at SSRN 3489963*.

Douwe Kiela, Suvrat Bhooshan, Hamed Firooz, and Davide Testuggine. 2022. Supervised multimodal bitransformers for classifying images and text. In *Proceedings of the NeurIPS 2019 Workshop on Visually Grounded Interaction and Language (VIGIL@NeurIPS'19*.

Douwe Kiela, Hamed Firooz, Aravind Mohan, Vedanuj Goswami, Amanpreet Singh, Pratik Ringshia, and Davide Testuggine. 2020. The hateful memes challenge: Detecting hate speech in multimodal memes. In *Proceedings of the Annual Conference on Neural Information Processing Systems (NeurIPS '20)*.

Tama Leaver. 2013. Olympic trolls: Mainstream memes and digital discord. *Fibreculture Journal*, 1(22):216–233.

Liunian Harold Li, Mark Yatskar, Da Yin, Cho-Jui Hsieh, and Kai-Wei Chang. Visualbert: A simple and performant baseline for vision and language. *arXiv:1908.03557*.

Y. Liu, M. Ott, N. Goyal, J. Du, M. Joshi, D. Chen, O. Levy, M. Lewis, L. Zettlemoyer, and V. Stoyanov. 2019. Roberta: A robustly optimized BERT pretraining approach. *CoRR*, abs/1907.11692.

Jiasen Lu, Dhruv Batra, Devi Parikh, and Stefan Lee. 2019. Vilbert: Pretraining task-agnostic visiolinguistic representations for vision-and-language tasks. In *Proceedings of the Annual Conference on Neural Information Processing Systems (NeurIPS '19)*, pages 13–23.

Martin Müller, Marcel Salathé, and Per E Kummervold. 2020. Covid-twitter-bert: A natural language processing model to analyse covid-19 content on twitter.

Dat Quoc Nguyen, Thanh Vu, and Anh Tuan Nguyen. 2020. BERTweet: A pre-trained language model for English Tweets. In *Proceedings of the 2020 Conference on Empirical Methods in Natural Language Processing: System Demonstrations*, pages 9–14.

F. Pedregosa, G. Varoquaux, A. Gramfort, V. Michel, B. Thirion, O. Grisel, M. Blondel, P. Prettenhofer, R. Weiss, V. Dubourg, J. Vanderplas, A. Passos, D. Cournapeau, M. Brucher, M. Perrot, and E. Duchesnay. 2011. Scikit-learn: Machine learning in Python. *Journal of Machine Learning Research*, 12:2825–2830.

Shivam Sharma, Tharun Suresh, Atharva Jitendra, Himanshi Mathur, Preslav Nakov, Md. Shad Akhtar, and Tanmoy Chakraborty. 2022. Findings of the constraint 2022 shared task on detecting the hero, the villain, and the victim in memes. In *Proceedings of the Workshop on Combating Online Hostile Posts in Regional Languages during Emergency Situations - CONSTRAINT 2022, Collocated with ACL 2022*.

Cynthia Van Hee, Els Lefever, and Veronique Hoste. 2018. SemEval-2018 task 3 : irony detection in English tweets. In *Proceedings of The 12th International Workshop on Semantic Evaluation*, pages 39–50. Association for Computational Linguistics.

Detecting the Role of an Entity in Harmful Memes: Techniques and Their Limitations

Rabindra Nath Nandi[1], **Firoj Alam**[2], **Preslav Nakov**[2]
[1]BJIT Limited, Dhaka, Bangladesh
[2]Qatar Computing Research Institute, HBKU, Doha, Qatar
rabindra.nath@bjitgroup.com, {falam,pnakov}@hbku.edu.qa

Abstract

Harmful or abusive online content has been increasing over time, raising concerns for social media platforms, government agencies, and policymakers. Such harmful or abusive content can have major negative impact on society, e.g., cyberbullying can lead to suicides, rumors about COVID-19 can cause vaccine hesitance, promotion of fake cures for COVID-19 can cause health harms and deaths. The content that is posted and shared online can be textual, visual, or a combination of both, e.g., in a meme. Here, we describe our experiments in detecting the roles of the entities (hero, villain, victim) in harmful memes, which is part of the CONSTRAINT-2022 shared task, as well as our system for the task. We further provide a comparative analysis of different experimental settings (i.e., unimodal, multimodal, attention, and augmentation). For reproducibility, we make our experimental code publicly available.[1]

1 Introduction

Social media have become one of the main communication channels for sharing information online. Unfortunately, they have been abused by malicious actors to promote their agenda using manipulative content, thus continuously plaguing political events, and the public debate, e.g., regarding the ongoing COVID-19 infodemic (Alam et al., 2021d; Nakov et al., 2022). Such type of content includes harm and hostility (Brooke, 2019; Joksimovic et al., 2019), hate speech (Fortuna and Nunes, 2018), offensive language (Zampieri et al., 2019; Rosenthal et al., 2021), abusive language (Mubarak et al., 2017), propaganda (Da San Martino et al., 2019, 2020), cyberbullying (Van Hee et al., 2015), cyberaggression (Kumar et al., 2018), and other kinds of harmful content (Pramanick et al., 2021; Sharma et al., 2022b).

The propagation of such content is often done by coordinated groups (Hristakieva et al., 2022) using automated tools and targeting specific individuals, communities, and companies. There have been many research efforts to develop automated tools to detect such kind of content. Several recent surveys have highlighted these aspects, which include fake news (Zhou and Zafarani, 2020), misinformation and disinformation (Alam et al., 2021c; Nakov et al., 2021; Hardalov et al., 2022), rumours (Bondielli and Marcelloni, 2019), propaganda (Da San Martino et al., 2020), hate speech (Fortuna and Nunes, 2018; Schmidt and Wiegand, 2017), cyberbullying (Haidar et al., 2016), offensive (Husain and Uzuner, 2021) and harmful content (Sharma et al., 2022b).

The content shared on social media comes in different forms: textual, visual, or audio-visual. Among other social media content, recently, *internet memes* became popular. Memes are defined as "a group of digital items sharing common characteristics of content, form, or stance, which were created by associating them and were circulated, imitated, or transformed via the Internet by many users" (Shifman, 2013). Memes typically consist of images containing some text (Shifman, 2013; Suryawanshi et al., 2020a,b). They are often shared for the purpose of having fun. However, memes can also be created and shared with bad intentions. This includes attacks on people based on characteristics such as ethnicity, race, sex, gender identity, disability, disease, nationality, and immigration status (Zannettou et al., 2018; Kiela et al., 2020). There has been research effort to develop computational methods to detect such memes, such as detecting hateful memes (Kiela et al., 2020), propaganda (Dimitrov et al., 2021a), offensiveness (Suryawanshi et al., 2020a), sexist memes (Fersini et al., 2019), troll memes (Suryawanshi and Chakravarthi, 2021), and generally harmful memes (Pramanick et al., 2021; Sharma et al., 2022a).

[1]https://github.com/robi56/harmful_memes_block_fusion

Proceedings of the Workshop on Combating Online Hostile Posts in Regional Languages during Emergency Situations, pages 43 - 54
May 27, 2022 ©2022 Association for Computational Linguistics

Harmful memes often target individuals, organizations, or social entities. Pramanick et al. (2021) developed a dataset where the annotation consists of (*i*) whether a meme is harmful or not, and (*ii*) whether it targets an individual, an organization, a community, or society. The CONSTRAINT-2022 shared task follows a similar line of research (Sharma et al., 2022c). The entities in a meme are first identified and then the task asks participants to predict which entities are glorified, vilified, or victimized in the meme. The task is formulated as *"Given a meme and an entity, determine the role of the entity in the meme: hero vs. villain vs. victim vs. other."* More details are given in Section 3.

Memes are multimodal in nature, but the textual and the visual content in a meme are sometimes unrelated, which can make them hard to analyze for traditional multimodal approaches. Moreover, context (e.g., where the meme was posted) plays an important role for understanding its content. Another important factor is that since the text in the meme is overlaid on top of the image, the text needs to be extracted using OCR, which can result in errors that require additional manual post-editing (Dimitrov et al., 2021a).

Here, we address a task about entity role labeling for harmful memes based on the dataset released in the CONSTRAINT-2022 shared task; see the task overview paper for more detail (Sharma et al., 2022c). This task is different from traditional semantic role labeling in NLP (Palmer et al., 2010), where understanding *who* did *what* to *whom*, *when*, *where*, and *why* is typically addressed as a sequence labeling problem (He et al., 2017). Recently, this has also been studied for visual content (Sadhu et al., 2021), i.e., situation recognition (Yatskar et al., 2016; Pratt et al., 2020), visual semantic role labeling (Gupta and Malik, 2015; Silberer and Pinkal, 2018; Li et al., 2020), and human-object interaction (Chao et al., 2015, 2018).

To address the entity role labeling for a potentially harmful meme, we investigate textual, visual, and multimodal content using different pretrained models such as BERT (Devlin et al., 2019), VGG16 (Simonyan and Zisserman, 2015), and other vision–language models (Ben-younes et al., 2019). We further explore different textual data augmentation techniques and attention methods. For the shared task participation, we used only the image modality, which resulted in an underperforming system in the leaderboard.

Further studies using other modalities and approaches improved the performance of our system, but it is still lower (0.464 macro F1) than the best system (0.586). Yet, our investigation might be useful to understand which approaches are useful for detecting the role of an entity in harmful memes.

Our contributions can be summarized as follows:

- we addressed the problem both as sequence labeling and as classification;
- we investigated different pretrained models for text and images;
- we explored several combinations of multimodal models, as well as attention mechanisms, and various augmentation techniques.

The rest of the paper is organized as follows: Section 2 presents previous work, Section 3 describes the task and the dataset, Section 4 formulates our experiments, Section 5 discusses the evaluation results. Finally, Section 6 concludes and points to possible directions for future work.

2 Related Work

Below, we discuss previous work on semantic role labeling and harmful content detection, both in general and in a multimodal context.

2.1 Semantic Role Labeling

Textual semantic role labeling has been widely studied in NLP, where the idea is to understand who did what to whom, when, where, and why. Traditionally, the task has been addressed using sequence labeling, e.g., FitzGerald et al. (2015) used local and structured learning, experimenting with PropBank and FrameNet, and Larionov et al. (2019) investigated recent transformer models.

Visual semantic role labeling has been explored for images and video. Yatskar et al. (2016) addressed situation recognition, and developed a large-scale dataset containing over 500 activities, 1,700 roles, 11,000 objects, 125,000 images, and 200,000 unique situations. The images were collected from Google and the authors addressed the task as a situation recognition problem. Pratt et al. (2020) developed a dataset for situation recognition consisting of 278,336 bounding-box groundings to the 11,538 entity classes. Gupta and Malik (2015) developed a dataset of 16K examples in 10K images with actions and associated objects in the scene with different semantic roles for each action.

Yang et al. (2016) worked on integrating language and vision with explicit and implicit roles. Silberer and Pinkal (2018) learned frame–semantic representations of the images. Sadhu et al. (2021) approached the same problem for video, developing a dataset of 29K 10-second movie clips, annotated with verbs and semantics roles for every two seconds of video content.

2.2 Harmful Content Detection in Memes

There has been significant effort for identifying misinformation, disinformation, and malinformation online (Schmidt and Wiegand, 2017; Bondielli and Marcelloni, 2019; Zhou and Zafarani, 2020; Da San Martino et al., 2020; Alam et al., 2021c; Afridi et al., 2020; Hristakieva et al., 2022; Nakov et al., 2022). Most of these studies focused on textual and multimodal content. Compared to that, modeling the harmful aspects of memes has not received much attention.

Recent effort in this direction include categorizing hateful memes (Kiela et al., 2020), detecting antisemitism (Chandra et al., 2021), detecting the propagandistic techniques used in a meme (Dimitrov et al., 2021a), detecting harmful memes and the target of the harm (Pramanick et al., 2021), identifying the protected categories that were attacked (Zia et al., 2021), and identifying offensive content (Suryawanshi et al., 2020a). Among these studies, the most notable low-level efforts that advanced research by providing high-quality datasets to experiment with include shared tasks such as the *Hateful Memes Challenge* (Kiela et al., 2020), the SemEval-2021 shared task on detecting persuasion techniques in memes (Dimitrov et al., 2021b), and the troll meme classification task (Suryawanshi and Chakravarthi, 2021).

Chandra et al. (2021) investigated antisemitism along with its types as a binary and a multi-class classification problem using pretrained transformers and convolutional neural networks (CNNs) as modality-specific encoders along with various multimodal fusion strategies. Dimitrov et al. (2021a) developed a dataset with 22 propaganda techniques and investigated the different state-of-the-art pretrained models, demonstrating that joint vision–language models performed better than unimodal ones. Pramanick et al. (2021) addressed two tasks: detecting harmful memes and identifying the social entities they target, using a multimodal model with local and global information.

Zia et al. (2021) went one step further than a binary classification of hateful memes, focusing on a more fine-grained categorization based on the protected category that was being attacked (i.e., race, disability, religion, nationality, sex) and the type of attack (i.e., contempt, mocking, inferiority, slurs, exclusion, dehumanizing, inciting violence) using the dataset released in the WOAH 2020 Shared Task.[2] Fersini et al. (2019) studied sexist memes and investigated the textual cues using late fusion. They also developed a dataset of 800 misogynistic memes covering different manifestations of hatred against women (e.g., body shaming, stereotyping, objectification, and violence), collected from different social media (Gasparini et al., 2021).

Kiela et al. (2021) summarized the participating systems in the Hateful Memes Challenge, where the best systems fine-tuned unimodal and multimodal pre-training transformer models such as VisualBERT (Li et al., 2019) VL-BERT (Su et al., 2020), UNITER (Chen et al., 2020), VILLA (Gan et al., 2020), and built ensembles on top of them.

The SemEval-2021 propaganda detection shared task (Dimitrov et al., 2021b) focused on detecting the use of propaganda techniques in the meme, and the participants' systems showed that multimodal cues were very important.

In the troll meme classification shared task (Suryawanshi and Chakravarthi, 2021), the best system used ResNet152 and BERT with multimodal attention, and most systems used pretrained transformers for the text, CNNs for the images, and early fusion to combine the two modalities.

Combining modalities causes several challenges, which arise due to representation issues (i.e., symbolic representation for language vs. signal representation for the visual modality), misalignment between the modalities, and fusion and transferring knowledge between the modalities. In order to address multimodal problems, a lot of effort has been paid to developing different fusion techniques such as (*i*) *early fusion*, where low-level features from different modalities are learned, fused, and fed into a single prediction model (Jin et al., 2017b; Yang et al., 2018; Zhang et al., 2019; Singhal et al., 2019; Zhou et al., 2020; Kang et al., 2020), (*ii*) *late fusion*, where unimodal decisions are fused with some mechanisms such as averaging and voting (Agrawal et al., 2017; Qi et al., 2019),

[2] `http://github.com/facebookresearch/fine_grained_hateful_memes`

and (*iii*) *hybrid fusion*, where a subset of the learned features are passed to the final classifier (early fusion), and the remaining modalities are fed to the classifier later (late fusion) (Jin et al., 2017a). Here, we use early fusion and joint learning for fusion.

3 Task and Dataset

Below, we describe the CONSTRAINT 2022 shared task and the corresponding dataset provided by the task organizers. More detail can be found in the shared task report (Sharma et al., 2022c).

3.1 Task

The CONSTRAINT 2022 shared task asked participating systems to detect the role of the entities in the meme, given the meme and a list of these entities. Figure 1 shows an example of an image with the extracted OCR text, implicit (image showing Salman Khan, who is not mentioned in the text), and explicit entities and their roles. The example illustrates various challenges: (*i*) an implicit entity, (*ii*) text extracted from the label of the vial, which has little connection to the overlaid written text, (*iii*) unclear target entity in the meme (*Vladimir Putin*). Such complexities are not common in the multimodal tasks we discussed above. The textual representation of the entities and their roles are different than for typical CoNLL-style semantic role labeling tasks (Carreras and Màrquez, 2005), which makes it more difficult to address the problem in the same formulation.

By observing these challenges, we first attempted to address the problem in the same formulation: as a sequence labeling problem by converting the data to CoNLL format (see Section 4.1). Then, we further tried to address it as a classification task, i.e., predict the role of each entity in a given meme–entity pair.

3.2 Data

We use the dataset provided for the CONSTRAINT 2022 shared task. It contains harmful memes, OCR-extracted text from these memes, and manually annotated entities with four roles: *hero*, *villian*, *victim*, and *other*. The datasets cover two domains: COVID-19 and US Politics. The COVID-19 domain consists of 2,700 training and 300 validation examples, while US Politics has 2,852 training and 350 validation examples. The test dataset combines examples from both domains, COVID-19 and US Politics, and has a total of 718 examples.

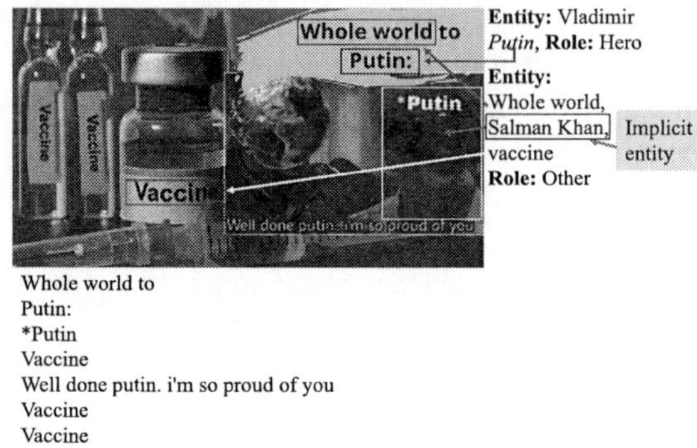

Figure 1: An example image showing the implicit (*Salman Khan*) and the explicit entities (from a text perspective) and their roles.

Class label	Train		Val		Test	
	Count	%	Count	%	Count	%
Hero	475	2	224	3	52	2
Villain	2,427	10	886	10	350	14
Victim	910	5	433	5	114	5
Others	13,702	83	6,937	82	1,917	79
Total	17,514		8,480		2,433	

Table 1: Distribution of the entity roles in the combined COVID-19 + US politics datasets.

For the experiments, we combined the two domains, COVID-19 and US Politics, which resulted in 5,552 training and 650 validation examples.

The class distribution of the entity roles, aggregated over all memes, in the combined COVID-19 + US Politics dataset is highly imbalanced as shown in Table 1. We can see that overall the role of *hero* represents only 2%, and the role of *victim* covers only 5% of the entities. We can further see that the vast majority of the entities are labeled with the *other* role. This skewed distribution adds additional complexity to the modeling task.

4 Experiments

Settings: We addressed the problem both as a sequence labeling and as a classification task. Below, we discuss each of them in detail.

Evaluation measures: In our experiments, we used accuracy, macro-average precision, recall, and F_1 score. The latter was the official evaluation measure for the shared task.

Provided JSON

{"OCR": "Bernie or Elizabeth?\nBe informed.Compare them on the issues that matter.\nIssue: Who makes the dankest memes?\n", "image": "covid_memes_18.png", "hero": [], "villain": [], "victim": [], "other": ["bernie sanders", "elizabeth warren"]}

Converted into IOB format

bernie	or	elizabeth	?	be	...	dankest	memes	?	sanders	warren
B-other	O	B-other	O	O	...	O	O	O	B-other	I-other

Figure 2: Example with text in BIO format.

4.1 Sequence Labeling

For the sequence labeling experiments, we first converted the OCR text and the entities to the CoNLL BIO-format. An example is shown in Figure 2. To convert them, we matched the entities in the text and we assigned the same tag (role label) to the token in the text. For the implicit entity that is not in the text, we added them at the end of the text and we assigned them the annotated role; we labeled all other tokens with the O-tag.

We trained the model using Conditional Random Fields (CRFs) (Lafferty et al., 2001), which has been widely used in earlier work. As features, we used part-of-speech tags, token length, tri-grams, presence of digits, use of special characters, token shape, w2vcluster, LDA topics, words present in a vocabulary list built on the training set, and in a name list, etc.[3] We ran two sets of experiments: (*i*) using the same format, and (*ii*) using only entities as shown in Figure 2.

4.2 Classification

For the classification experiments, we first converted the dataset into a classification problem. As it contains all examples with one or more entities, we reorganized the dataset so that an example contains an entity, OCR text, image, and entity role. Hence, the dataset size is now the same as the number of entity instances rather than memes. We ended up with 17,514 training examples, which is the number of training entities as shown in Table 1.

We then ran different unimodal and multimodal experiments: (*i*) only text, (*ii*) only meme, and (*iii*) text and meme together. For each setting, we also ran several baseline experiments. We further ran advanced experiments such as adding attention to the network and text-based data augmentation. Figure 3 shows our experimental pipeline for this classification task. For the unimodal experiments, we used individual modalities, and we trained them using different pre-trained models.

[3]More details about the feature set can be found at `https://github.com/moejoe95/crf-vs-rnn-ner`

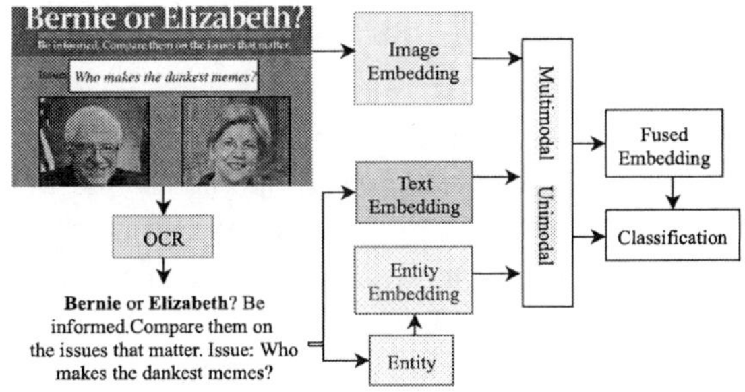

Figure 3: Diagram of our experimental pipeline.

Note that for the text modality, we ran several combinations of fusion (e.g., text and entity) experiments. For the multimodal experiments, we combined embedding from both modalities, and we ran the classification on the fused embedding, as shown in Figure 3.

4.2.1 Text Modality

For the text modality, we experimented using BERT (Devlin et al., 2019) and XLM-RoBERTa (Liu et al., 2019). We performed ten reruns for each experiment using different random seeds, and then we picked the model that performed best on the development set. We used a batch size of 8, a learning rate of 2e-5, a maximum sequence length of 128, three epochs, and categorical cross-entropy as the loss function. We used the Transformer toolkit to train the transformer-based models.

Using the text-only modality, we also ran a different combination of experiments using the text and the entities, where we used bilinear fusion to combine them. We discuss this fusion technique in more detail in Section 4.2.3.

4.2.2 Image Modality

For our experiments using the image modality, we extract features from a pre-trained model, and then we trained an SVM classifier using these features. In particular, we extracted features from the penultimate layer of the EfficientNet-b1 (EffNet) model (Tan and Le, 2019), which was trained using the ImageNet dataset. For training the model using the extracted features, we used SVM with its default parameter settings, with no further optimization of its hyper-parameter values. We chose EffNet as it was shown to achieve better performance for some social media image classification tasks (Alam et al., 2021a,b).

4.2.3 Multimodal: Text and Image

For the multimodal experiments, we used the BLOCK Fusion (Ben-younes et al., 2019) approach, which was originally proposed for question answering (QA). Our motivation is that an entity can be seen like a question about the meme context, asking for its role as an answer. In a QA setting, there are three elements: (*i*) a context (image or text), (*ii*) a question, and (*iii*) a list of answers. The goal is to select the right answer from the answer list. Similarly, we have four types of answers (i.e., roles). The task formation is that for an entity and a context (image or text), we need to determine the role of the entity in that context.

BLOCK fusion is a multi-modal framework based on block-superdiagonal tensor decomposition, where tensor blocks are decomposed into blocks of smaller sizes, with the size characterized by a set of mode-n ranks (De Lathauwer, 2008). It is a bilinear model that takes two vectors $x^1 \in R^I$ and $x^2 \in R^J$ as input and then projects them to a K-dimensional space with tensor products: $y = \mathcal{T} \times x^1 \times x^2$, where $y \in R^K$. Each component of y is a quadratic form of the inputs, $\forall k \in [1; K]$:

$$y_k = \sum_{i=1}^{I} \sum_{j=1}^{J} \mathcal{T}_{ijk} x_i^1 x_2^j \tag{1}$$

BLOCK fusion can model bilinear interactions between groups of features, while limiting the complexity of the model, but keeping expressive high dimensional mono-model representations (Ben-younes et al., 2019). We used BLOCK fusion in different settings: (*i*) for image and entity, (*ii*) for text and entity, and (*iii*) for text, image with entity.

Text and entity: We extracted embedding representation for the entity and the text using a pre-trained BERT model. We then fed both embedding representations into linear layers of 512 neurons each. The output of two linear layers is taken as input to the trainable block fusion network. Then, a regularization layer and linear layer are used before the final layer.

Image and entity: To build embedding representations for the image and the entity, we used a vision transformer (ViT) (Dosovitskiy et al., 2021) and BERT pretrained models. The output of two different modalities was then used as input to the block fusion network.

Image, text, and entity: In this setting, we first built embedding representations for the text and the image using a pretraind BERT and ViT models, respectively. Then, we concatenated these representations (text + image) and we passed them to a linear layer with 512 neurons. We then extracted embedding representation for the target entity using the pretraind BERT model. Afterwards, we merged the text + image and the entity representations and we fed them into the fusion layer. In this way, we combined the image and the text representations as a unified context, aiming to predict the role of the target entity in this context.

In all the experiments, we uses a learning rate of $1e^{-6}$, a batch size of 8, and a maximum length of the text of 512.

4.2.4 Additional Experiments

We ran two additional sets of experiments using attention mechanism and augmentation, as using such approaches has been shown to help in many natural language processing (NLP) tasks.

Attention: In the entity + image block fusion network, we used block fusion to merge the entity and the image representations. Instead of using the image representation directly, we used attention mechanism on the image and then we fed the attended features along with the entity representation into the entity + image block. To compute the attention, we used the PyTorchNLP library.[4] In a similar fashion, we applied the attention mechanism to the text and to the combined text + image representation.

Augmentation: Text data augmentation has recently gained a lot of popularity as a way to address data scarceness and class imbalance (Feng et al., 2021). We used three types of text augmentation techniques to balance the distribution of the different class: (*i*) synonym augmentation using WordNet, (*ii*) word substitution using BERT, and (*iii*) a combination thereof. In our experiments, we used the NLPAug data augmentation package.[5] Note that we applied six times augmentation for the *hero* class, twice for the *villain* class, and three times for the *victim* class. These numbers were empirically set and require further investigation in future work.

[4] `http://github.com/PetrochukM/PyTorch-NLP`

[5] `https://github.com/makcedward/nlpaug`

Exp.	Acc	P	R	F1
All tokens	0.51	0.32	0.21	0.24
Only entities	0.77	0.40	0.27	0.25

Table 2: Evaluation results on the test set for the sequence labeling reformulation of the problem.

5 Results and Discussion

Below, we first discuss our sequence labeling and classification experiments. We then perform some analysis, and finally, we put our results in a broader perspective in the context of the shared task.

5.1 Sequence Labeling Results

Table 2 shows the evaluation results on the test set for our sequence labeling reformulation of the problem. We performed two experiments: one where we used as input the entire meme text (i.e., all tokens), and another one where we used the concatenation of the target entities only. We can see that the latter performed marginally better, but overall the macro-F1 score is quite low in both cases.

5.2 Classification Results

Table 3 shows the evaluation results on the test set for our classification reformulation of the problem. We computed the *majority class* baseline (row 0), which always predicts the most frequent label in the training set. Due to time limitations, our official submission used the image modality only, which resulted in a very low macro-F1 score of 0.23, as shown in row 1. For our text modality experiments, we used the meme text and the entities. We experimented with BERT and XLM-RoBERTa, obtaining better results using the former. Using the BLOCK fusion technique on unimodal (text + entity) and multimodality (text + image + entity) yielded sizable improvements. The combination of image + text (rows 6 and 9) did not yield much better results compared to using text only (row 4). Next, we added attention on top of block fusion, which improved the performance, but there was no much difference between the different combinations (rows 7–9). Considering only the text and the entity, we observe an improvement using text augmentation. Among the different augmentation techniques, there was no performance difference between WordNet and BERT, and combining them yielded worse results.

Exp.	Acc	P	R	F1
Baseline				
0 Majority	0.79	0.20	0.25	0.22
Image modality				
1 EffNet feat + SVM	*0.72*	*0.24*	*0.25*	*0.23*
Text modality				
2 BERT	0.76	0.42	0.36	0.37
3 XLM-RoBERTa	0.75	0.38	0.32	0.32
Multimodality/Fusion				
BLOCK fusion				
4 Entity + Text	0.74	0.44	0.43	0.43
5 Entity + Image	0.74	0.39	0.39	0.39
6 Entity + (Text + Image)	0.75	0.43	0.42	0.41
Attention				
7 Entity + Text	0.72	0.42	0.48	0.44
8 Entity + Image	0.71	0.42	0.48	0.44
9 Entity + (Text + Image)	0.71	0.42	0.49	0.44
Augmentation				
10 Entity + Text (WordNet aug)	0.76	0.48	0.46	**0.46**
11 Entity + Text (BERT aug)	0.74	0.46	0.46	**0.46**
12 Entity + Text (Mix aug)	0.77	0.49	0.41	0.43

Table 3: Evaluation results on the test set for our classification reformulation of the problem. Our official submission for the shared task is shown in *italic*.

5.3 Role-Level Analysis

Next, we studied the impact of using attention and data augmentation on the individual entity roles: *hero*, *villain*, *victim*, and *other*.

Table 4 shows the impact of using attention on (a) entity + image (left side), and (b) entity + [image + text] (right side) combinations. We can observe a sizable gain for the *hero* (+0.09), the *villain* (+0.06), and the *victim* (+0.07) roles in the former case (a). However, for case (b), there is an improvement for the *victim* role only; yet, this improvement is quite sizable: +0.16.

Table 5 shows the impact of data augmentation using WordNet or BERT on the individual roles. We can observe sizable performance gains of +0.11 for the *hero* role, and +0.04 for the *villain* role, when using WordNet-based data augmentation. Similarly, BERT-based data augmentation yields +0.12 for the *hero* role, and +0.02 for the *villain* role. However, the impact of either augmentation on the *victim* and on the *other* role is negligible.

	E+I, w/o Att.			E+I, w/ Att.			E+[I+T], w/o Att.			E+[I+T], w/ Att.		
Role	**P**	**R**	**F1**	**P**	**R**	**F1**	**P**	**R**	**F1**	**P**	**R**	**F1**
Hero	0.06	0.02	0.03	0.09	0.15	**0.12**	0.22	0.12	0.15	0.09	0.21	0.12
Villain	0.35	0.44	0.39	0.40	0.51	**0.45**	0.39	0.54	0.45	0.39	0.54	0.45
Victim	0.30	0.25	0.28	0.33	0.39	**0.35**	0.23	0.18	0.20	0.31	0.45	**0.36**
Other	0.86	0.84	0.85	0.88	0.81	0.84	0.87	0.84	0.85	0.89	0.77	0.82

Table 4: Role-level results on the test set with (w/) or without (w/o) attention between the context (text, image) and the entity. (E: Entity, I: Image, Att.: Attention, T: Text)

	No Aug.			Aug. WordNet			Aug. BERT		
Role	**P**	**R**	**F1**	**P**	**R**	**F1**	**P**	**R**	**F1**
Hero	0.21	0.12	0.15	0.33	0.21	**0.26**	0.30	0.25	**0.27**
Villain	0.36	0.49	0.42	0.41	0.52	**0.46**	0.39	0.51	**0.44**
Victim	0.31	0.27	0.29	0.30	0.27	0.29	0.29	0.27	0.28
Other	0.87	0.83	0.85	0.87	0.84	0.86	0.87	0.83	0.85

Table 5: Role-level results on the test set for the entity + text combination with and without augmentation.

5.4 Official Submission

For our official submission for the task, we used the image modality system from line 1 in Table 3, which was quite weak, with a macro-F1 score of 0.23. Our subsequent experiments and analysis pointed to several promising directions: (*i*) combining the textual and the image modalities, (*ii*) using attention, (*iii*) performing data augmentation. As a result, we managed to improve our results to 0.46. Yet, this is still far behind the F1-score of the winning system: 0.5867.

6 Conclusion and Future Work

We addressed the problem of understanding the role of the entities in harmful memes, as part of the CONSTRAINT-2022 shared task. We presented a comparative analysis of the importance of different modalities: the text and the image. We further experimented with two task reformulations —sequence labeling and classification—, and we found the latter to work better. Overall, we obtained improvements when using BLOCK fusion, attention between the image and the text representations, and data augmentation.

In future work, we plan to combine the sequence and the classification formulations in a joint multimodal setting. We further want to experiment with multi-task learning using other meme analysis tasks and datasets. Last but not least, we plan to develop better data augmentation techniques to improve the performance on the low-frequency roles.

Acknowledgments

The work is part of the Tanbih mega-project, which is developed at the Qatar Computing Research Institute, HBKU, and aims to limit the impact of "fake news," propaganda, and media bias by making users aware of what they are reading, thus promoting media literacy and critical thinking.

References

Tariq Habib Afridi, Aftab Alam, Muhammad Numan Khan, Jawad Khan, and Young Koo Lee. 2020. A multimodal memes classification: A survey and open research issues. In *Proceedings of the 5th International Conference on Smart City Applications*, SCA '20, pages 1451–1466, Online. Springer.

Taruna Agrawal, Rahul Gupta, and Shrikanth Narayanan. 2017. Multimodal detection of fake social media use through a fusion of classification and pairwise ranking systems. In *Proceedings of the 25th European Signal Processing Conference*, EUSIPCO '17, pages 1045–1049. IEEE.

Firoj Alam, Tanvirul Alam, Md Hasan, Abul Hasnat, Muhammad Imran, Ferda Ofli, et al. 2021a. MEDIC: a multi-task learning dataset for disaster image classification. *arXiv:2108.12828*.

Firoj Alam, Tanvirul Alam, Muhammad Imran, and Ferda Ofli. 2021b. Robust training of social media image classification models for rapid disaster response. *arXiv:2104.04184*.

Firoj Alam, Stefano Cresci, Tanmoy Chakraborty, Fabrizio Silvestri, Dimiter Dimitrov, Giovanni Da San

Martino, Shaden Shaar, Hamed Firooz, and Preslav Nakov. 2021c. A survey on multimodal disinformation detection. *arXiv preprint arXiv:2103.12541*.

Firoj Alam, Shaden Shaar, Fahim Dalvi, Hassan Sajjad, Alex Nikolov, Hamdy Mubarak, Giovanni Da San Martino, Ahmed Abdelali, Nadir Durrani, Kareem Darwish, Abdulaziz Al-Homaid, Wajdi Zaghouani, Tommaso Caselli, Gijs Danoe, Friso Stolk, Britt Bruntink, and Preslav Nakov. 2021d. Fighting the COVID-19 infodemic: Modeling the perspective of journalists, fact-checkers, social media platforms, policy makers, and the society. In *Findings of the Association for Computational Linguistics*, EMNLP (Findings) '21, pages 611–649, Punta Cana, Dominican Republic. Association for Computational Linguistics.

Hedi Ben-younes, Remi Cadene, Nicolas Thome, and Matthieu Cord. 2019. BLOCK: Bilinear superdiagonal fusion for visual question answering and visual relationship detection. In *Proceedings of the AAAI Conference on Artificial Intelligence*, AAAI '19, Honolulu, Hawaii, USA. AAAI Press.

Alessandro Bondielli and Francesco Marcelloni. 2019. A survey on fake news and rumour detection techniques. *Information Sciences*, 497:38–55.

Sian Brooke. 2019. "Condescending, Rude, Assholes": Framing gender and hostility on Stack Overflow. In *Proceedings of the Third Workshop on Abusive Language Online*, pages 172–180, Florence, Italy. Association for Computational Linguistics.

Xavier Carreras and Lluís Màrquez. 2005. Introduction to the CoNLL-2005 shared task: Semantic role labeling. In *Proceedings of the 9th Conference on Computational Natural Language Learning*, CoNLL '05, pages 152–164, Ann Arbor, Michigan, USA.

Mohit Chandra, Dheeraj Reddy Pailla, Himanshu Bhatia, AadilMehdi J. Sanchawala, Manish Gupta, Manish Shrivastava, and Ponnurangam Kumaraguru. 2021. "Subverting the Jewtocracy": Online antisemitism detection using multimodal deep learning. In *Proceedings of the 13th ACM Web Science Conference 2021*, WebSci '21, pages 148–157. ACM.

Yu-Wei Chao, Yunfan Liu, Xieyang Liu, Huayi Zeng, and Jia Deng. 2018. Learning to detect human-object interactions. In *Proceedings of the 2018 IEEE Winter Conference on Applications of Computer Vision*, WACV '18, pages 381–389, Lake Tahoe, Nevada, USA. IEEE.

Yu-Wei Chao, Zhan Wang, Yugeng He, Jiaxuan Wang, and Jia Deng. 2015. HICO: A benchmark for recognizing human-object interactions in images. In *Proceedings of the IEEE International Conference on Computer Vision*, ICCV '15, pages 1017–1025, Santiago, Chile. IEEE.

Yen-Chun Chen, Linjie Li, Licheng Yu, Ahmed El Kholy, Faisal Ahmed, Zhe Gan, Yu Cheng, and Jingjing Liu. 2020. UNITER: UNiversal Image-TExt Representation learning. In *Proceedings of the European Conference on Computer Vision*, ECCV '20, pages 104–120, Cham. Springer International Publishing.

Giovanni Da San Martino, Stefano Cresci, Alberto Barrón-Cedeño, Seunghak Yu, Roberto Di Pietro, and Preslav Nakov. 2020. A survey on computational propaganda detection. In *Proceedings of the Twenty-Ninth International Joint Conference on Artificial Intelligence*, IJCAI '20, pages 4826–4832, Online. IJCAI.

Giovanni Da San Martino, Seunghak Yu, Alberto Barrón-Cedeño, Rostislav Petrov, and Preslav Nakov. 2019. Fine-grained analysis of propaganda in news article. In *Proceedings of the 2019 Conference on Empirical Methods in Natural Language Processing and the 9th International Joint Conference on Natural Language Processing*, EMNLP-IJCNLP '19, pages 5636–5646, Hong Kong, China. Association for Computational Linguistics.

Lieven De Lathauwer. 2008. Decompositions of a higher-order tensor in block terms—part ii: Definitions and uniqueness. *SIAM Journal on Matrix Analysis and Applications*, 30(3):1033–1066.

Jacob Devlin, Ming-Wei Chang, Kenton Lee, and Kristina Toutanova. 2019. BERT: Pre-training of deep bidirectional transformers for language understanding. In *Proceedings of the 2019 Conference of the North American Chapter of the Association for Computational Linguistics: Human Language Technologies*, NAACL-HLT '19, pages 4171–4186, Minneapolis, Minnesota, USA. Association for Computational Linguistics.

Dimitar Dimitrov, Bishr Bin Ali, Shaden Shaar, Firoj Alam, Fabrizio Silvestri, Hamed Firooz, Preslav Nakov, and Giovanni Da San Martino. 2021a. Detecting propaganda techniques in memes. In *Proceedings of the 59th Annual Meeting of the Association for Computational Linguistics and the 11th International Joint Conference on Natural Language Processing*, ACL-IJCNLP '21, pages 6603–6617, Online. Association for Computational Linguistics.

Dimitar Dimitrov, Bishr Bin Ali, Shaden Shaar, Firoj Alam, Fabrizio Silvestri, Hamed Firooz, Preslav Nakov, and Giovanni Da San Martino. 2021b. Task 6 at SemEval-2021: Detection of persuasion techniques in texts and images. In *Proceedings of the 15th International Workshop on Semantic Evaluation*, SemEval '21, Bangkok, Thailand. Association for Computational Linguistics.

Alexey Dosovitskiy, Lucas Beyer, Alexander Kolesnikov, Dirk Weissenborn, Xiaohua Zhai, Thomas Unterthiner, Mostafa Dehghani, Matthias Minderer, Georg Heigold, Sylvain Gelly, Jakob Uszkoreit, and Neil Houlsby. 2021. An image is worth 16x16 words: Transformers for image recognition at scale. In *Proceedings of the International*

Conference on Learning Representations, ICLR '21, Online.

Steven Y Feng, Varun Gangal, Jason Wei, Sarath Chandar, Soroush Vosoughi, Teruko Mitamura, and Eduard Hovy. 2021. A survey of data augmentation approaches for NLP. In *Findings of the Association for Computational Linguistics: ACL-IJCNLP 2021*, pages 968–988, Online. Association for Computational Linguistics.

Elisabetta Fersini, Francesca Gasparini, and Silvia Corchs. 2019. Detecting sexist MEME on the web: A study on textual and visual cues. In *Proceedings of the 8th International Conference on Affective Computing and Intelligent Interaction*, ACIIW '19, pages 226–231, Cambridge, UK. IEEE.

Nicholas FitzGerald, Oscar Täckström, Kuzman Ganchev, and Dipanjan Das. 2015. Semantic role labeling with neural network factors. In *Proceedings of the 2015 Conference on Empirical Methods in Natural Language Processing*, EMNLP '15, pages 960–970, Lisbon, Portugal. Association for Computational Linguistics.

Paula Fortuna and Sérgio Nunes. 2018. A survey on automatic detection of hate speech in text. *ACM Computing Surveys*, 51(4):1–30.

Zhe Gan, Yen-Chun Chen, Linjie Li, Chen Zhu, Yu Cheng, and Jingjing Liu. 2020. Large-scale adversarial training for vision-and-language representation learning. *Advances in Neural Information Processing Systems*, 33:6616–6628.

Francesca Gasparini, Giulia Rizzi, Aurora Saibene, and Elisabetta Fersini. 2021. Benchmark dataset of memes with text transcriptions for automatic detection of multi-modal misogynistic content. *arXiv:2106.08409*.

Saurabh Gupta and Jitendra Malik. 2015. Visual semantic role labeling. *arXiv:1505.04474*.

Batoul Haidar, Maroun Chamoun, and Fadi Yamout. 2016. Cyberbullying detection: A survey on multilingual techniques. In *Proceedings of the 2016 European Modelling Symposium*, EMS '2016, pages 165–171, Pisa, Italy. IEEE.

Momchil Hardalov, Arnav Arora, Preslav Nakov, and Isabelle Augenstein. 2022. A survey on stance detection for mis- and disinformation identification. In *Proceedings of the 2022 Conference of the North American Chapter of the Association for Computational Linguistics: Human Language Technologies*, NAACL-HLT '2022, Seattle, Washington, USA.

Luheng He, Kenton Lee, Mike Lewis, and Luke Zettlemoyer. 2017. Deep semantic role labeling: What works and what's next. In *Proceedings of the 55th Annual Meeting of the Association for Computational Linguistics*, ACL '17, pages 473–483, Vancouver, Canada. Association for Computational Linguistics.

Kristina Hristakieva, Stefano Cresci, Giovanni Da San Martino, Mauro Conti, and Preslav Nakov. 2022. The spread of propaganda by coordinated communities on social media. In *Proceedings of the 14th International ACM Conference on Web Science*, WebSci '2022, Barcelona, Spain. ACM.

Fatemah Husain and Ozlem Uzuner. 2021. A survey of offensive language detection for the arabic language. *ACM Transactions on Asian and Low-Resource Language Information Processing (TALLIP)*, 20(1):1–44.

Zhiwei Jin, Juan Cao, Han Guo, Yongdong Zhang, and Jiebo Luo. 2017a. Multimodal fusion with recurrent neural networks for rumor detection on microblogs. In *Proceedings of the 25th ACM international conference on Multimedia*, MM '17, pages 795–816, California, USA. ACM.

Zhiwei Jin, Juan Cao, Yongdong Zhang, Jianshe Zhou, and Qi Tian. 2017b. Novel visual and statistical image features for microblogs news verification. *IEEE Transactions on Multimedia*, 19(3):598–608.

Srecko Joksimovic, Ryan S. Baker, Jaclyn Ocumpaugh, Juan Miguel L. Andres, Ivan Tot, Elle Yuan Wang, and Shane Dawson. 2019. Automated identification of verbally abusive behaviors in online discussions. In *Proceedings of the Third Workshop on Abusive Language Online*, pages 36–45, Florence, Italy. Association for Computational Linguistics.

SeongKu Kang, Junyoung Hwang, and Hwanjo Yu. 2020. Multi-modal component embedding for fake news detection. In *Proceedings of the 14th International Conference on Ubiquitous Information Management and Communication*, IMCOM '20, pages 1–6, Taichung, Taiwan. IEEE.

Douwe Kiela, Hamed Firooz, Aravind Mohan, Vedanuj Goswami, Amanpreet Singh, Casey A Fitzpatrick, Peter Bull, Greg Lipstein, Tony Nelli, Ron Zhu, et al. 2021. The hateful memes challenge: competition report. In *Proceedings of the 35th International Conference on Neural Information Processing Systems: Competition and Demonstration Track*, NeurIPS '21, pages 344–360, Online.

Douwe Kiela, Hamed Firooz, Aravind Mohan, Vedanuj Goswami, Amanpreet Singh, Pratik Ringshia, and Davide Testuggine. 2020. The hateful memes challenge: Detecting hate speech in multimodal memes. In *Proceedings of the 34th International Conference on Neural Information Processing Systems*, NIPS '20, NY, USA. Curran Associates Inc.

Ritesh Kumar, Atul Kr. Ojha, Shervin Malmasi, and Marcos Zampieri. 2018. Benchmarking aggression identification in social media. In *Proceedings of the First Workshop on Trolling, Aggression and Cyberbullying*, TRAC'2018, pages 1–11, Santa Fe, New Mexico, USA. Association for Computational Linguistics.

John D. Lafferty, Andrew McCallum, and Fernando C. N. Pereira. 2001. Conditional random fields: Probabilistic models for segmenting and labeling sequence data. In *Proceedings of the Eighteenth International Conference on Machine Learning*, ICML '01, pages 282–289, San Francisco, California, USA. Morgan Kaufmann Publishers Inc.

Daniil Larionov, Artem Shelmanov, Elena Chistova, and Ivan Smirnov. 2019. Semantic role labeling with pretrained language models for known and unknown predicates. In *Proceedings of the International Conference on Recent Advances in Natural Language Processing*, RANLP '2019, pages 619–628, Varna, Bulgaria. INCOMA Ltd.

Liunian Harold Li, Mark Yatskar, Da Yin, Cho-Jui Hsieh, and Kai-Wei Chang. 2019. VisualBERT: A simple and performant baseline for vision and language. *arXiv:1908.03557*.

Manling Li, Alireza Zareian, Qi Zeng, Spencer Whitehead, Di Lu, Heng Ji, and Shih-Fu Chang. 2020. Cross-media structured common space for multimedia event extraction. In *Proceedings of the 58th Annual Meeting of the Association for Computational Linguistics*, ACL '20, pages 2557–2568, Online. Association for Computational Linguistics.

Yinhan Liu, Myle Ott, Naman Goyal, Jingfei Du, Mandar Joshi, Danqi Chen, Omer Levy, Mike Lewis, Luke Zettlemoyer, and Veselin Stoyanov. 2019. RoBERTa: A robustly optimized BERT pretraining approach. *arXiv preprint arXiv:1907.11692*.

Hamdy Mubarak, Kareem Darwish, and Walid Magdy. 2017. Abusive language detection on Arabic social media. In *Proceedings of the First Workshop on Abusive Language Online*, WALO '17, pages 52–56, Vancouver, BC, Canada. Association for Computational Linguistics.

Preslav Nakov, Alberto Barrón-Cedeño, Giovanni Da San Martino, Firoj Alam, Julia Maria Struß, Thomas Mandl, Rubén Míguez, Tommaso Caselli, Mucahid Kutlu, Wajdi Zaghouani, Chengkai Li, Shaden Shaar, Gautam Kishore Shahi, Hamdy Mubarak, Alex Nikolov, Nikolay Babulkov, Yavuz Selim Kartal, and Javier Beltrán. 2022. The CLEF-2022 CheckThat! lab on fighting the COVID-19 infodemic and fake news detection. In *Advances in Information Retrieval*, CLEF '2022, pages 416–428. Springer International Publishing.

Preslav Nakov, Husrev Taha Sencar, Jisun An, and Haewoon Kwak. 2021. A survey on predicting the factuality and the bias of news media. *arXiv:2103.12506*.

Martha Palmer, Daniel Gildea, and Nianwen Xue. 2010. Semantic role labeling. *Synthesis Lectures on Human Language Technologies*, 3(1):1–103.

Shraman Pramanick, Shivam Sharma, Dimitar Dimitrov, Md. Shad Akhtar, Preslav Nakov, and Tanmoy Chakraborty. 2021. MOMENTA: A multimodal framework for detecting harmful memes and their targets. In *Findings of the Association for Computational Linguistics*, EMNLP (Findings) '21, pages 4439–4455, Punta Cana, Dominican Republic. Association for Computational Linguistics.

Sarah Pratt, Mark Yatskar, Luca Weihs, Ali Farhadi, and Aniruddha Kembhavi. 2020. Grounded situation recognition. In *Proceedings of the European Conference on Computer Vision*, ECCV '20, pages 314–332, Online. Springer.

Peng Qi, Juan Cao, Tianyun Yang, Junbo Guo, and Jintao Li. 2019. Exploiting multi-domain visual information for fake news detection. In *Proceedings of the IEEE International Conference on Data Mining*, ICDM '19, pages 518–527, Beijing, China. IEEE.

Sara Rosenthal, Pepa Atanasova, Georgi Karadzhov, Marcos Zampieri, and Preslav Nakov. 2021. SOLID: A Large-Scale Semi-Supervised Dataset for Offensive Language Identification. In *Findings of the Association for Computational Linguistics*, ACL-IJCNLP (Findings) '21, pages 915–928, Online. Association for Computational Linguistics.

Arka Sadhu, Tanmay Gupta, Mark Yatskar, Ram Nevatia, and Aniruddha Kembhavi. 2021. Visual semantic role labeling for video understanding. In *Proceedings of the IEEE/CVF Conference on Computer Vision and Pattern Recognition*, CVPR '21, pages 5589–5600, Online. IEEE.

Anna Schmidt and Michael Wiegand. 2017. A survey on hate speech detection using natural language processing. In *Proceedings of the Fifth International Workshop on Natural Language Processing for Social Media*, pages 1–10, Valencia, Spain. Association for Computational Linguistics.

Shivam Sharma, Md Shad Akhtar, Preslav Nakov, and Tanmoy Chakraborty. 2022a. DISARM: Detecting the victims targeted by harmful memes. In *Findings of North American Chapter of the Association for Computational Linguistics*, EMNLP (Findings) '22, Seattle, Washington, USA. Association for Computational Linguistics.

Shivam Sharma, Firoj Alam, Md. Shad Akhtar, Dimitar Dimitrov, Giovanni Da San Martino, Hamed Firooz, Alon Halevy, Fabrizio Silvestri, Preslav Nakov, and Tanmoy Chakraborty. 2022b. Detecting and understanding harmful memes: A survey. In *Proceedings of the 31st International Joint Conference on Artificial Intelligence*, IJCAI-ECAI '22, Vienna, Austria.

Shivam Sharma, Tharun Suresh, Atharva Jitendra, Himanshi Mathur, Preslav Nakov, Md. Shad Akhtar, and Tanmoy Chakraborty. 2022c. Findings of the constraint 2022 shared task on detecting the hero, the villain, and the victim in memes. In *Proceedings of the Workshop on Combating Online Hostile Posts in Regional Languages during Emergency Situations*, CONSTRAINT '22, Dublin, Ireland. Association for Computational Linguistics.

Limor Shifman. 2013. *Memes in digital culture*. MIT press.

Carina Silberer and Manfred Pinkal. 2018. Grounding semantic roles in images. In *Proceedings of the 2018 Conference on Empirical Methods in Natural Language Processing*, EMNLP '18, pages 2616–2626, Brussels, Belgium. Association for Computational Linguistics.

Karen Simonyan and Andrew Zisserman. 2015. Very deep convolutional networks for large-scale image recognition. In *Proceedings of the 3rd International Conference on Learning Representations*, ICLR '15, San Diego, CA, USA.

Shivangi Singhal, Rajiv Ratn Shah, Tanmoy Chakraborty, Ponnurangam Kumaraguru, and Shin'ichi Satoh. 2019. SpotFake: A multi-modal framework for fake news detection. In *Proceedings of the 2019 IEEE fifth international conference on multimedia big data*, BigMM '19, pages 39–47. IEEE.

Weijie Su, Xizhou Zhu, Yue Cao, Bin Li, Lewei Lu, Furu Wei, and Jifeng Dai. 2020. VL-BERT: pre-training of generic visual-linguistic representations. In *Proceedings of the 8th International Conference on Learning Representations*, ICLR '20, Addis Ababa, Ethiopia. OpenReview.net.

Shardul Suryawanshi and Bharathi Raja Chakravarthi. 2021. Findings of the shared task on Troll Meme Classification in Tamil. In *Proceedings of the First Workshop on Speech and Language Technologies for Dravidian Languages*, Kyiv. Association for Computational Linguistics.

Shardul Suryawanshi, Bharathi Raja Chakravarthi, Mihael Arcan, and Paul Buitelaar. 2020a. Multimodal meme dataset (MultiOFF) for identifying offensive content in image and text. In *Proceedings of the Second Workshop on Trolling, Aggression and Cyberbullying*, pages 32–41, Marseille, France. European Language Resources Association.

Shardul Suryawanshi, Bharathi Raja Chakravarthi, Pranav Verma, Mihael Arcan, John Philip McCrae, and Paul Buitelaar. 2020b. A dataset for troll classification of TamilMemes. In *Proceedings of the 5th Workshop on Indian Language Data: Resources and Evaluation*, WILDRE '20, pages 7–13, Marseille, France. European Language Resources Association.

Mingxing Tan and Quoc Le. 2019. EfficientNet: Rethinking model scaling for convolutional neural networks. In *Proceedings of the International Conference on Machine Learning*, ICLR '19, pages 6105–6114, CA, USA.

Cynthia Van Hee, Els Lefever, Ben Verhoeven, Julie Mennes, Bart Desmet, Guy De Pauw, Walter Daelemans, and Veronique Hoste. 2015. Detection and fine-grained classification of cyberbullying events. In *Proceedings of the International Conference Recent Advances in Natural Language Processing*, RANLP '15, pages 672–680, Hissar, Bulgaria. INCOMA Ltd. Shoumen, Bulgaria.

Shaohua Yang, Qiaozi Gao, Changsong Liu, Caiming Xiong, Song-Chun Zhu, and Joyce Chai. 2016. Grounded semantic role labeling. In *Proceedings of the 2016 Conference of the North American Chapter of the Association for Computational Linguistics: Human Language Technologies*, NAACL-HLT '16, pages 149–159, San Diego, California. Association for Computational Linguistics.

Yang Yang, Lei Zheng, Jiawei Zhang, Qingcai Cui, Zhoujun Li, and Philip S Yu. 2018. TI-CNN: Convolutional neural networks for fake news detection. *arXiv:1806.00749*.

Mark Yatskar, Luke Zettlemoyer, and Ali Farhadi. 2016. Situation recognition: Visual semantic role labeling for image understanding. In *Proceedings of the IEEE Conference on Computer Vision and Pattern Recognition*, CVPR '16, San Juan, PR, USA. IEEE.

Marcos Zampieri, Shervin Malmasi, Preslav Nakov, Sara Rosenthal, Noura Farra, and Ritesh Kumar. 2019. Predicting the type and target of offensive posts in social media. In *Proceedings of the 2019 Conference of the North American Chapter of the Association for Computational Linguistics: Human Language Technologies*, NAACL '19, pages 1415–1420, Minneapolis, Minnesota, USA. Association for Computational Linguistics.

Savvas Zannettou, Tristan Caulfield, Jeremy Blackburn, Emiliano De Cristofaro, Michael Sirivianos, Gianluca Stringhini, and Guillermo Suarez-Tangil. 2018. On the origins of memes by means of fringe web communities. In *Proceedings of the Internet Measurement Conference*, IMC '18, pages 188–202, Boston, USA. ACM.

Huaiwen Zhang, Quan Fang, Shengsheng Qian, and Changsheng Xu. 2019. Multi-modal knowledge-aware event memory network for social media rumor detection. In *Proceedings of the 27th ACM International Conference on Multimedia*, MM '19, page 1942–1951, Nice, France. ACM.

Xinyi Zhou, Jindi Wu, and Reza Zafarani. 2020. SAFE: Similarity-aware multi-modal fake news detection. In *Proceedings of the Pacific-Asia Conference on Knowledge Discovery and Data Mining*, PAKDD '20, pages 354–367, Singapore. Springer.

Xinyi Zhou and Reza Zafarani. 2020. A survey of fake news: Fundamental theories, detection methods, and opportunities. *ACM Computing Surveys*, 53(5):1–40.

Haris Bin Zia, Ignacio Castro, and Gareth Tyson. 2021. Racist or sexist meme? Classifying memes beyond hateful. In *Proceedings of the 5th Workshop on Online Abuse and Harms*, WOAH '21, pages 215–219, Online. Association for Computational Linguistics.

Fine-tuning and Sampling Strategies for Multimodal Role Labeling of Entities under Class Imbalance

Syrielle Montariol[†*] and **Étienne Simon**[‡*] and **Arij Riabi**[†] and **Djamé Seddah**[†]

[†]INRIA Paris
F-75012 Paris, France
firstname.lastname@inria.fr

[‡]Sorbonne Université, CNRS, ISIR
F-75005 Paris, France
etienne.simon@isir.upmc.fr

Abstract

We propose our solution to the multimodal semantic role labeling task from the CONSTRAINT'22 workshop. The task aims at classifying entities in memes into classes such as "hero" and "villain". We use several pre-trained multi-modal models to jointly encode the text and image of the memes, and implement three systems to classify the role of the entities. We propose dynamic sampling strategies to tackle the issue of class imbalance. Finally, we perform qualitative analysis on the representations of the entities.

1 Introduction

Social media memes can be defined as "*pieces of culture, typically jokes, which gain influence through online transmission*" (Davison, 2012). More specifically, memes are visual templates usually associated with a textual caption. Analysing memes involves many unique challenges that differ from classical multimodal tasks such as image captioning and visual question answering. While unimodal models can often perform well on multimodal datasets (Agrawal et al., 2018), memes involve a lot of entanglement – stylistic or semantic – between the two modalities, such as the caption contradicting the image. This makes memes intrinsically multimodal. Furthermore, pragmatics – the context's contribution to meaning – plays a key role in the interpretation of memes. In particular, phenomenons such as irony are challenging to detect. Even human annotators have difficulties in interpreting a meme correctly without knowledge of the community in which the meme was shared.

In this paper, we tackle the shared task on multimodal semantic role labeling of the CONSTRAINT'22 workshop (Sharma et al., 2022). Given a (meme, entity) pair,[1] the goal is to classify the entity's role in the meme into one of four classes (`hero`, `villain`, `victim` or `other`) from the perspective of the author of the meme. The multimodality of the problem stems from the meme, which is given as an (image, OCR) pair, where OCR (for Optical Character Recognition) is the caption extracted from the image. The dataset covers one language, English, and two domains, COVID-19 and US politics. Figure 1 shows a sample from the training set.

Understanding memes involves a lot of commonsense and cultural knowledge on the political stance of the entities. Thus, it requires models pre-trained on a large amount of data, capable of recognising key entities such as political figures in both modalities, and of inferring their relationship, their role and the public opinion of a community on them. To evaluate the task's difficulty, we manually annotate a set of samples. With 5 annotators, we reach an average Macro-F_1 of 0.65 (see details in Appendix A), less than 10 points above the best system submitted to the shared task.

We propose systems relying on several multimodal (vision–language) pre-trained models: One For All (OFA, Wang et al., 2022), CLIP (Radford et al., 2021) and VisualBERT (Li et al., 2019). We use these models as encoders to extract multimodal meme representations. These *encoders* are introduced in Section 3. We then design several neural network classifiers to handle these representations in a task-specific fashion. These *classifiers* are presented in Section 4.1.

The CONSTRAINT'22 dataset is characterised by a large class imbalance, with the most frequent class gathering 78% of the samples in the train set, while the least frequent one is conveyed by less than 3% of the samples. However, the challenge is evaluated using a Macro-F_1 metric and calls for balanced performances across all classes. To handle this discrepancy, we developed several sub-

*These authors contributed equally.

[1]We take each (meme, entity) pair as independent samples, thus considering all entities of a meme independently during training and inference.

Proceedings of the Workshop on Combating Online Hostile Posts in Regional Languages during Emergency Situations, pages 55 - 65
May 27, 2022 ©2022 Association for Computational Linguistics

Figure 1: In this meme, the OCR is: "WEARS A MASK THE SAME WAY\nEXIT\nHE HANDLES THE\nPANDEMIC \nmakeameme.org\n". There are two entities, "Donald trump" labeled as `villain` and "mask" labeled as `other`.

sampling strategies that we present in Section 4.2.

Our best results are obtained by ensembling predictions from all of our models, using various ensembling methods. The details of the ensembling methods are given in Section 4.3. Finally, we present our performance in Section 5 along with a qualitative analysis of our models. We highlight the limitations of the dataset, task and methods in Section 6.

To summarise, our whole architecture is built on freely available pre-trained models. We only fine-tune these models for the multimodal semantic role labeling task. This makes computational training cost particularly low. Our system can be characterised by:

- Simple classifier design on top of deep pre-trained model.
- Handling of class imbalance through carefully-designed sampling strategies.

Our code is available at: `https://github.com/smontariol/mmsrl_constraint`.

2 Related Work

Multimodal semantic role detection in memes is a relatively unique task, compared to other language–image multimodal task such as object classification and entity action detection, it requires a lot more contextual and cultural background. In this section, we list some related problems before introducing tools to tackle the task at hand in the next section.

In recent years, social media platforms have seen a wave of multimodal data in diverse media types. This attracted the interest of researchers to combine modalities to solve various tasks with joint representations, where the model's encoder takes all the modalities as input, or separated representations, where all modalities are encoded separately (Baltrušaitis et al., 2018).

In the CONSTRAINT'22 challenge, we tackle multimodal semantic role labeling (SRL). SRL is originally a Natural Language Processing (NLP) task which consists in labeling words in a sentence with different semantics roles to determine Who did What to Whom, When and Where (Gildea and Jurafsky, 2002; Carreras and Màrquez, 2005); these roles are also known as thematic relations. It was extended to the computer vision domain through Visual SRL. Visual SRL benchmarks focus on situation recognition in images (Silberer and Pinkal, 2018; Pratt et al., 2020); these tasks heavily rely on object detection systems for visual groundings (Yang et al., 2019). This differs from the methods we need to implement for the shared task, where the entities do not necessarily appear in the image. Moreover, in our case, the semantic role is taken from the point of view of a political argumentative: the perception of the entity by the author of the meme. This involves completely different features compared to labeling the thematic relations of the entity; in particular, cultural and contextual knowledge on the background of the meme.

Another similar task is multimodal named entity recognition, which aims at identifying and classifying named entities in texts and images. It requires more in-domain knowledge compared to multimodal SRL; but most multimodal NER datasets are text-centric, with the image being an additional feature for the text-based prediction (Arshad et al., 2019; Chen et al., 2021), while our task is more symmetrical or even image-centric.

Finally, many shared task on memes have been proposed in recent years, with a large variety of tasks: emotion classification (e.g. MEMOTION task at SemEval 2020 Sharma et al., 2020); hateful meme detection (e.g. the Hateful Meme Challenge Kiela et al., 2020) event clustering (e.g. DANKMEMES at EVALITA 2020 (Miliani et al., 2020)); more fine-grained hateful content analysis (Fine-Grained Hateful Memes Detection Mathias et al., 2021, aiming at classifying the target attacked by the meme and the type of attack); or and detection of persuasion techniques (e.g. Semeval 2021 Task 6, Dimitrov et al., 2021).

3 Multimodal Encoding

Since we experiment with deep neural networks, we need to obtain distributed representations of our inputs. To this end, we use pre-trained models with good performances on popular datasets. These models are multimodal transformers, that we use to encode image and caption's OCR into a common latent space. While transformers were originally developed for natural language processing (Vaswani et al., 2017; Devlin et al., 2019), they subsequently became ubiquitous in computer vision models as well (Dosovitskiy et al., 2021). To process an image, it is first cut into a sequence of $P \times P \times C$ patches. These patches are then projected into the transformer input dimension, either using a single linear layer, or using a full-fledged CNN architecture.

The output of a transformer has the same length as its input. We call this length N; it is the number of patches in the image, the number of tokens in the OCR, or the sum of the two for multimodal transformers. Thereafter, we refer to an encoded meme image i and OCR o as $\text{enc}_{\text{full}}(o, i) \in \mathbb{R}^{N \times d}$. This output can be further pooled into a fixed-size representation $\text{enc}_{\text{pool}}(o, i) \in \mathbb{R}^{d}$. We now describe what models are behind these encoder functions.

3.1 CLIP and VisualBERT

The multi-modal features are extracted from the caption's OCR and the meme image using two vision-language models, CLIP and VisualBERT.

CLIP (Contrastive Language–Image Pre-training, Radford et al., 2021) is trained using text as supervision to encode images, with 400 million image–text pairs available on the internet. The training task is to predict which text is associated with an image, from all text snippets of the batch, using a contrastive objective instead of a predictive one for computational efficiency. CLIP trains an image encoder and a text encoder jointly, maximizing the cosine similarity of the image and text embeddings in the joint representation space for positive pairs, and minimizing similarity of negative pairs. The strength of this task is to offer large robustness and zero-shot capability to the model, to transfer to many classification tasks. Image encoding is done using a variation of the Vision Transformer (ViT, Dosovitskiy et al., 2021). Text encoding is done using a GPT-like language model (Radford et al., 2019).[2]

Similar to CLIP, we use a VisualBERT model (Li et al., 2019) trained on visual commonsense reasoning and image captioning. VisualBERT uses self-attention to align parts of the text with regions of the image and build a joint representation. It mostly differs from CLIP in its training procedure in three phases: task-agnostic pre-training, task-specific pre-training, and task-specific fine-tuning. Moreover, VisualBERT does not include an image encoder; the patch features are extracted beforehand with pre-trained image classification and segmentation models. We extract features using FasterRCNN (Ren et al., 2015), EfficientNet (Tan and Le, 2019) and VGG (Simonyan and Zisserman, 2015). Bucur et al. (2022) showed that EfficientNet features prove useful for sentiment and emotion analyses of meme, while Pramanick et al. (2021) prove the efficiency of VGG for detecting harmful memes and identifying their target.

The output of both CLIP and VisualBERT can either be pooled (enc_{pool}) or be used as-is (enc_{full}).

3.2 OFA

A second method we experiment with to obtain a distributed representation of text and images is OFA (One For All, Wang et al., 2022). OFA is based on an encoder–decoder architecture pre-trained on several visual, textual and cross-modal tasks. A key point of OFA is to leverage a diverse set of training tasks to obtain good zero-shot performances. Despite this claim, we did not obtain satisfactory zero-shot results. We hypothesize that this is due to the noisy OCR and to the nature of meme role labeling which is radically different from what OFA was pre-trained on.

All tasks are expressed as sequence-to-sequence problems, such that a single OFA model can be used without the need of task-specific layers. For example, one of the pretraining task is image captioning; for this task, the model is trained to predict the caption given the image and the text "What does the image describe?" as inputs.

The input image and text are fed jointly to the encoding transformer using modality-specific positional embeddings. The image representation is built from 16×16 patches embedded by a ResNet (He et al., 2016). The decoding transformer is trained as a causal language model conditioned on the encoder's output with a standard cross-entropy loss. When the output is constrained on a small number of classes, the model is trained and evaluated on the task's output domain, not on the whole output vocabulary.

[2]The sequence length is limited to 76 byte-pairs. In the CONSTRAINT task corpus, 76 byte-pairs corresponds to the 95th quantile of OCR text length in the test set, and slightly more in the train set.

For the meme role labeling task, we feed OFA with the image as well as the following instruction:

"What is the category of ENTITY *between hero, villain and victim?* OCR*"*

As we detail in the next Section 4, we train OFA either as a sequence to sequence problem (resulting in a pair of models enc_{OFA}–dec_{OFA}) or by adding a classification head on top of the decoder (which can be used as a standard enc_{pool}).[3]

4 Models

We now describe how we use the encoded text and images for semantic role labeling.

4.1 Classification

We experiment with three different methods to classify a (meme, entity) pair, depending on what kind of representation we get from the encoder. The representation of the meme is composed of the image's representation along with the encoded caption's OCR, and any extra features such as the list of entities related to the meme. For ease of notation, we group under "OCR" all extra features which were extracted from the meme, and we refer to them using a single variable $o = (\text{OCR}, \text{caption}, \dots)$. Image features are referred to by i and the encoded list of entities by e. All classifiers are illustrated in Figure 2.

Multilayer perceptron (MLP) When the output of the encoder is of fixed size, we use a 2-layers MLP classifier. The input of the classifier is made from the encoding of the OCR, image and entity. The representation of the entity is obtained using the same transformer used to process the OCR. The output of the model is a softmax on the four possible roles:

$$P(r \mid o, i, e) \propto \exp \text{MLP} \left(\begin{bmatrix} \text{enc}_{\text{pool}}(o, i) \\ \text{enc}_{\text{pool}}(e) \end{bmatrix} \right)_r .$$

This model is trained using a standard cross-entropy loss. Depending on the encoder, we either train the MLP alone, or the MLP and the encoder jointly.

Attention When the representations of the OCR and image are not pooled along the sequence's length, we use an attention mechanism. In this case, the query of the attention is the entity we wish to classify, while the memory is built from a concatenation of the image and OCR encoded by CLIP or VisualBERT:

$$\alpha_j \propto \exp \left(\text{enc}_{\text{pool}}(e)^{\mathsf{T}} \boldsymbol{W}_k \, \text{enc}_{\text{full}}(o, i)_j \right),$$

$$\boldsymbol{a} = \text{ReLU} \left(\sum_j \alpha_j \boldsymbol{W}_v \, \text{enc}_{\text{full}}(o, i)_j \right),$$

where $\boldsymbol{W}_k$ and $\boldsymbol{W}_v$ are parameters used to project the encoded meme for use as attention key and value. We classify the attention output $\boldsymbol{a}$, using a softmax layer $P(r \mid o, i, e) \propto \exp(\boldsymbol{W}_p \boldsymbol{a})_r$.

Since the encoders already use positional embeddings, we do not add this information to our classifier's attention. However, we do use segment embeddings to distinguish the vectors encoding the image, OCR or entity list in the encoder's output. We use different MLP layers depending on whether a vector correspond to an input image, OCR or entity list. This model is also trained by minimizing the cross-entropy with gold labels.

Seq2seq When using an OFA encoder, we also attempt to stay in the sequence to sequence framework and train the model to generate the class labels. In this case, if we denote the label's tokens by $\boldsymbol{\ell}$, the model is trained to maximize the likelihood that the meme (o, i) has the gold target $\boldsymbol{\ell}$:

$$P(\ell_k \mid \boldsymbol{\ell}_{<k}, o, i) \propto \text{dec}_{\text{ofa}}(\text{enc}_{\text{ofa}}(o, i), \boldsymbol{\ell}_{<k})_{\ell_k},$$

where $\boldsymbol{\ell}_{<k} = [\ell_1, \ell_2, \dots, \ell_{k-1}]^{\mathsf{T}}$ refers to the list of previous tokens. To evaluate this model, the log-likelihood of the possible labels are summed along sequence length:

$$\hat{r} = \arg\max_r P(r \mid o, i) \propto \prod_k P(\ell_k^{(r)} \mid \boldsymbol{\ell}_{<k}^{(r)}, o, i),$$

where $\boldsymbol{\ell}^{(r)}$ designates the list of tokens for the label r, such as $[\texttt{vil}, \texttt{lain}]^{\mathsf{T}}$.

Additional features As explained in Section 2, our task is quite different from most multimodal tasks on which the encoders were trained; it is much more abstract and requires a lot of additional background knowledge. Thus, when using CLIP and VisualBERT, we add supplementary features as input to the classification model (MLP and attention).

We add as textual features the list of entities associated with the meme, this list is directly available in the dataset. We encode the entities' names

[3]For the OFA model, enc_{pool} refers to the output of the penultimate layer of OFA's decoder, while we use enc_{OFA} to reference only the OFA's encoder.

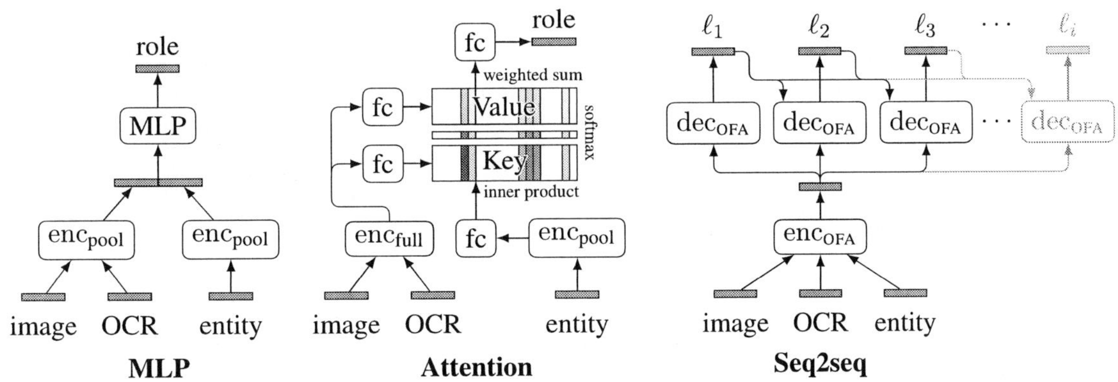

Figure 2: Our three classifiers. Note that each classifier uses a different combination of encoders. MLP is used with $\mathrm{enc}_{\mathrm{pool}}$, Attention requires $\mathrm{enc}_{\mathrm{full}}$, while Seq2seq requires an $\mathrm{enc}_{\mathrm{OFA}}$–$\mathrm{dec}_{\mathrm{OFA}}$ pair.

using the same encoder as the system (CLIP or VisualBERT).[4] We also add to the system the image features that were extracted using VGG, EfficientNET and FRCNN.

4.2 Dealing with Class Imbalance

The dataset faces a large class imbalance, with the class `other` being over-represented (78% in the train set) and classes `hero` and `victim` consisting of only 2.7% and 5.2% of the train set respectively. Thus, training on the raw dataset might lead to overfitting and over-predicting the majority class. Moreover, recall that the evaluation metric is Macro-F_1, which weighs each class equally; hence the importance of solving the class imbalance issue.

Our first solution was to weight labels in the loss. This loss penalisation led to poor performances; we suspect this is due to the working of the optimization algorithm we used. Adam and its variants estimate the distribution of the gradients using exponential moving averages; these estimates are faulty when the magnitude of the loss changes often.

A common strategy is over-sampling the low-frequency classes and under-sampling the high-frequency ones. Each (meme, entity) pair is dropped with a pre-defined probability, following various class sampling strategies. We evaluated 6 different sampling strategies illustrated in Figure 3:

Micro does not subsample. This optimize the Micro-F_1, which puts more weight on samples labeled `other` due to their sheer number.

Macro subsamples memes such that the label distribution is uniform. This implies dropping a large amount of `other` samples in order to lower their frequency.

In-between is a compromise between *micro* and *macro*, balancing between matching the evaluation loss and seeing a more diverse set of samples.

Interpolate drifts from *micro* to *macro* during training. For the first epoch, the memes are sampled according to the empirical distribution (*micro*); while the last epoch is sampled to have a uniform label distribution (*macro*).

Cycle alternates between *micro* and *macro* (2-epoch *short cycle*) or between *micro*, *macro* and two different *in-between* (4-epoch *long cycle*).

For the last two strategies, the sampling rates are updated at the end of each epoch during training. In general, these *dynamic* sampling strategies performed better than sampling strategies with a fixed rate for the whole training duration.

4.3 Ensembling

In order to further improve our results, we build several ensemble of our models. We filter-out models with a low validation macro-F_1 and experiment with several ensembling techniques. Due to the small size of the dataset, we did not create an additional split to evaluate our ensembling approach. In

[4]We also experiment with adding generated captions as features. We generate them using an OFA model trained for automatic caption generation. However, the captions are very generic and descriptive; for example the entities names are not captured by the model. This features does not improve the systems, hence we do not further develop it in the results section.

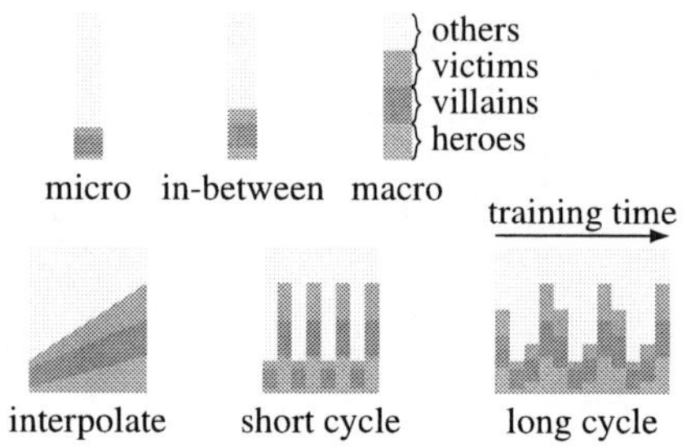

Figure 3: Target frequencies of the various strategies during training. The *micro* strategy corresponds to using the empirical class distribution in the dataset, that is hero 2.7%, villain 13.9%, victim 5.2% and other 78.2%.

this context, overfitting the validation set is a risk. Two of the ensembling methods we evaluate are therefore non-parametric. These non-parametric strategies take the average or the median probability assigned to each class by all models.

Preliminary results indicate that training a linear model to weight the output of our various models is tedious and does not improve over non-parametric strategies. We therefore turn towards gradient boosted trees (Friedman, 2001) trained by XGBoost (Chen and Guestrin, 2016). XGBoost builds an ensemble of decision trees, whose internal nodes correspond to conditions on our models' output, and whose leaves correspond to a predicted semantic role. Boosted trees have the potential to outperform non-parametric methods by better capturing the scale of various models' output, however it has the downside of being very prone to overfitting.

5 Results

5.1 Experimental process

The train set consists of 17 514 (meme, entity) pairs, the validation set 2 069 pairs and the test set 2 433 pairs. We did all the training on the datasets from the two domains, COVID-19 and US politics jointly. The test set contains examples from both domains. The evaluation is done with Macro-F_1 score; the OCR and the list of entities are provided along with the image of the meme. We run all experiments 5 times to check for the robustness of results and perform statistical testing.

For CLIP, we use the biggest `L/14` CLIP-ViT model built on the Vision Transformers (Dosovitskiy et al., 2021). Both preliminary self-supervised fine-tuning and fine-tuning while doing the classification failed. This is probably due to the size and the format of the shared task dataset, much smaller and quite different from the training data of the pre-trained model; any fine-tuning leads the model to forget the knowledge it learned during pre-training. Consequently, we freeze all layers and tune only the classifier, with the architectures described in Section 4.

For VisualBERT, we fine-tune the `visualbert-vcr-coco-pre` model trained on caption generation and visual commonsense reasoning.

For OFA enc_{pool} with an MLP classifier, we obtained better results by fine-tuning the whole model from the `vqa_large_best` checkpoint[5] using a small 0.1 label smoothing and feeding the OCR and entity both to the encoder – along with the image – and to the decoder. Our OFA seq2seq model follows the same setup using the `ofa_base` checkpoint.

In the dataset, several entities are associated with more that one label. As this situation is infrequent, we consider the small amount of samples with multiple labels does not warrant a full-fledged multi-label classification setup. Thus, our models output a single categorical distribution. When multiple labels ought to be predicted for an entity (the entity appears twice in the list of entities associated with the meme), we predict them in order of likelihood.

5.2 Quantitative results

Classifier results. Table 1 compares our main models on the CONSTRAINT'22 test set. We measure the statistical significance of our results using a one-sided Welch's unequal variances t-test (Welch, 1947) under the null hypothesis that the macro-F_1 are equals. Some hyperparameters are optimized on a per-model basis. In particular, using the list of entities as additional feature improves the performance for VisualBERT and CLIP-attention but not for our best CLIP-MLP model.

A CLIP enc_{pool} together with an MLP classifier reached the best performances among our non-ensembling model pool, significantly ($p < 0.0004$) improving over the OFA MLP combination. Using the unpooled features of the transformers (enc_{full}) with an attention classifier underperform compared to the enc_{pool}+MLP approach. However this difference is not significant in the case of VisualBERT ($p < 0.3$). In particular, attention-based

[5]This refers to an OFA model pre-trained on 8 tasks then fine-tuned on VQA from the official OFA repository.

Encoder	Classifier	Macro-F_1	
		mean	std
OFA	MLP	44.6	0.5
OFA	Seq2seq	44.0	0.9
CLIP	MLP	**47.0**	0.5
CLIP*	Attention	42.3	1.7
VisualBERT*	MLP	43.1	0.2
VisualBERT*	Attention	42.3	1.8
Ensemble mean		47.9	-
Ensemble median		47.5	-
Ensemble XGBoost		47.6	-
Challenge's top score		58.7	-
Human		65.5	4.6

Table 1: Comparison of the best systems with the different encoders and classification architectures. All systems are run 5 times with 25 epochs. Encoders with a * in exponent are augmented with the list of entities as feature.

Sampling	Macro-F_1	
	mean	std
micro	38.3	1.0
in-between	44.1	0.3
macro	42.3	0.6
interpolate	46.3	0.8
short cycle	**47.0**	0.5
long cycle	46.5	0.5

Table 2: Sampling results with the CLIP model and MLP classifier, with 500 batch per epoch.

approaches have more variance than their MLP counterpart. The OFA seq2seq model reaches performances within the error margin of the OFA MLP model ($p < 0.14$), which is not surprising since the two models are relatively close. The gap between VisualBERT and OFA is somewhat significant with p-values between 0.001 and 0.07 depending on the pairwise comparison. As expected, ensembling leads to the best result, regardless of the ensembling strategy; human annotators far exceed current model performances. We further develop human annotation in Section 6.

Sampling results. Table 2 compares the different sampling strategies represented in Figure 3 for training a CLIP encoder with MLP model. As expected, using the empirical class distribution (*micro* strategy) leads to the worse score. While the *macro* strategy is in theory what we should maximise to improve the Macro-F_1, it is second worst among all strategies. The dynamic strategies, which use evolving sampling frequencies during training clearly outperform static strategies. In particular, for training CLIP, the *short cycle* strategy outperforms the other ones, but the difference with *long cycle* and *interpolate* is not statistically significant (p-values > 0.05). We observe similar tendencies with systems based on OFA and VisualBERT, with a slight advantage to the *interpolate* strategy over the *cycling* ones for the former.

Despite the different subsampling strategies, the per-class performances vary widely, see for example the results for the CLIP MLP model with a *short cycling* subsampling strategy:

%	hero	villain	victim	other
F_1	20	50	33	84
Precision	15	46	26	90
Recall	33	56	45	79

We observe similar results with all hyperparameter combination. These performances somewhat follow the empirical distribution of the classes, with the rarest class `hero` having the worst performance, and `victim` being not much better. This makes us consider sub-sampling `other` even below 25%. However, this observation-inspired "*super-macro*" strategy did not prove successful, reaching an average Macro-F_1 or 40.0, higher than the *micro* strategy but lower than the *macro* one.

5.3 Qualitative analysis

We extract the embeddings of all entities in the train set as their are embedded by the CLIP model, right before being fed into the MLP or being used as query for the attention mechanism. Keeping only the ones occurring more than 30 times, we perform a PCA on their embeddings and represent the first two components in Figure 4. Each point represents an entity, its colour depends on the distribution of labels that are attributed to the entity, normalised by the global frequency of each label in the full dataset. We keep only the two most frequent labels associated with the entity for colouring. We can see that inanimate objects tend to be labeled as `other`. On the other hand, large political parties are nearly always portrayed as `villain` with America as a `victim`. The somewhat unexpected heroic status of the libertarian party can be explained by the pres-

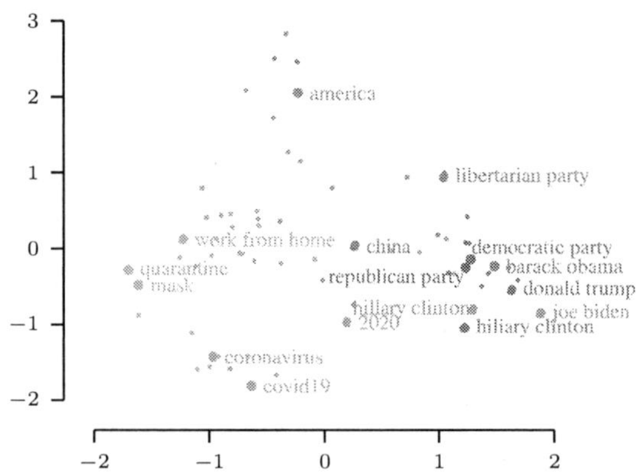

Figure 4: PCA of entity embeddings from CLIP. The explained variance is 33%+18%. The entities appearing more than 30 times, with labels attached to the 16 most frequent ones. The color of the embeddings reflect the role attached to the entity in the train set (▮ `hero`, ▮ `villain`, ▮ `victim`, ▮ `other`). When the entity is assigned different roles, the color are mixed together; e.g. covid19 ▮ appears twice as often as `other` as it does as `villain`.

ence of advertisements in the form of memes in the dataset. We can see that CLIP was able to separate the entities according to their probable class even before processing the meme. Still, the model can't clearly distinguish between most heroes and villains without seeing the meme, which is to be expected.

6 Discussion

The multimodal aspect is crucial in this task. When looking at entity names, only 15% have an exact surface form match in the caption's OCR; moreover, the OCR is often incomplete or noisy (see example in Figure 1 with the "Exit" sign popping in the middle of the caption). Thus, using only the text is far from sufficient. On the other hand, recognising the entities in the image of the meme is not an easy task. As stated in the introduction, the image and the text are often not directly related. Moreover, the image often contains elements not seen in common image datasets; for example, meme creators often perform montages like swapping faces and objects. Overall, a lot of commonsense and cultural knowledge is needed for the model to understand what the meme is about.

The absence of contextual information also makes the task difficult for humans. To evaluate the difficulty of the task, we performed human annotation of a sample of 100 (image, entity) pairs with five annotators. Details of annotation process can be found in Appendix A. The average pairwise Cohen's κ (Cohen, 1960), used to measure the inter-annotator agreement, is 0.47. It indicates a "moderate" agreement according to Cohen (1960). However, it also shows that less than one third of the annotations are reliable (McHugh, 2012). Moreover, the macro-F_1 scores are relatively low: the average is 0.65 and the maximum 0.69. Having metadata such as source website and date of publication of the meme would help human and algorithmic annotators alike.

Finally, from a real-world point of view, this task is not entirely complete: the OCR and the list of entities are already provided in the dataset, and we only have to perform the classification. In a real-life setting, we would create a multi-task system jointly extracting the caption, detecting entities and classifying them; the three tasks complementing each other.

7 Conclusion

In this work, we propose several systems to solve the task of classifying entity roles in memes. We focus on comparing classification models – MLP, Attention and Seq2seq systems – on top of pre-trained multimodal encoder: CLIP, VisualBERT and OFA. Our best standalone system uses the CLIP encoder with MLP classifier, but our best score is obtained using ensembling of a large number of models. We also compare several sampling strategies to deal with the class imbalance issue, proposing dynamic sampling methods that outperform the standard uniform ("*macro*") sampling.

As a preliminary future work, more or less straightforward processing can be performed on the dataset, at the entity-level (using an entity linker to resolve surface forms to entity identifiers, e.g. merging entities "US" and "United States" together); at the OCR-level (performing lexical normalization (Samuel and Straka, 2021) to deal with OCR errors and meme-specific syntax); and at the image-level (removing the text from the image, for a less noisy image embedding).

To improve the model, entity representation is key. We wish to train global entity embedding, shared across the whole dataset, and contextualised entity embeddings, aligning the entity's vector representation in the image and in the OCR of the meme (when there is an explicit mention of it).

8 Acknowledgments

We want to express our strong gratitude to Matt Post for the time he took providing manual annotation for our validation process. We also warmly thank the reviewers for their very valuable feedback. This work received funding from the European Union's Horizon 2020 research and innovation programme under grant agreement No. 101021607 and the last author acknowledges the support of the French Research Agency via the ANR ParSiTi project (ANR16-CE33-0021).

References

Aishwarya Agrawal, Dhruv Batra, Devi Parikh, and Aniruddha Kembhavi. 2018. Don't just assume; look and answer: Overcoming priors for visual question answering. In *Proceedings of the IEEE Conference on Computer Vision and Pattern Recognition (CVPR)*.

Omer Arshad, Ignazio Gallo, Shah Nawaz, and Alessandro Calefati. 2019. Aiding intra-text representations with visual context for multimodal named entity recognition. In *2019 International Conference on Document Analysis and Recognition (ICDAR)*, pages 337–342. IEEE.

Tadas Baltrušaitis, Chaitanya Ahuja, and Louis-Philippe Morency. 2018. Multimodal machine learning: A survey and taxonomy. *IEEE transactions on pattern analysis and machine intelligence*, 41(2):423–443.

Ana-Maria Bucur, Adrian Cosma, and Ioan-Bogdan Iordache. 2022. Blue at memotion 2.0 2022: You have my image, my text and my transformer. *arXiv preprint arXiv:2202.07543*.

Xavier Carreras and Lluís Màrquez. 2005. Introduction to the conll-2005 shared task: Semantic role labeling. In *Proceedings of the ninth conference on computational natural language learning (CoNLL-2005)*, pages 152–164.

Shuguang Chen, Gustavo Aguilar, Leonardo Neves, and Thamar Solorio. 2021. Can images help recognize entities? a study of the role of images for multimodal NER. In *Proceedings of the Seventh Workshop on Noisy User-generated Text (W-NUT 2021)*, pages 87–96, Online. Association for Computational Linguistics.

Tianqi Chen and Carlos Guestrin. 2016. Xgboost: A scalable tree boosting system. In *Proceedings of the 22nd acm sigkdd international conference on knowledge discovery and data mining*, pages 785–794.

Jacob Cohen. 1960. A coefficient of agreement for nominal scales. *Educational and Psychological Measurement*, 20(1):37–46.

Patrick Davison. 2012. *9. The Language of Internet Memes*, pages 120–134. New York University Press.

Jacob Devlin, Ming-Wei Chang, Kenton Lee, and Kristina Toutanova. 2019. Bert: Pre-training of deep bidirectional transformers for language understanding. In *Proceedings of the 2019 Conference of the North American Chapter of the Association for Computational Linguistics: Human Language Technologies, Volume 1 (Long and Short Papers)*, pages 4171–4186, Minneapolis, Minnesota. Association for Computational Linguistics.

Dimitar Dimitrov, Bishr Bin Ali, Shaden Shaar, Firoj Alam, Fabrizio Silvestri, Hamed Firooz, Preslav Nakov, and Giovanni Da San Martino. 2021. SemEval-2021 task 6: Detection of persuasion techniques in texts and images. In *Proceedings of the 15th International Workshop on Semantic Evaluation (SemEval-2021)*, pages 70–98, Online. Association for Computational Linguistics.

Alexey Dosovitskiy, Lucas Beyer, Alexander Kolesnikov, Dirk Weissenborn, Xiaohua Zhai, Thomas Unterthiner, Mostafa Dehghani, Matthias Minderer, Georg Heigold, Sylvain Gelly, Jakob Uszkoreit, and Neil Houlsby. 2021. An image is worth 16x16 words: Transformers for image recognition at scale. In *International Conference on Learning Representations*.

Jerome H Friedman. 2001. Greedy function approximation: a gradient boosting machine. *Annals of statistics*, pages 1189–1232.

Daniel Gildea and Daniel Jurafsky. 2002. Automatic labeling of semantic roles. *Computational linguistics*, 28(3):245–288.

Kaiming He, Xiangyu Zhang, Shaoqing Ren, and Jian Sun. 2016. Deep residual learning for image recognition. In *2016 IEEE Conference on Computer Vision and Pattern Recognition (CVPR)*, pages 770–778.

Douwe Kiela, Hamed Firooz, Aravind Mohan, Vedanuj Goswami, Amanpreet Singh, Pratik Ringshia, and Davide Testuggine. 2020. The hateful memes challenge: Detecting hate speech in multimodal memes. In *Advances in Neural Information Processing Systems*, volume 33, pages 2611–2624. Curran Associates, Inc.

Liunian Harold Li, Mark Yatskar, Da Yin, Cho-Jui Hsieh, and Kai-Wei Chang. 2019. Visualbert: A simple and performant baseline for vision and language. *arXiv preprint arXiv:1908.03557*.

Lambert Mathias, Shaoliang Nie, Aida Mostafazadeh Davani, Douwe Kiela, Vinodkumar Prabhakaran, Bertie Vidgen, and Zeerak Waseem. 2021. Findings of the WOAH 5 shared task on fine grained hateful memes detection. In *Proceedings of the 5th Workshop on Online Abuse and Harms (WOAH 2021)*, pages 201–206, Online. Association for Computational Linguistics.

Mary L McHugh. 2012. Interrater reliability: the kappa statistic. *Biochemia medica*, 22(3):276–282.

Martina Miliani, Giulia Giorgi, Ilir Rama, Guido Anselmi, and Gianluca E Lebani. 2020. Dankmemes@ evalita 2020: The memeing of life: Memes, multimodality and politics. In *EVALITA*.

Shraman Pramanick, Shivam Sharma, Dimitar Dimitrov, Md. Shad Akhtar, Preslav Nakov, and Tanmoy Chakraborty. 2021. MOMENTA: A multimodal framework for detecting harmful memes and their targets. In *Findings of the Association for Computational Linguistics: EMNLP 2021*, pages 4439–4455, Punta Cana, Dominican Republic. Association for Computational Linguistics.

Sarah Pratt, Mark Yatskar, Luca Weihs, Ali Farhadi, and Aniruddha Kembhavi. 2020. Grounded situation recognition. In *European Conference on Computer Vision*, pages 314–332. Springer.

Alec Radford, Jong Wook Kim, Chris Hallacy, Aditya Ramesh, Gabriel Goh, Sandhini Agarwal, Girish Sastry, Amanda Askell, Pamela Mishkin, Jack Clark, et al. 2021. Learning transferable visual models from natural language supervision. In *International Conference on Machine Learning*, pages 8748–8763. PMLR.

Alec Radford, Jeff Wu, Rewon Child, David Luan, Dario Amodei, and Ilya Sutskever. 2019. Language models are unsupervised multitask learners.

Shaoqing Ren, Kaiming He, Ross Girshick, and Jian Sun. 2015. Faster r-cnn: Towards real-time object detection with region proposal networks. *Advances in neural information processing systems*, 28.

David Samuel and Milan Straka. 2021. ÚFAL at MultiLexNorm 2021: Improving multilingual lexical normalization by fine-tuning ByT5. In *Proceedings of the Seventh Workshop on Noisy User-generated Text (W-NUT 2021)*, pages 483–492, Online. Association for Computational Linguistics.

Chhavi Sharma, Deepesh Bhageria, William Scott, Srinivas PYKL, Amitava Das, Tanmoy Chakraborty, Viswanath Pulabaigari, and Björn Gambäck. 2020. SemEval-2020 task 8: Memotion analysis- the visuolingual metaphor! In *Proceedings of the Fourteenth Workshop on Semantic Evaluation*, pages 759–773, Barcelona (online). International Committee for Computational Linguistics.

Shivam Sharma, Tharun Suresh, Atharva Kulkarni, Himanshi Mathur, Preslav Nakov, Md. Shad Akhtar, and Tanmoy Chakraborty. 2022. Findings of the constraint 2022 shared task on detecting the hero, the villain, and the victim in memes. In *Proceedings of the Workshop on Combating Online Hostile Posts in Regional Languages during Emergency Situations - CONSTRAINT 2022, Collocated with ACL 2022.*

Carina Silberer and Manfred Pinkal. 2018. Grounding semantic roles in images. In *Proceedings of the 2018 Conference on Empirical Methods in Natural Language Processing*, pages 2616–2626, Brussels, Belgium. Association for Computational Linguistics.

Karen Simonyan and Andrew Zisserman. 2015. Very deep convolutional networks for large-scale image recognition. In *3rd International Conference on Learning Representations, ICLR 2015, San Diego, CA, USA, May 7-9, 2015, Conference Track Proceedings*.

Mingxing Tan and Quoc Le. 2019. Efficientnet: Rethinking model scaling for convolutional neural networks. In *International conference on machine learning*, pages 6105–6114. PMLR.

Ashish Vaswani, Noam Shazeer, Niki Parmar, Jakob Uszkoreit, Llion Jones, Aidan N Gomez, Łukasz Kaiser, and Illia Polosukhin. 2017. Attention is all you need. In *Advances in Neural Information Processing Systems*, volume 30. Curran Associates, Inc.

Peng Wang, An Yang, Rui Men, Junyang Lin, Shuai Bai, Zhikang Li, Jianxin Ma, Chang Zhou, Jingren Zhou, and Hongxia Yang. 2022. Unifying architectures, tasks, and modalities through a simple sequence-to-sequence learning framework.

Bernard Lewis Welch. 1947. The generalization of 'student's' problem when several different population variances are involved. *Biometrika*, 34(1-2):28–35.

Hao Yang, Hao Wu, and Hao Chen. 2019. Detecting 11k classes: Large scale object detection without fine-grained bounding boxes. In *Proceedings of the IEEE/CVF International Conference on Computer Vision*, pages 9805–9813.

A Human Annotations

To assess the quality of the dataset and put our results into perspective, we hand labeled part of the datasets. The team of five annotators is composed of researchers in Natural Language Processing. One of them is American native and the other 4 are European. Two of them are in the 40-50s age range and three of them are in the 20-30s. The annotators were all given the same 100 samples to label. To have a better estimate of the macro-F_1, we sampled 25 memes for each gold role. The annotator were given the class definitions and were informed that the labels had a uniform distribution. The annotation script as well as the answers of the annotators are available with the remainder of our code at `https://github.com/smontariol/mmsrl_constraint`.

We compute the macro-F_1 score of each annotator, resulting in an average score of 0.65. The minimum score was 0.57 and the maximum 0.69.

These scores show the difficulty of the task for a human. For comparison, the best score during the challenge was 0.58, still considerably lower than the human best score.

To measure the inter-annotator agreement, we compute the average pair-wise Cohen's κ (Cohen, 1960). It is similar to measuring the percentage of agreement, but taking into account the possibility of the agreement between two annotators to occur by chance for each annotated sample. The average Cohen's κ is 0.47, indicating a "moderate" agreement according to Cohen (1960). However, it also indicates that less than one third of the annotations are reliable (McHugh, 2012).

Document Retrieval and Claim Verification to Mitigate COVID-19 Misinformation

Megha Sundriyal[1], Ganeshan Malhotra[2], Md Shad Akhtar[1], Shubhashis Sengupta[3], Andrew Fano[3], Tanmoy Chakraborty[1]
[1]*IIIT-Delhi, India*, [2]*BITS Pilani, Goa, India*, [3]*Accenture Labs, India*
meghas@iiitd.ac.in, f20170512g@alumni.bits-pilani.ac.in, shad.akhtar@iiitd.ac.in,
shubhashis.sengupta@accenture.com, andrew.e.fano@accenture.com, tanmoy@iiitd.ac.in

Abstract

During the COVID-19 pandemic, the spread of misinformation on online social media has grown exponentially. Unverified bogus claims on these platforms regularly mislead people, leading them to believe in half-baked truths. The current vogue is to employ manual fact-checkers to verify claims to combat this avalanche of misinformation. However, establishing such claims' veracity is becoming increasingly challenging, partly due to the plethora of information available, which is difficult to process manually. Thus, it becomes imperative to verify claims automatically without human interventions. To cope up with this issue, we propose an automated claim verification solution encompassing two steps – document retrieval and veracity prediction. For the retrieval module, we employ a hybrid search-based system with BM25 as a base retriever and experiment with recent state-of-the-art transformer-based models for re-ranking. Furthermore, we use a BART-based textual entailment architecture to authenticate the retrieved documents in the later step. We report experimental findings, demonstrating that our retrieval module outperforms the best baseline system by 10.32 NDCG@100 points. We escort a demonstration to assess the efficacy and impact of our suggested solution. As a byproduct of this study, we present an open-source, easily deployable, and user-friendly Python API that the community can adopt.

1 Introduction

The escalating drift of online social media platforms has led to a massive rise in online content consumers. Participation in these platforms has swung into another correspondence, which is no longer limited by physical barriers. Because of their speed and focused information, these platforms facilitate the dissemination of personal thoughts and information to a much larger audience. However, at the same time, these platforms have enriched an equally docile environment for malicious users to promulgate fake news, bogus claims, rumors and misinformation. There have been numerous cases where the propagation of malicious unverified content has influenced the entire society. One such concrete example is the 2016 Presidential Elections in the United States, which witnessed the alarming impact of false news, with many citizens swayed by a fraudulent website (Grave et al., 2018). Allcott and Gentzkow (2017) revealed that nearly 25% of American citizens visited a fake news website that aimed at manipulating the general public's cognitive process and consequently clouted the eventual conclusion of the election. Another recent example is the global pandemic of COVID-19. When the entire world went into lockdown, the virtual world encountered a great closeness transforming social media platforms into the primary conduits for information consumption and dissemination. Consequently, there has been an accretion of 50%-70% in total Internet hits in the year 2020 (Beech, 2020). Around the same time, enormous social media posts with unverified bogus claims about the pandemic began to arise, frequently spurring life-threatening remedies (Naeem and Bhatti, 2020). Such claims had an unprecedented impact, resulting in monetary damage and the loss of priceless human lives. A study revealed that at least 800 individuals died worldwide in the first quarter of 2020 due to misinformation about COVID-19 (Coleman, 2020).

Motivation: A slew of such incidents has continued to emerge from the worldwide community in recent years. Thousands of people read these unverified claims online and spread misinformation if the claims' integrity is not corroborated. As a result, a variety of manual fact-checking organizations have evolved to

Proceedings of the Workshop on Combating Online Hostile Posts in Regional Languages during Emergency Situations, pages 66 - 74
May 27, 2022 ©2022 Association for Computational Linguistics

address this concerning issue. Unfortunately, the enormity of misinformation floating around on the Internet has developed into a global *infodemic*[1] making their efforts untenable. To alleviate this bottleneck, the process of automating fact-checking has recently garnered a lot of consideration in the research world. Vlachos and Riedel (2014) formalized the task of fact-checking and claim verification as a series of components – identifying claims to be evaluated, extracting relevant shreds of evidence, and delivering verdicts. As a result, this facilitated the establishment of automated fact-checking pipelines composed of subcomponents that can be mapped to tasks well-studied in the NLP community. The task of retrieving relevant information has gained a lot of impetus in recent years, especially with the introduction of tools like PYSERINI[2] and BEIR[3]. Furthermore, advancements were made by establishing datasets of either claims acquired from fact-checking websites (Wang, 2017) or datasets curated specifically for research (Thorne et al., 2018a). The recent release of the CORD-19 dataset[4], consisting of more than 500,000 articles, has provided access to thousands of scientific articles on the prevention techniques, spread, transmission, and cures of the COVID-19. The dataset consists of more than 500,000 articles.

State-of-the-art and Challenges: Previous research in the realm of claim verification and fact-checking has primarily concentrated on structured data, often in the form of subject-predicate-object statements (Dong et al., 2015; Nakashole and Mitchell, 2014). Several research on detecting false claims on social media included network metadata such as user profile characteristics, user-user interactions, popularity attributes based on the number of likes or followers, etc (Kumar et al., 2016; Qazvinian et al., 2011). Most notably, all of these procedures use black-box approaches, and hence, do not articulate why a statement is considered verified. Another pressing issue is that the input claim does not coexist naturally with the corresponding review articles. As a result, obtaining the relevant articles via internet is critical. There is, however, a disparity between the human—crafted review articles generated specifically for claim verification in the fact database and the report articles gathered from the web. Meanwhile, methods such as ClaimBuster[5] and Google's Fact Check Explorer[6] have been developed to check the legitimacy of the statement by assessing trust criteria utilizing internet. However, these existing methods are not intended to investigate the veracity of the evidence and hence fail to meet the previously identified issues.

Our Contributions: To address the aforementioned issues, we create an end-to-end claim verification system capable of establishing the integrity of a query claim and explaining its decisions with supporting evidence. Our model takes in as input the claim whose veracity is to be verified. Due to the diversity of natural language idioms, the first major problem in developing such a system is identifying connected snippets of a claim. Thus, we utilize well-known retrieval systems for this task. The system selects relevant articles from either the CORD-19 dataset or our in-house dataset, `ClaVer`, using a host of different models ranging from BM25 to intricate hybrid searchers. Users can additionally opt to retrieve more fine-grained results where the model selects relevant snippets in the article. Eventually, the model verifies the claim by calculating the entailment of the input claim concerning the retrieved articles.

Through this work, we make the following contributions:

1. To allay the unavailability of a COVID-19 centric annotated dataset for claim verification in Twitter, we develop `ClaVer`, a new dataset of claim-evidence pairs based on a subset of COVID-19-related claims reaped from a recently released large-scale claim-detection dataset, LESA (Gupta et al., 2021).

2. We propose an end-to-end claim verification system encompassing two steps to validate the claims proffered online provided high-quality editorial review articles and Twitter posts.

[1] https://www.who.int/health-topics/infodemic

[2] https://github.com/castorini/pyserini

[3] https://github.com/UKPLab/beir

[4] https://allenai.org/data/cord-19

[5] https://idir.uta.edu/claimbuster/api/

[6] https://toolbox.google.com/factcheck/explorer

3. We evaluate our retrieval model against multiple state-of-the-art systems concerning our dataset, `ClaVer`. According to the comparison, BM25 surpasses all other existing systems by a wide margin.

4. We provide an open-source, easily deployable, and user-friendly Python API based on our proposed solution for claim verification. We also accompany a demonstration to evaluate the efficacy and usage of the API.

2 Related Work

The challenge of verifying claims on online social media has garnered considerable attention in the last several years. Initially, the task of automatic claim verification and fact-checking were investigated in the context of computational journalism (Cohen et al., 2011; Flew et al., 2012), and journalists and professional fact-debunkers manually verified claims utilizing various information sources. However, that was not just time-consuming but also introduced substantial human bias in it. The recent advancement in NLP and information retrieval (IR) has equipped journalists and online social media users with tools enabling automatic claim verification. In the past few years, plenty of work has been proposed to fact-check online claims. Vlachos and Riedel (2014) presented the initial pioneering work in this domain. They published the first claim verification dataset, which included 106 statements taken from fact-checking websites like PolitiFact. However, they lacked justification for the verdict, which verification systems typically require. To address this issue, Wang (2017) prolonged this approach by introducing 12.8K claims from PolitiFact along with their explanations. The Fact Extraction and Verification (FEVER) shared task was launched to advance research in this direction (Thorne et al., 2018b). The organizers of the FEVER shared task constructed a large-scale dataset of 185445 claims based on Wikipedia articles, each of which comes with several evidence sets.

Traditionally, the existing claim verification systems primarily rely on textual content and/or social context. The content-based methods essentially acquire the n-grams (Wang, 2017), semantics (Khattar et al., 2019), writing styles (Gröndahl and Asokan, 2019), etc. Besides textual-content, auxiliary knowledge around social-context has also been extensively examined for verification tasks. These context-based methods emphasize collecting user profile-based (Shu et al., 2019), propagation structure-based (Wei et al., 2019), source-based (Pennycook and Rand, 2019), etc. Zhi et al. (2017) introduced ClaimVerif that provides a credibility score for a user given a claim and also gives supporting evidences that justify the credibility score. Hanselowski et al. (2018) presented their approach to the FEVER task (Thorne et al., 2018b) which was introduced to expedite the development of fact verification systems, in which they used entity linking for document retrieval and Enhanced Sequential Inference Model for determining the entailment. Ma et al. (2019) used Hierarchical Attention Networks with sentence-level evidence embeddings. Despite the fact that these tactics produce good performance results, it is challenging for these approaches to provide adequate reasons for claim verification outcomes.

As a result, current research has focused on interpretable claim verification, which develops interactive models to examine the distinction. Attention-based interaction models (Popat et al., 2018), gate fusion interactive models (Wu and Rao, 2020), coherence modelling interactive models (Ma et al., 2019), and graph-aware interaction models are among the interactive models. The granularity of captured semantic conflicts involves word-level (Popat et al., 2018), sentence-level (Ma et al., 2019), and multi-feature (Wu and Rao, 2020) conflicts. Su et al. (2020) came up with a question-answering-based model that mines relevant articles from the CORD-19 dataset and summarizes them to answer pressing questions about the COVID-19 pandemic. Recently, Pradeep et al. (2021) proposed a T5[7] transformer-based architecture for abstract retrieval, sentence selection and label prediction and perform claim verification. Similar to us, they also utilized the CORD-19 (Wang et al., 2020) corpus as the knowledge base to retrieve shreds of evidences. These methods, which employ semantic conflicts to verify claims, reflect a certain degree of interpretability. But not all conflicts can be used as valid evidence to reasonably explain the results, and they also include considerable conflicts unrelated to claims or even interfere with the verified results. It is difficult for automatic claim verification to provide reasonable explanations for the

[7] https://huggingface.co/transformers/model_doc/t5.html

Table 1: Examples from ClaVer dataset along with the evidence and corresponding labels.[8]

Evidence	Label
Claim: 1 *@CNN Boosting our immune systems will help deter the virus. It's our only defense aside from n95 masks and goggles*	
*First, there's the not-so-great news. Despite claims you may have seen on the Internet, there's no magic food or pill that is guaranteed to boost your immune system and protect you against coronavirus...**There are ways to keep your immune system functioning optimally, which can help to keep you healthy and give you a sense of control in an uncertain time**...For a starter dose of immune-boosting vitamins, minerals and antioxidants, fill half of your plate with vegetables and fruits.*	SUPPORTED
Claim: 2 *@AFP @EvelDick It's much more than a coincidence that China has a bioweapons lab with sloppy protocols in Wuhan. Wonder if this is another booboo? Seems like a very bad place to have a bioweapons lab. The whole "this came from snakes" Chinese party line makes me think the virus was manufactured.*	
*As the Covid-19 pandemic continues its destructive course, two theories are being widely aired...**The lab is one of 20 such facilities under the Chinese Academy of Sciences, but is the only one dealing with virology. Fully compliant with ISO standards, the Wuhan facility interacts regularly with a host of outside experts. Like other labs, its aim is to protect populations against new viruses**...*	REFUTED

verification results; the demand for interpretable claim verification is growing, with the goal of providing end-users with grounds to debunk rumours by showing the incorrect elements of claims. Existing methods in this assignment investigate semantic conflicts between claims and relevant articles by creating various interactive models to explain verification results.

3 Description of the Datasets

For our experiments, we adopt two datasets. Their details are shown as follows:

1. **CORD-19 Dataset** (Wang et al., 2020): CORD-19 dataset consists of over $\sim 500,000$ articles (over $\sim 200,000$ containing full text) taken from various scientific publications about COVID-19, SARS-COV2 and other viruses. This dataset provides access to trustworthy scientific sources of information to mitigate the spread of misinformation.

2. **LESA Dataset** (Gupta et al., 2021): LESA dataset consists of $\sim 10,000$ tweets that were mined from various sources and were manually annotated for the binary classification task of claim detection. Furthermore, we develop a validation set – **Cla**im **Ver**ification (ClaVer) by selecting a subset of claims from the LESA dataset and annotating those claims with relevant articles that provide additional context for the claim, as shown in Table 1. These articles are gathered from reliable online news sources and contain additional extensive information that may be used to verify the authenticity of the claim. The articles can "*Refute*" or "*Support*" the claim. In other circumstances, the claim may be that the annotated article does not give conclusive evidence. These articles lack sufficient information to support or reject the claim's veracity and hence labelled for "*Not Enough Information*". These articles are also stored in our global knowledge base of articles along with the articles taken from the CORD-19 dataset.

4 Our Approach

Adhering to the standard of automated claim verification and fact-checking systems (Thorne et al., 2018b), our proposed approach also consists of a two-step pipeline – Document Retrieval and Veracity Prediction. In this section, we present the techniques employed for retrieval and veracity prediction components. Besides the current approach, we had also employ alternative techniques using Rapid Automatic Keyword Extraction or RAKE (Rose et al., 2010) and SciSpacy (Neumann et al., 2019) for keyword extraction and searching our corpus using the extracted keywords. Figure 1 illustrates the general architecture of our proposed claim verification approach. Once a textual claim is submitted, the document retrieval module extracts the top-k relevant documents from the knowledge base. The retrieved documents are then passed to the veracity prediction module that figures out an

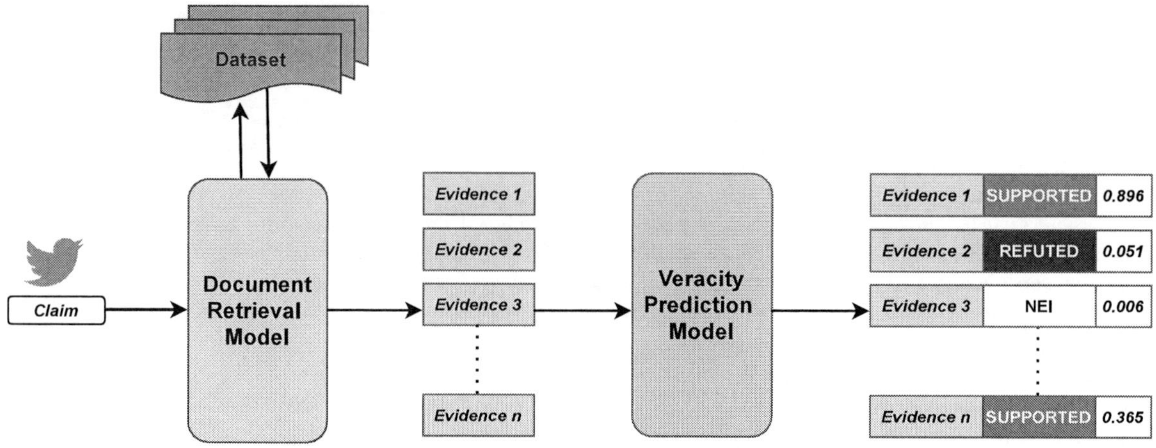

Figure 1: An overview of the proposed evidence-based claim verification pipeline. The significant components have been highlighted to correspond to the two stages of our experimental setup: (a) a document retrieval module that uses one of the given datasets to retrieve top-k relevant documents for the corresponding input claim, and (b) a veracity prediction module that seeks to establish the retrieved documents' credibility against the input claim.

entailment decision for the claim with respect to the retrieved evidences.

4.1 Document Retrieval

Inspired by IR systems, the retrieval problem we attempt to address is defined as follows: Given a textual claim c and a set of documents D, we aim to retrieve the top-k documents from D relevant to c. Our retrieval pipeline consists of two broad categories of retrieval systems, namely Sparse Retrieval and Dense Retrieval.

1. **Sparse Retrieval Model:** Over the years, lexical approaches like TF-IDF and BM25 have dominated textual information retrieval. We also utilize the BM25 scoring function (Robertson et al., 1995) as the backbone model for sparse retrieval. We use the sparse retrievers for both the `ClaVer` as well as CORD-19 datasets. In this case, we also provide an extra option of getting finer-grained results. This step scans through the retrieved article and provides a relevant part of the article. We use a BioBERT (Lee et al., 2019) language model which is pre-trained on large-scale bio-medical corpora. We compute the hidden representation of each paragraph in the article using the language model and calculate its cosine similarity with the hidden representation of the claim. The paragraph with the highest value is then selected.

2. **Dense and Hybrid Retrieval Models:** More recently, dense retrieval approaches were proposed to get better retrieval results. They are capable of capturing semantic matches and try to overcome the (potential) lexical gap. Dense retrievers map queries and documents in a shared, dense vector space (Gillick et al., 2018). This allowed the document representation to be pre-computed and indexed. We provide the option of dense retrievers specifically for our `ClaVer` dataset. Using dense indexes for CORD-19 dataset is difficult because of the huge size of the corpora. To use the dense and hybrid searchers, we first index our `ClaVer` data using the FAISS (Johnson et al., 2017) library. For our dense retriever, we use the simple dense searcher provided by the PYSERINI (Lin et al., 2021) library while initializing it with COVID-BERT weights. The hybrid searcher uses a combination of sparse and dense retrievers and computes a weighted interpolation of the individual results to arrive at the final rankings. We use the TCT-ColBERT (Lin et al., 2020) architecture to encode our queries into the same representation space as the encoded documents.

4.2 Veracity Prediction

Given a claim and the evidence gathered through document retrieval system, veracity prediction module seeks to establish the evidence's credibility in terms of a veracity score. To verify the veracity of our retrieved articles, we leverage a BART-based

Table 2: Sample response generated by our proposed system leveraging `ClaVer` dataset for extraction.

Claim

Story about how #HydroxyChloroquine likely help people recover from #Coronavirus. IMO, it was never touted as the cure but as option for treatment doctors should consider and it appears to work in some cases....39 in one place.

Outputs			
Technique	**Evidence Retrieved**[8]	**Label**	**Veracity**
Ours	*Chloroquine and hydroxychloroquine, a pair of old drugs used to treat and prevent malaria, are the latest compounds to be thrust into the limelight as people tout them as treatments for the novel coronavirus. On Sunday, March 29, the US Department of Health and Human Services accepted 30 million doses of hydroxychloroquine sulfate from Novartis and 1 million doses of chloroquine phosphate from Bayer...The World Health Organization is sponsoring a large international clinical trial called SOLIDARITY to study six drugs that could be rapidly deployed for the fight the coronavirus, including chloroquine and hydroxychloroquine.*	CONTRADICTION	0.82737
Dense	*As of now, no study says coronavirus can be cured by drinking lots of water or gargling with warm saltwater. Though it is true that warm salt water has long been used as a home remedy to soothe a sore throat, but till now, there is no evidence that it can also ward off the novel coronavirus. A report by fact-check website "Snopes" also says that there is no proof that coronavirus remains in the throat for four days as mentioned in the viral post.*	NEUTRAL	0.99825
Hybrid	*As of now, no study says coronavirus can be cured by drinking lots of water or gargling with warm saltwater. Though it is true that warm salt water has long been used as a home remedy to soothe a sore throat, but till now, there is no esidence that it can also ward off the novel coronavirus. A report by fact-check website "Snopes" also says that there is no proof that coronavirus remains in the throat for four days as mentioned in the viral post.*	NEUTRAL	0.99825

(Lewis et al., 2020) Natural Language Inference (NLI) model that returns one of the three classes for each claim-evidence pair: Entailment, Neutral and Contradiction (as shown in Table 2). The mapping of these labels with our use case is done in the following way:

- If the model outputs 'Entailment', it means that the given claim's veracity can be positively supported by the retrieved article.
- If the model outputs 'Contradiction', it means that the given claim's veracity is refuted by the retrieved article which makes the claim dubious.
- If the model outputs 'Neutral', it means the retrieved article does not provide enough evidence to either support or refute the claim.

5 Evaluation

We compare the findings of our retrieval system BM25 to those of other existing systems. We employ a collection of claims and ground-truth labels from our `ClaVer` dataset for quantitative evaluation. The test data set consists of claims excluded from the knowledge base in the retrieval phase. For this, we develop a manually annotated dataset with $\sim$ 1000 claims obtained from Twitter and build a knowledge-base of $\sim$ 400 articles from reliable sources, equipping a testing ground to validate the results. Table 3 presents experimental results based on Normalized Discounted Cumulative Gain (NDCG@k) scores, Mean Average Precision (MAP@k) and Mean Average Recall (MAR@k) scores for different values of k. We find that using BM25 outperforms all other baseline systems for retrieval task. The NDCG@100 score of the BM25

Table 3: Performance of various retrieval techniques on `ClaVer` dataset. (NDCG: Normalized Discounted Cumulative Gain, MAP: Mean Average Precision and MAR: Mean Average Recall)

Technique	NDCG@1	NDCG@10	NDCG@100	MAP@1	MAP@10	MAR@1	MAR@10
Ours	**24.71**	**36.75**	**45.73**	**24.71**	**32.14**	**24.71**	**51.72**
CrossEncoder MS Marco	22.99	35.41	35.41	22.99	31.12	22.99	48.85
CrossEncoder CovidBERT	3.41	15.04	15.04	3.41	3.41	3.49	36.36
SentenceBERT MS Marco	18.97	32.09	32.58	18.97	26.83	18.97	49.43

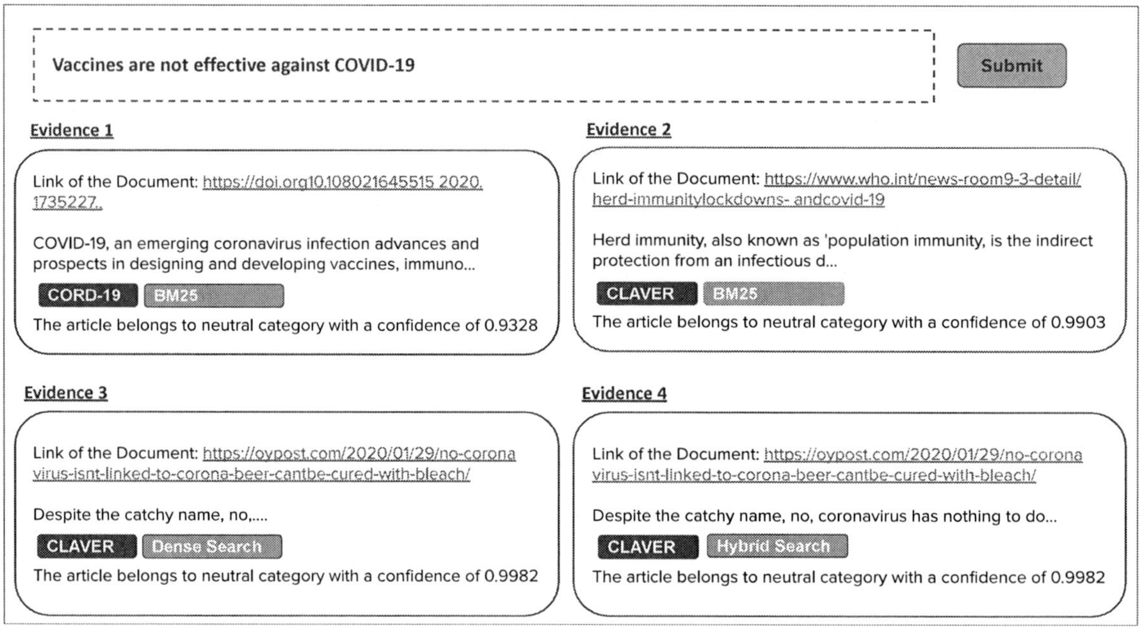

Figure 2: User-interface of our proposed tool after the claim has been submitted.

retrieval model improves the baseline method by more than 10% out of the whole testing set. We find that BM25 detects relevant snippets with higher precision and recall than other existing retrieval systems.

6 Demonstration

In this section, we demonstrate how our proposed claim verification pipeline works. Figure 2 depicts an example claim as well as the model's output results. Users enter a claim into our system as a query, and the system evaluates whether or not it is a validated claim. In practice, the system takes somewhere around 20 and 80 seconds to execute a single user query, depending on the number and length of articles obtained by the search engine.

The input section of our tool, as shown in Figure 2, provides a query text box where the user can enter any natural language text as an input claim for evaluation, as well as a specific configuration to limit the number of articles to be retrieved. Following the submission of the claim, the tool's back-end server does its analysis. It returns three sets of outputs: (i) a set of articles employing the various approaches, (ii) a claim category, and (iii) a veracity score. The output also presents the technique utilized for retrieval (pink) and from which knowledge base the shreds of evidence were extracted (blue). The most intriguing aspect of the system is that it links resources from the web, where the article was retrieved, allowing individuals to make their own decisions based on them.

Not all information is equally reliable, and sometimes even the trusted sources contradict one another. This calls into question the assumptions behind most current fact-checking research, which relies on a single authoritative source. As a result, we offer results for a common claim from several models and knowledge bases. For demonstration, we practice the widely spread claim *"Vaccines are not effective against COVID-19"* as an input as shown in Figure 2, and the tool returned the top-

[8]Links of article sources can be found at: `https://cutt.ly/lFwsxXa`

ranked shreds of evidence. The first two pieces of evidence come from the BM25 model, which was run on the CORD-19 dataset and our data, respectively. Furthermore, evidences 3 and 4 collected articles from our dataset using a dense and hybrid retrieval strategy, respectively. We can see that all four pieces of evidence assigned the same label to the claim, but their truthfulness scores differed from each other.

7 Conclusion

In this work, we verged upon claim verification on online social media towards coping with misinformation. We bestowed a claim verification system that evaluates the authenticity of a user-supplied query claim and justifies the verdict corroborating evidence. We explored multiple retrieval methodologies and published user research findings, demonstrating the utility of the BM25 method. Unlike other tools, our system learns the distributed representations to encapsulate the semantic relations between the claim and the evidence. Our approach uses a two-step training process to provide a high-quality veracity score as well as best-suited articles, leveraging data from formal articles and web-based informal texts. We have made the source codes and the dataset public at the following link: `https://github.com/LCS2-IIITD/claim_verification`.

Acknowledgements

T. Chakraborty would like to acknowledge the support of the Ramanujan Fellowship, and ihub-Anubhuti-iiitd Foundation set up under the NM-ICPS scheme of the Department of Science and Technology, India. M. S. Akhtar and T. Chakraborty thank Infosys Centre for AI at IIIT-Delhi for the valuable support.

References

Hunt Allcott and Matthew Gentzkow. 2017. Social media and fake news in the 2016 election. *Journal of economic perspectives*, 31(2):211–36.

Mark Beech. 2020. Covid-19 pushes up internet use 70% and streaming more than 12%, first figures reveal.

Sarah Cohen, Chengkai Li, Jun Yang, and Cong Yu. 2011. Computation al journalism: A call to arms to database research-ers. In *5th Biennial Conference on Innovative Data Systems Research, ACM*.

Alistair Coleman. 2020. 'hundreds dead' because of covid-19 misinformation.

Xin Luna Dong, Evgeniy Gabrilovich, Kevin Murphy, Van Dang, Wilko Horn, Camillo Lugaresi, Shaohua Sun, and Wei Zhang. 2015. Knowledge-based trust: Estimating the trustworthiness of web sources.

Terry Flew, Christina Spurgeon, Anna Daniel, and Adam Swift. 2012. The promise of computational journalism. *Journalism practice*, 6(2):157–171.

Daniel Gillick, Alessandro Presta, and Gaurav Singh Tomar. 2018. End-to-end retrieval in continuous space. *arXiv preprint arXiv:1811.08008*.

Edouard Grave, Piotr Bojanowski, Prakhar Gupta, Armand Joulin, and Tomas Mikolov. 2018. Learning word vectors for 157 languages. *arXiv preprint arXiv:1802.06893*.

Tommi Gröndahl and N Asokan. 2019. Text analysis in adversarial settings: Does deception leave a stylistic trace? *ACM Computing Surveys (CSUR)*, 52(3):1–36.

Shreya Gupta, Parantak Singh, Megha Sundriyal, Md Shad Akhtar, and Tanmoy Chakraborty. 2021. Lesa: Linguistic encapsulation and semantic amalgamation based generalised claim detection from online content. In *Proceedings of the 16th Conference of the EACL: Main Volume*, pages 3178–3188.

Andreas Hanselowski, Hao Zhang, Zile Li, Daniil Sorokin, Benjamin Schiller, Claudia Schulz, and Iryna Gurevych. 2018. UKP-athene: Multi-sentence textual entailment for claim verification. In *Proceedings of the First Workshop on Fact Extraction and VERification (FEVER)*, Brussels, Belgium. ACL.

Jeff Johnson, Matthijs Douze, and Hervé Jégou. 2017. Billion-scale similarity search with gpus. *arXiv preprint arXiv:1702.08734*.

Dhruv Khattar, Jaipal Singh Goud, Manish Gupta, and Vasudeva Varma. 2019. Mvae: Multimodal variational autoencoder for fake news detection. In *The world wide web conference*, pages 2915–2921.

Srijan Kumar, Robert West, and Jure Leskovec. 2016. Disinformation on the web: Impact, characteristics, and detection of wikipedia hoaxes. In *Proceedings of the 25th international conference on World Wide Web*, pages 591–602.

Jinhyuk Lee, Wonjin Yoon, Sungdong Kim, Donghyeon Kim, Sunkyu Kim, Chan Ho So, and Jaewoo Kang. 2019. BioBERT: a pre-trained biomedical language representation model for biomedical text mining. *Bioinformatics*, 36(4):1234–1240.

Mike Lewis, Yinhan Liu, Naman Goyal, Marjan Ghazvininejad, Abdelrahman Mohamed, Omer Levy, Veselin Stoyanov, and Luke Zettlemoyer. 2020. BART: Denoising sequence-to-sequence pre-training for natural language generation, translation, and comprehension. In *Proceedings of the 58th Annual Meeting of the ACL*, Online. ACL.

Jimmy Lin, Xueguang Ma, Sheng-Chieh Lin, Jheng-Hong Yang, Ronak Pradeep, and Rodrigo Nogueira. 2021. Pyserini: An easy-to-use python toolkit to support replicable ir research with sparse and dense representations.

Sheng-Chieh Lin, Jheng-Hong Yang, and Jimmy Lin. 2020. Distilling dense representations for ranking using tightly-coupled teachers.

Jing Ma, Wei Gao, Shafiq Joty, and Kam-Fai Wong. 2019. Sentence-level evidence embedding for claim verification with hierarchical attention networks. ACL.

Salman Bin Naeem and Rubina Bhatti. 2020. The covid-19 'infodemic': a new front for information professionals. *Health Information & Libraries Journal*, 37(3):233–239.

Ndapandula Nakashole and Tom Mitchell. 2014. Language-aware truth assessment of fact candidates. In *Proceedings of the 52nd Annual Meeting of the ACL (Volume 1: Long Papers)*, pages 1009–1019.

Mark Neumann, Daniel King, Iz Beltagy, and Waleed Ammar. 2019. ScispaCy: Fast and Robust Models for Biomedical Natural Language Processing. In *Proceedings of the 18th BioNLP Workshop and Shared Task*, pages 319–327, Florence, Italy. ACL.

Gordon Pennycook and David G Rand. 2019. Fighting misinformation on social media using crowdsourced judgments of news source quality. *Proceedings of the National Academy of Sciences*, 116(7):2521–2526.

Kashyap Popat, Subhabrata Mukherjee, Andrew Yates, and Gerhard Weikum. 2018. Declare: Debunking fake news and false claims using evidence-aware deep learning. *arXiv preprint arXiv:1809.06416*.

Ronak Pradeep, Xueguang Ma, Rodrigo Nogueira, and Jimmy Lin. 2021. Scientific claim verification with VerT5erini. In *Proceedings of the 12th International Workshop on Health Text Mining and Information Analysis*, online. ACL.

Vahed Qazvinian, Emily Rosengren, Dragomir Radev, and Qiaozhu Mei. 2011. Rumor has it: Identifying misinformation in microblogs. In *Proceedings of the 2011 Conference on Empirical Methods in Natural Language Processing*, pages 1589–1599.

Stephen E Robertson, Steve Walker, Susan Jones, Micheline M Hancock-Beaulieu, Mike Gatford, et al. 1995. Okapi at trec-3. *Nist Special Publication Sp*, 109:109.

Stuart Rose, Dave Engel, Nick Cramer, and Wendy Cowley. 2010. *Automatic Keyword Extraction from Individual Documents*, chapter 1. John Wiley Sons, Ltd.

Kai Shu, Suhang Wang, and Huan Liu. 2019. Beyond news contents: The role of social context for fake news detection. In *Proceedings of the twelfth ACM international conference on web search and data mining*, pages 312–320.

Dan Su, Yan Xu, Tiezheng Yu, Farhad Bin Siddique, Elham J. Barezi, and Pascale Fung. 2020. Caire-covid: A question answering and query-focused multi-document summarization system for covid-19 scholarly information management.

James Thorne, Andreas Vlachos, Christos Christodoulopoulos, and Arpit Mittal. 2018a. Fever: a large-scale dataset for fact extraction and verification. *arXiv preprint arXiv:1803.05355*.

James Thorne, Andreas Vlachos, Oana Cocarascu, Christos Christodoulopoulos, and Arpit Mittal. 2018b. The fact extraction and VERification (FEVER) shared task. In *Proceedings of the First Workshop on Fact Extraction and VERification (FEVER)*, Brussels, Belgium. ACL.

Andreas Vlachos and Sebastian Riedel. 2014. Fact checking: Task definition and dataset construction. In *Proceedings of the ACL 2014 Workshop on Language Technologies and Computational Social Science*, Baltimore, MD, USA. ACL.

Lucy Lu Wang, Kyle Lo, Yoganand Chandrasekhar, Russell Reas, Jiangjiang Yang, Doug Burdick, Darrin Eide, Kathryn Funk, Yannis Katsis, Rodney Kinney, Yunyao Li, Ziyang Liu, William Merrill, Paul Mooney, Dewey Murdick, Devvret Rishi, Jerry Sheehan, Zhihong Shen, Brandon Stilson, Alex Wade, Kuansan Wang, Nancy Xin Ru Wang, Chris Wilhelm, Boya Xie, Douglas Raymond, Daniel S. Weld, Oren Etzioni, and Sebastian Kohlmeier. 2020. Cord-19: The covid-19 open research dataset.

William Yang Wang. 2017. "liar, liar pants on fire": A new benchmark dataset for fake news detection. In *Proceedings of the 55th Annual Meeting of the ACL (Volume 2: Short Papers)*, Vancouver, Canada. ACL.

Penghui Wei, Nan Xu, and Wenji Mao. 2019. Modeling conversation structure and temporal dynamics for jointly predicting rumor stance and veracity. *arXiv preprint arXiv:1909.08211*.

Lianwei Wu and Yuan Rao. 2020. Adaptive interaction fusion networks for fake news detection. *arXiv preprint arXiv:2004.10009*.

Shi Zhi, Yicheng Sun, Jiayi Liu, Chao Zhang, and Jiawei Han. 2017. Claimverif: a real-time claim verification system using the web and fact databases. In *Proceedings of the 2017 ACM on Conference on Information and Knowledge Management*, pages 2555–2558.

M-BAD: A Multilabel Dataset for Detecting Aggressive Texts and Their Targets

Omar Sharif[Ψ], **Eftekhar Hossain**[$] and **Mohammed Moshiul Hoque**[Ψ]
[Ψ]Department of Computer Science and Engineering
[$]Department of Electronics and Telecommunication Engineering
[$Ψ]Chittagong University of Engineering & Technology, Chattogram-4349, Bangladesh
{omar.sharif, eftekhar.hossain, moshiul_240}@cuet.ac.bd

Abstract

Recently, detection and categorization of undesired (e. g., aggressive, abusive, offensive, hate) content from online platforms has grabbed the attention of researchers because of its detrimental impact on society. Several attempts have been made to mitigate the usage and propagation of such content. However, most past studies were conducted primarily for English, where low-resource languages like Bengali remained out of the focus. Therefore, to facilitate research in this arena, this paper introduces a novel multilabel Bengali dataset (named ***M-BAD***) containing 15650 texts to detect aggressive texts and their targets. Each text of M-BAD went through rigorous two-level annotations. At the primary level, each text is labelled as either *aggressive* or *non-aggressive*. In the secondary level, the aggressive texts have been further annotated into five fine-grained target classes: *religion*, *politics*, *verbal*, *gender* and *race*. Baseline experiments are carried out with different machine learning (ML), deep learning (DL) and transformer models, where Bangla-BERT acquired the highest weighted f_1-score in both detection (0.92) and target identification (0.83) tasks. Error analysis of the models exhibits the difficulty to identify context-dependent aggression, and this work argues that further research is required to address these issues.

1 Introduction

Social media platforms have become a powerful tool to spontaneously connect people and share information with effortless access to the internet. These platforms provide users with a cloak of anonymity that allows them to speak their opinions publicly. Unfortunately, this power of anonymity is misused to disseminate aggressive, abusive, hatred and illegal content. In the recent past, these mediums have been used to incite religious, political and communal violence (Hartung et al., 2017). A significant portion of such incidents has been communicated through textual content (Kumar et al., 2020a; Feldman et al., 2021). Therefore, it has become crucial to develop automated systems to restrain the proliferation of such undesired or aggressive texts. This issue has been taken seriously in English, German, and other high-resource languages (Caselli et al., 2021; Aksenov et al., 2021). However, minimal research effort has been made in low-resource languages, including Bengali. Systems developed in English or other languages can not detect detrimental texts written in Bengali due to the significant variations in language constructs and morphological features. Nevertheless, people use their regional language to communicate over social media. Therefore, developing benchmark datasets and regional language tools is monumental to tackle the undesired text detection challenges. This work develops M-BAD containing 15650 texts using a two-level hierarchical annotation schema. In level-1, texts are categorized into binary classes: aggressive or non-aggressive. In level-2, 8289 aggressive texts are further annotated with multilabel targets. These labels are used to identify aggression's target into five fine-grained classes, such as *religion*, *gendered*, *race*, *verbal* and *politics* (detailed taxonomy discussed in Section 3). Proper annotation guidelines and the detailed statistics of the dataset is described to ensure M-BAD's quality. Several experiments are performed using ML, DL and transformer models to assess the task. The experiments demonstrate that (i) transformer models are more effective in detecting aggressive texts and their targets than ML/DL counterparts, (ii) covert propagation of aggression using ambiguous, context-dependent and sarcastic words is difficult to identify. The significant contributions of this work can be summarized as follows,

- Study two new problems from the perspective of low-resource language (i.e. Bengali), *(i)* detecting aggressive texts and *(ii)* identifying the multilabel targets of aggression.

Proceedings of the Workshop on Combating Online Hostile Posts in Regional Languages during Emergency Situations, pages 75 - 85
May 27, 2022 ©2022 Association for Computational Linguistics

- Release a new benchmark aggressive dataset labelled with the target of aggression and detailed annotation steps.

- Perform baseline experimentation on the developed dataset (M-BAD) to benchmark the two problems, providing the first insight into this challenging task.

Reproducibility: The resources to reproduce the results are available at https://github.com/omar-sharif03/M-BAD. The appendix contains details about data sources, annotators and a few samples of M-BAD.

2 Related Work

This section briefly describes the past studies related to aggression and other undesired content detection concerning non-Bengali and Bengali languages.

Non-Bengali aggressive text classification: Kumar et al. (2018a) compiled a dataset of 15000 aggression annotated comments in English and Hindi with three classes: *overtly aggressive, covertly aggressive, non-aggressive*. In their subsequent work (Kumar et al., 2020b), Bengali aggressive comments were added in the corpus. Early works with neural network techniques such as LSTM (Nikhil et al., 2018), CNN (Kumari and Singh, 2020), combination of shallow and deep network (Golem et al., 2018) achieved good accuracy. However, with the arrival of BERT based models, it acquired superior performance and outperformed all the models on these datasets (Risch and Krestel, 2020; Gordeev and Lykova, 2020; Sharif et al., 2021). Bhardwaj et al. (2020) developed a multilabel dataset in Hindi with five hostile classes: *fake, defamation, offensive, hate, non-hostile*. Their baseline system was implemented with m-BERT embedding and SVM. Leite et al. (2020) introduced a multilabel toxic language dataset. The dataset contains 21k tweets manually annotated into seven categories: *insult*, *LGBTQ+phobia*, *obscene*, *misogyny*, *racism*, *non-toxic* and *xenophobia*. They also performed baseline evaluation with the variation of BERT models. In a similar work, Moon et al. (2020) developed a corpus to detect toxic speech in Korean online news comments.

Bengali aggressive text classification: No significant research has been conducted yet to detect multilabel aggression in Bengali. The scarcity of benchmark corpora is the primary reason behind this. Few works have been conducted to develop datasets and models in other correlated domains such as hate, abuse, fake and offence. Karim et al. (2021) developed a hate speech dataset of 3000 samples with four categories: *political*, *personal*, *religious*, *geopolitical*. Emon et al. (2019) presented a dataset comprised of 4.7k abusive Bengali texts collected from online platforms. They proposed LSTM based classifier to categorize texts into seven classes. However, they did not investigate other DL models' performance, which might get similar accuracy with less computational cost. To detect the threat and abusive language, a dataset of 5.6k Bengali comments is created by Chakraborty and Seddiqui (2019). In recent work, Sharif and Hoque (2021a) introduced a benchmark Bengali aggressive text dataset. They employed a hierarchical annotation schema to divide the dataset into two coarse-grained (aggressive, non-aggressive) and four fine-grained (political, religious, verbal, gendered) aggression classes. In their later work (Sharif and Hoque, 2021b), they extended the dataset from 7.5k texts to 14k texts.

Differences with existing studies: As far as we are concerned, very few works have been accomplished to detect aggressive texts and identify the target of aggression (e.g. religion, gender, race). Existing works (Sharif and Hoque, 2021b; Zampieri et al., 2019; Kumar et al., 2018b) have framed it as a multi-class classification problem and ignored the overlapping phenomena of classes. However, a text can express aggression towards multiple targets simultaneously. Suppose a text has an aggressive write up against political women, expressing political and gendered aggressions. The proposed work addresses the issues that are previously overlooked and differs from the existing research in the following ways, (i) develop a novel Bengali aggressive text dataset annotated with the multiple targets of an aggressive text. As our knowledge goes, this is the first attempt to develop such a dataset in Bengali, (ii) illustrate a detailed annotation guideline which can be followed to develop resources for the similar domains in Bengali and other low-resource languages, (iii) perform experimentation with multilabel classes with various ML, DL and transformer-based models.

3 Dataset Development Taxonomy

This work presents a two-level hierarchical annotation schema to develop a novel multilabel aggression dataset in Bengali (M-BAD). Level-1 has two coarse-grained categories: aggressive and non-aggressive. In contrast, level-2 has five fine-grained multilabel target classes (religion, politics, verbal, gender, race). This work differs from previous work done by Sharif and Hoque (2021b) in two ways; (i) overlapping phenomena between aggression targets are considered, (ii) a new target class (i.e., racial aggression) is added into the M-BAD. Figure 1 illustrates the taxonomic structure of M-BAD.

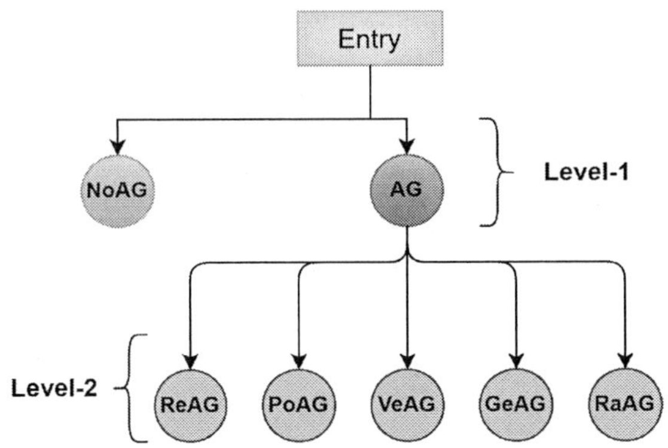

Figure 1: Taxonomic structure

Because of the subjective nature of the dataset, it is crucial to have a clear understanding of the categories. It helps develop a quality dataset by mitigating annotation biases and reducing ambiguities. After analyzing past studies (Sharif and Hoque, 2021b; Bhardwaj et al., 2020; Zampieri et al., 2019; Vidgen et al., 2021) on textual aggression and other related phenomena, we differentiate between the coarse-grained and fine-grained categories.

Coarse-grained Aggression Classes : The system initially identifies an input text as aggressive (AG) or non-aggressive (NoAG) classes.

- **(AG)**: excite, attack or seek harm to the individual, group or community based on a few criteria such as gender identity, political ideology, sexual orientation, religious belief, race, ethnicity and nationality.
- **(NoAG)**: do not contain any aggressive statements or express any evil intention to harm others.

Fine-grained Target Classes: An AG text is further classified into five fine-grained categories: religious aggression (ReAG), political aggression (PoAG), verbal aggression (VeAG), gendered aggression (GeAG) and racial aggression (RaAG). Each of the classes is defined in the following:

- **ReAG**: excite violence by attacking religion, religious organization or religious belief (Catholic, Hindu, Jew, or Islam, etc.) of a community
- **PoAG**: demean political ideology, provoke followers of political parties, or incite people in against law enforcement agencies and state.
- **VeAG**: seek to do evil or harm others, denounce the social status by using curse words, obscene words, outrageous and other threatening languages.
- **GeAG**: attack an individual or group by making aggressive reference to sexual orientation, sexuality, body parts, or other lewd contents.
- **RaAG**: insult or attack some and promote aggression based on race.

4 M-BAD: Multilabel Aggression Dataset

As far as we are concerned, no dataset is available to date for detecting or classifying multilabel aggressive texts and their targets in Bengali. However, the availability of a benchmark dataset is the prerequisite to developing any deep learning-based intelligent text classification system. This drawback motivates us to construct **M-BAD**: a novel multilabel Bengali aggressive text dataset. This work follows the guidelines and directions given by (Sharif and Hoque, 2021b; Vidgen and Derczynski, 2021) to ensure the quality of the dataset. This section briefly describes the data collection and annotation steps with detailed statistics of M-BAD.

4.1 Data Collection

We have manually accumulated **16000** aggressive and non-aggressive texts from different social platforms within the duration from 16 June to 27 December 2021. During this period, we only collected those texts that were posted, composed or shared after 1 January 2020. Potential texts were accumulated from YouTube channels and Facebook pages affiliated with political organizations, religion, newsgroups, artists, authors, celebrities, etc. Appendix A presents detailed statistics of the data collection sources.

Aggressive texts were cumulated from comments and posts that express aggression or excite violence. User profiles were also scanned who promoted, shared, or glorified aggression information to acquire additional texts. On the other hand, non-aggressive posts have been collected from news/comments/posts related to sports, education, entertainment, science and technology. Furthermore, while collecting aggressive texts, many data samples were found that did not express any aggression. Such texts were added to the corpus. We did not store any personal information (name, phone number, birth date, location) of the users during data accumulation. Each sample text is anonymized in the dataset. Thus, we do not know who has posted or created the collected texts. Finally, a few preprocessing filters are applied to remove inappropriate texts. 255 samples are discarded based on the following filtering criteria, (i) contains non-Bengali texts, (ii) has length fewer than three words, (iii) duplication. Remaining **15745** texts passed to the annotators for manual labelling.

4.2 Annotation Process

Section 3 describes the annotation schema and class definitions used to annotate the texts. Six annotators carried the annotation: four undergraduate and two graduate students. An expert verified the label in case of disagreement. Appendix B illustrates the detailed demographics of annotators. Annotators were split into three groups (two in each), and each group labelled a different subset of processed texts. To achieve quality annotations, we trained the annotators to define classes and associated examples. We tried to ensure that annotators understood what an aggressive text is and how to determine the target of aggression. Moreover, annotators are carefully guided in the weekly lab meetings.

Two annotators annotated each text, and the final label was assigned based on the agreement between the annotators. In case of disagreement, an expert resolve the issue through deliberations with the annotators. During the final label assignment, we found 95 texts that did not fall into any defined aggression categories and subsequently discarded them. Finally, we get M-BAD, an aggression dataset annotated with their targets containing **15650** texts. Appendix C shows few samples of M-BAD.

We measure the inter-annotator agreement using kappa score (Cohen, 1960) to check the validity of annotations. Table 1 presents the κ-*score* on both coarse-grained and fine-grained classes. The table shows that agreement is higher (0.77) in coarse-grained classes. The agreement is consistently 'moderate' (≈ 0.62) among the fine-grained classes but a bit lower in ReAG. Scores indicate difficulty in detecting targets of aggression by the annotators. Analysis reveals that sarcastic, implicit and ambiguous words made this difficult.

		κ-score	**Average**
Level-1	AG	0.85	0.77
	NoAG	0.69	
Level-2	ReAG	0.55	0.62
	PoAG	0.61	
	VeAG	0.62	
	GeAG	0.67	
	RaAG	0.65	

Table 1: Kappa (κ) score on each annotation level

4.3 Dataset Statistics

For training and evaluation purposes, the developed M-BAD is divided into the train (80%), test (10%), and validation (10%) split using a stratified strategy. The identical split ratio is used for both coarse-grained and multilabel fine-grained experiments. Table 2 presents the class-wise distribution of the texts for both Level-1 and Level-2. It is noticed that the distributions are slightly imbalanced with Level-2, which will be very challenging to handle in a multilabel setup.

Class	**Train**	**Test**	**Valid**	**Total**
ReAG	2391	327	305	3023
PoAG	2408	310	275	2993
VeAG	3939	498	472	4909
GeAG	1306	148	167	1621
RaAG	175	21	28	224
NoAG	5893	710	758	7361
AG	6642	840	807	8289

Table 2: Number of instances in train, test and validation sets for each category

	Class	**#Words**	**#Unique words**	**Avg. #words/text**
Level-1	AG	80553	17413	12.12
	NoAG	106573	24617	18.08
Level-2	ReAG	30748	9093	12.85
	PoAG	28410	8496	11.79
	VeAG	42342	11587	10.74
	GeAG	13817	4796	10.57
	RaAG	1711	1206	9.77

Table 3: Training set statistics in each level and class

To obtain in-depth insights, training set is further analyzed which is reported in Table 3. The statistics illustrated that in Level-1, NoAG class has the highest number of words ($\approx$106k) and unique words ($\approx$24k) compared to the AG class. Meanwhile, in Level-2, VeAG has the maximum number of words ($\approx$42k) and unique words ($\approx$11k) while RaAG class has the lowest ($\approx$1.7k, $\approx$1.2k). However, the average number of words per text ranges from 10 to 12 among the aggression categories. Figure 2 shows the histogram of the texts length of each category. It is observed that $\approx$5000 texts of NoAG class have a length between $\approx$15-40. On the other hand, most of the length of the texts falls between 5-30 in VeAG class while $\approx$ 1000 texts of RaAG class has a length < 20. It is also noticed that only a small number of texts have length > 50.

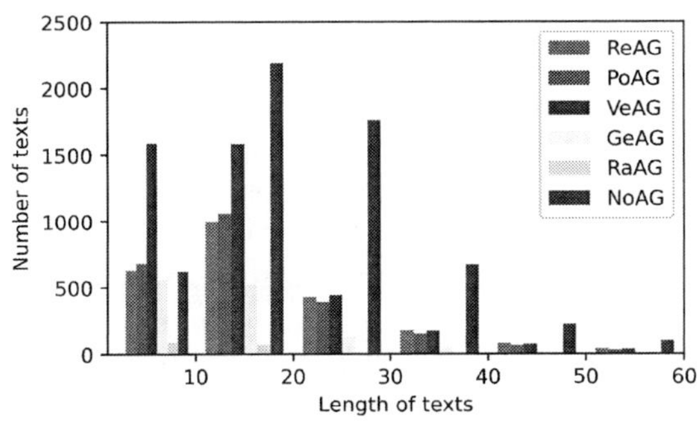

Figure 2: Histogram of the text length for each categories

	PoAG	VeAG	GeAG	RaAG
ReAG	0.38	0.47	0.36	0.18
PoAG		0.42	0.29	0.16
VeAG			0.50	0.25
GeAG				0.23
	NoAG			
AG	0.22			

Table 4: Jaccard similarity of 400 most frequent words between each pair of classes

We calculated the Jaccard similarity scores between the most 400 frequent words for quantitative analysis. Table 4 presents the similarity values among each pair of categories from Level-1 and Level-2. The VeAG-GeAG pair obtained the highest similarity score (0.50), while the PoAG-RaAG pair got the lowest score (0.16). It is observed that VeAG class has maximum similarity with almost all the classes except RaAG.

5 Methodology

Several computational models are investigated to develop the target aware aggression identification system. At first, the investigation is carried out for classifying the aggressive texts, and then we develop models for categorizing the target of the aggression (ReAG, PoAG, VeAG, GeAG, RaAG) considering the multilabel scenario. Machine learning and deep learning-based methods are employed to build the system. This section briefly discussed the techniques and methods used to develop the system.

5.1 ML-based methods

Two ML-based methods, Logistic Regression (LR) (Sharif and Hoque, 2019) and Naive Bayes with Support Vector Machine (NBSVM) (Wang and Manning, 2012) have been investigated for the classification task. Bag of words (BoW) features are used to train these models. The LR model is built with the 'lbfgs' optimizer and 'l2' regularization technique. Apart from this, the inverse regularization parameter C settled to 1.0. On the other hand, for NBSVM, the additive smoothing (α) and regularization parameters (C) are settled at 1.0 whereas the interpolation value is selected to $\beta = 0.25$.

5.2 DL-based Methods

Several popular DL methods are also investigated including BiGRU (Marpaung et al., 2021) and pretrained transformers (Vaswani et al., 2017) to identify the multi-label textual aggression.

BiGRU+FastText: The FastText (Joulin et al., 2016) embeddings are used as the input of the BiGRU model. Before that, a 1D spatial dropout technique is applied over the embedding features and then fed to a BiGRU layer with 80 hidden units. The last time step hidden output from the BiGRU is passed to a 1D global average pooling and a 1D global max-pooling layer. Subsequently, the two pooling layers outputs are concatenated and propagated to the classification layer.

Pretrained Transformers: In recent years, transformer (Vaswani et al., 2017) models trained on multilingual and monolingual settings achieved outstanding result in solving undesired text classification related tasks (Sharif and Hoque, 2021b; Hossain et al., 2021). As our task deals with a dataset of low-resource language, we employed three transformer-based models: (i) Multilingual

Bidirectional Encoder Representations for transformers (m-BERT) (Devlin et al., 2018) (ii) BERT for Bangla language (Bangla-BERT) (Bhattacharjee et al., 2021), and (iii) BERT for Indian languages (Indic-BERT) (Kakwani et al., 2020). The models have culled from the hugging face[1] transformers library and fine-tuned them with default arguments on the developed dataset.

Both ML and DL-based models are trained for two classification tasks: coarse-grained and multilabel fine-grained. To allow the reproducibility of the models and mitigate the training complexity, we use identical hyperparameters values for both classification tasks. We employed the Ktrain (Maiya, 2020) wrapper that provides easy training and implementation of the models. For multilabel classification, we enabled the Ktrain default multilabel settings. The BiGRU+FastText model is trained with a learning rate of $7e^{-3}$ while the transformer models with $8e^{-5}$. The models are trained using the triangular policy method (Smith, 2017) for 20 epochs with a batch size of 32. To save the best intermediate models, we utilized the early stopping criterion.

6 Experiments

The experiments were carried out in a google collaboratory platform with a GPU environment. The evaluation of the dataset is performed based on the weighted f_1-score. Due to the highly skewed distribution of the classes, we considered macro f_1-score (MF1) as our primary metric in multilabel evaluation. Besides, the individual class performance is measured through precision (P), recall (R), and f_1-score (F1) matrices.

6.1 Results

Table 5 presents the outcome of the different models on the test set concerning the coarse-grained classification. In terms of weighted f_1-score (WF1), both LR and NBSVM obtained an identical score of 0.91 while BiGRU + FastText and m-BERT model got a slightly low score (0.90). However, the Bangla-BERT model achieved the highest F1 across the two coarse-grained classes (AG/NoAG = 0.92) and thus outperformed all the models by achieving the highest WF1 score of 0.92.

Table 6 reports the evaluation results of the multilabel fine-grained classification. The outcome illustrates that the NBSVM obtained the lowest MF1 (0.61) and WF1 score (0.77). Both Indic-BERT and BiGRU+FastText models acquired identical WF1 of 0.79. Meanwhile, macro and weighted f_1-score is slightly (MF1 $\approx$4%, WF1 $\approx$ 1%) improved with the m-BERT model. However, the Bangla-BERT model exceeds all the models by achieving the highest MF1 (0.72) and WF1 (0.83). In terms of class-wise performance, Bangla-BERT obtained the highest f_1-score in four fine-grained aggression classes: ReAG (0.94), PoAG (0.92), VeAG (0.81), and GeAG (0.68). One interesting finding is that in RaAG class, some models (LR, NBSVM, Indic-BERT) did not identify a single instance correctly. Moreover, the models' performance degrades with the classes (GeAG, RaAG) having fewer training samples than other classes. Thus, a large dataset with balanced data distribution needs to be developed for classifying the problematic multilabel samples.

	AG			NoAG			
Method	P	R	F1	P	R	F1	WF1
LR	0.93	0.90	0.91	0.89	0.92	0.91	0.91
NBSVM	0.94	0.89	0.91	0.89	0.94	0.91	0.91
BG+FT	0.88	0.93	0.90	0.92	0.87	0.89	0.90
m-BERT	0.90	0.89	0.90	0.89	0.90	0.89	0.90
Indic-BERT	0.88	0.90	0.89	0.89	0.87	0.88	0.89
Bangla-BERT	0.93	0.91	0.92	0.91	0.93	0.92	**0.92**

Table 5: Performance of the Coarse-grained classification on the test set. Here, BG+FT represents BiGRU+FastText model

6.1.1 Error Analysis

The results confirmed that Bangla-BERT is the best performing model in both coarse-grained and fine-grained classification tasks (Table 5, 6). We perform a thorough error analysis to know the model mistakes across different classes.

Quantitative analysis: Figure 3 shows the confusion matrices for the Bangla-BERT model. Figure 3 (a) depicts that with coarse-grained classification, the model incorrectly identified 73 (out of 807) and 56 (out 758) instances as NoAG and AG texts, respectively. The confusion matrices for fine-grained classes are shown in Figure 3 (b)-(f). It is noticed that in ReAG and PoAG classes model misclassified 20 (out of 305) and 23 instances (out of 275), respectively. The model yields the most incorrect predictions (24 out of 28) with RaAG class. The reason might be that the model did not get enough samples for learning and thus failed to discern the correct class in the testing phase. Meanwhile, in the case of VeAG, the model gets confused and mis-

[1]https://huggingface.co/

	ReAG			PoAG			VeAG			GeAG			Racism				
Method	P	R	F1	P	R	F1	P	R	F1	P	R	F1	P	R	F1	MF1	WF1
LR	0.93	0.84	0.88	0.93	0.81	0.86	0.74	0.75	0.75	0.75	0.51	0.61	0.00	0.00	0.00	0.66	0.77
NBSVM	0.93	0.85	0.89	0.95	0.82	0.88	0.74	0.73	0.74	0.72	0.47	0.57	0.00	0.00	0.00	0.61	0.77
BG+FT	0.89	0.89	0.89	0.90	0.85	0.87	0.75	0.74	0.75	0.67	0.64	0.66	0.50	0.11	0.18	0.67	0.79
m-BERT	0.92	0.89	0.90	0.90	0.93	0.92	0.81	0.71	0.76	0.71	0.60	0.65	0.50	0.25	0.33	0.71	0.80
Indic-BERT	0.89	0.90	0.89	0.94	0.87	0.90	0.75	0.75	0.75	0.68	0.64	0.66	0.00	0.00	0.00	0.64	0.79
Bangla-BERT	0.94	0.93	0.94	0.93	0.92	0.92	0.79	0.82	0.81	0.70	0.66	0.68	0.67	0.14	0.24	**0.72**	**0.83**

Table 6: Fine-grained classification performance on the test set. Here, MF1 indicates the macro f_1-score

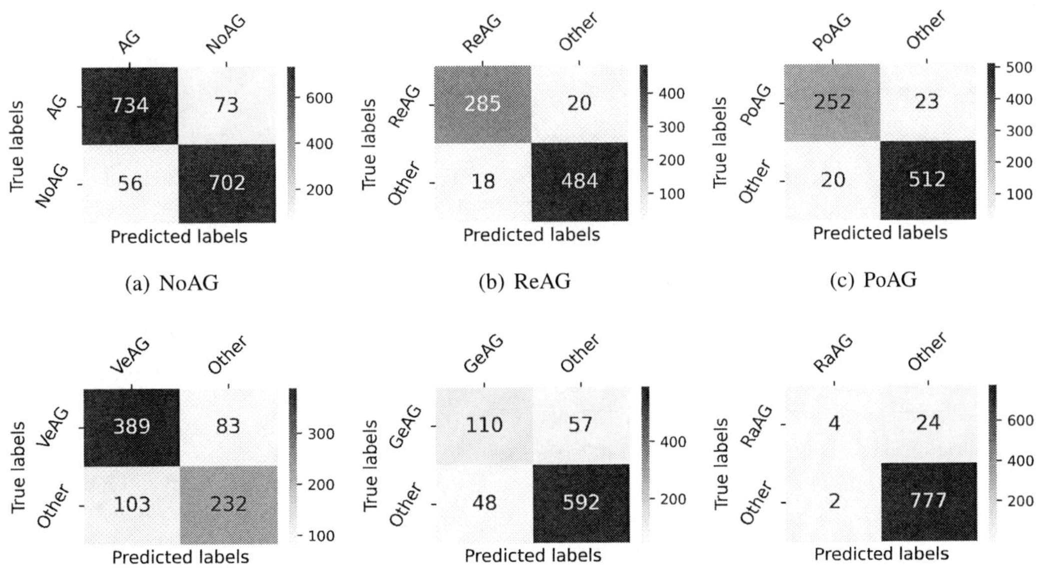

(a) NoAG (b) ReAG (c) PoAG

(d) VeAG (e) GeAG (f) RaAG

Figure 3: Confusion matrices of each category for Bangla-BERT model

classifies other classes instance (103 out of 232) as VeAG. The appearance of outrageous words in other fine-grained aggressive classes may be the reason for this confusion. Table 7 presents the false-negative rate (FNR) of the fine-grained categories. We noticed that the FNR is very high with GeAG (0.34) class while ReAG (0.065) and PoAG (0.08) classes FNR is deficient.

	False negative Rate
ReAG	20/305 (0.065)
PoAG	23/275 (0.08)
VeAG	83/472 (0.17)
GeAG	57/167 (0.34)
RaAG	4/28 (0.14)

Table 7: Error analysis for each fine-grained category

Qualitative Analysis: Figure 4 shows some correctly and misclassified sample texts from fine-grained classification tasks. The output predictions are obtained from the Bangla-BERT model. It is observed that the first two samples are correctly classified into different fine-grained aggression classes. However, in the third example, the model was only able to identify the text as **ReAG** and incorrectly predicted it as VeAG. Similarly, in the case of the last example model, it was not even able to classify it as RaAG. These examples illustrate the underlying difficulties of the multilabel classification problem. From the analysis, we found that the texts implicitly express aggression, which makes it arduous for the model to determine the multiple classes simultaneously. Moreover, some words have extensively appeared in the fine-grained classes. Perhaps, these words confuse the model to distinguish the classes and thus makes the task more difficult. Adding more training samples across all the classes might eradicate the problem to some extent.

7 Conclusion

This paper presented a multilabel aggression identification system for Bengali. To accomplish the purpose, this work introduced *M-BAD*, a multilabel

Text	Actual	Predicted
'ভারত আর বাংলাদেশের বিশ্ব বিদ্যালয়ে ধ**ণ কে পারফেক্ট করানোর কোর্স চালু হবে।' (Courses to make r**e perfect will be introduced in universities in India and Baladesh.)	PoAG, VeAG	PoAG, VeAG
'হিন্দুরা ভারতকে সাপোর্ট করে বাংলাদেশের চেয়ে বেশী। এই কু**র বাচ্চা হিন্দুদের দেশ হতে বের করে দেয়া দরকার' (Hindus support India more than Bangladesh. Get this Hindu bi**h out of the country)	ReAG, PoAG, VeAG	ReAG, PoAG, VeAG
'এই ধর্মান্ধ শালারা পরে সেক্স কন্ট্রোল করতে না পেরে ছাগল লাগাই' (These fanatical bastards can't control sex and then rape goats)	ReAG, RaAG	ReAG, VeAG
'পররাষ্ট্রমন্ত্রী এ সরিলে ভারতের হিন্দুর রক্ত আছে' (Foreign Minister has the blood of Hindus of India)	ReAG, PoAG, RaAG	ReAG, PoAG

Figure 4: Some correctly and incorrectly classified samples by the Bangla-BERT model

benchmark dataset consisting of 15650 texts. A two-level hierarchical annotation schema has been followed to develop the corpus. Among the levels, Level-1 is concerned with either aggressive or not aggressive, whereas Level-2 is concerned with the targets (religious, political, verbal, gender, racial) of the aggressive texts in a multilabel scenario. Several traditional and state of the art computational models have been investigated for benchmark evaluation. The results exhibit that the Bangla-BERT model obtained the highest weighted f_1-score of 0.83 for the multilabel classification. The error analysis revealed that it is challenging to identify the multiple targets of aggressive text as words are frequently overlapped across different classes. In future, we aim to mitigate this issue by exploring multitask learning and domain adaption approaches. Moreover, future work considers including more data samples with a significant period to minimize the bias towards a limited set of events.

Acknowledgements

This work supported by the ICT Innovation Fund, ICT Division, Ministry of Posts, Telecommunications and Information Technology, Bangladesh.

References

Dmitrii Aksenov, Peter Bourgonje, Karolina Zaczynska, Malte Ostendorff, Julian Moreno-Schneider, and Georg Rehm. 2021. Fine-grained classification of political bias in German news: A data set and initial experiments. In *Proceedings of the 5th Workshop on Online Abuse and Harms (WOAH 2021)*, pages 121–131, Online. Association for Computational Linguistics.

Mohit Bhardwaj, Md Shad Akhtar, Asif Ekbal, Amitava Das, and Tanmoy Chakraborty. 2020. Hostility detection dataset in hindi.

Abhik Bhattacharjee, Tahmid Hasan, Kazi Samin, Md Saiful Islam, M. Sohel Rahman, Anindya Iqbal, and Rifat Shahriyar. 2021. Banglabert: Combating embedding barrier in multilingual models for low-resource language understanding. *CoRR*, abs/2101.00204.

Tommaso Caselli, Valerio Basile, Jelena Mitrović, and Michael Granitzer. 2021. HateBERT: Retraining BERT for abusive language detection in English. In *Proceedings of the 5th Workshop on Online Abuse and Harms (WOAH 2021)*, pages 17–25, Online. Association for Computational Linguistics.

Puja Chakraborty and Md. Hanif Seddiqui. 2019. Threat and abusive language detection on social media in bengali language. In *2019 1st International Conference on Advances in Science, Engineering and Robotics Technology (ICASERT)*, pages 1–6.

Jacob Cohen. 1960. A coefficient of agreement for nominal scales. *Educational and Psychological Measurement*, 20(1):37–46.

Jacob Devlin, Ming-Wei Chang, Kenton Lee, and Kristina Toutanova. 2018. BERT: pre-training of deep bidirectional transformers for language understanding. *CoRR*, abs/1810.04805.

Estiak Ahmed Emon, Shihab Rahman, Joti Banarjee, Amit Kumar Das, and Tanni Mittra. 2019. A deep learning approach to detect abusive bengali text. In *2019 7th International Conference on Smart Computing Communications (ICSCC)*, pages 1–5.

Anna Feldman, Giovanni Da San Martino, Chris Leberknight, and Preslav Nakov, editors. 2021. *Proceedings of the Fourth Workshop on NLP for Internet Freedom: Censorship, Disinformation, and Propaganda*. Association for Computational Linguistics, Online.

Viktor Golem, Mladen Karan, and Jan Šnajder. 2018. Combining shallow and deep learning for aggressive text detection. In *Proceedings of the First Workshop on Trolling, Aggression and Cyberbullying (TRAC-2018)*, pages 188–198, Santa Fe, New Mexico, USA. Association for Computational Linguistics.

Denis Gordeev and Olga Lykova. 2020. BERT of all trades, master of some. In *Proceedings of the Second Workshop on Trolling, Aggression and Cyberbullying*, pages 93–98, Marseille, France. European Language Resources Association (ELRA).

Matthias Hartung, Roman Klinger, Franziska Schmidtke, and Lars Vogel. 2017. Ranking right-wing extremist social media profiles by similarity to democratic and extremist groups. In *Proceedings of the 8th Workshop on Computational Approaches to Subjectivity, Sentiment and Social Media Analysis*, pages 24–33, Copenhagen, Denmark. Association for Computational Linguistics.

Eftekhar Hossain, Omar Sharif, and Mohammed Moshiul Hoque. 2021. NLP-CUET@DravidianLangTech-EACL2021: Investigating visual and textual features to identify trolls from multimodal social media memes. In *Proceedings of the First Workshop on Speech and Language Technologies for Dravidian Languages*, pages 300–306, Kyiv. Association for Computational Linguistics.

Armand Joulin, Edouard Grave, Piotr Bojanowski, Matthijs Douze, Hérve Jégou, and Tomas Mikolov. 2016. Fasttext. zip: Compressing text classification models. *arXiv preprint arXiv:1612.03651*.

Divyanshu Kakwani, Anoop Kunchukuttan, Satish Golla, Gokul N.C., Avik Bhattacharyya, Mitesh M. Khapra, and Pratyush Kumar. 2020. IndicNLPSuite: Monolingual Corpora, Evaluation Benchmarks and Pre-trained Multilingual Language Models for Indian Languages. In *Findings of EMNLP*.

Md. Rezaul Karim, Sumon Kanti Dey, Tanhim Islam, Sagor Sarker, Mehadi Hasan Menon, Kabir Hossain, Bharathi Raja Chakravarthi, Md. Azam Hossain, and Stefan Decker. 2021. Deephateexplainer: Explainable hate speech detection in under-resourced bengali language.

Ritesh Kumar, Atul Kr. Ojha, Bornini Lahiri, Marcos Zampieri, Shervin Malmasi, Vanessa Murdock, and Daniel Kadar, editors. 2020a. *Proceedings of the Second Workshop on Trolling, Aggression and Cyberbullying*. European Language Resources Association (ELRA), Marseille, France.

Ritesh Kumar, Atul Kr. Ojha, Shervin Malmasi, and Marcos Zampieri. 2018a. Benchmarking aggression identification in social media. In *Proceedings of the First Workshop on Trolling, Aggression and Cyberbullying (TRAC-2018)*, pages 1–11, Santa Fe, New Mexico, USA. Association for Computational Linguistics.

Ritesh Kumar, Atul Kr. Ojha, Shervin Malmasi, and Marcos Zampieri. 2020b. Evaluating aggression identification in social media. In *Proceedings of the Second Workshop on Trolling, Aggression and Cyberbullying*, pages 1–5, Marseille, France. European Language Resources Association (ELRA).

Ritesh Kumar, Aishwarya N. Reganti, Akshit Bhatia, and Tushar Maheshwari. 2018b. Aggression-annotated corpus of Hindi-English code-mixed data. In *Proceedings of the Eleventh International Conference on Language Resources and Evaluation (LREC 2018)*, Miyazaki, Japan. European Language Resources Association (ELRA).

Kirti Kumari and Jyoti Prakash Singh. 2020. AI_ML_NIT_Patna @ TRAC - 2: Deep learning approach for multi-lingual aggression identification. In *Proceedings of the Second Workshop on Trolling, Aggression and Cyberbullying*, pages 113–119, Marseille, France. European Language Resources Association (ELRA).

João Augusto Leite, Diego Silva, Kalina Bontcheva, and Carolina Scarton. 2020. Toxic language detection in social media for Brazilian Portuguese: New dataset and multilingual analysis. In *Proceedings of the 1st Conference of the Asia-Pacific Chapter of the Association for Computational Linguistics and the 10th International Joint Conference on Natural Language Processing*, pages 914–924, Suzhou, China. Association for Computational Linguistics.

Arun S. Maiya. 2020. ktrain: A low-code library for augmented machine learning. *arXiv preprint arXiv:2004.10703*.

Angela Marpaung, Rita Rismala, and Hani Nurrahmi. 2021. Hate speech detection in indonesian twitter texts using bidirectional gated recurrent unit. In *2021 13th International Conference on Knowledge and Smart Technology (KST)*, pages 186–190. IEEE.

Jihyung Moon, Won Ik Cho, and Junbum Lee. 2020. BEEP! Korean corpus of online news comments for toxic speech detection. In *Proceedings of the Eighth International Workshop on Natural Language Processing for Social Media*, pages 25–31, Online. Association for Computational Linguistics.

Nishant Nikhil, Ramit Pahwa, Mehul Kumar Nirala, and Rohan Khilnani. 2018. LSTMs with attention for aggression detection. In *Proceedings of the First Workshop on Trolling, Aggression and Cyberbullying (TRAC-2018)*, pages 52–57, Santa Fe, New Mexico, USA. Association for Computational Linguistics.

Julian Risch and Ralf Krestel. 2020. Bagging BERT models for robust aggression identification. In *Proceedings of the Second Workshop on Trolling, Aggression and Cyberbullying*, pages 55–61, Marseille, France. European Language Resources Association (ELRA).

Omar Sharif and Mohammed Moshiul Hoque. 2019. Automatic detection of suspicious bangla text using logistic regression. In *International Conference on Intelligent Computing & Optimization*, pages 581–590. Springer.

Omar Sharif and Mohammed Moshiul Hoque. 2021a. Identification and classification of textual aggression in social media: Resource creation and evaluation. In *Combating Online Hostile Posts in Regional*

Languages during Emergency Situation, pages 1–12. Springer Nature Switzerland AG.

Omar Sharif and Mohammed Moshiul Hoque. 2021b. Tackling cyber-aggression: Identification and fine-grained categorization of aggressive texts on social media using weighted ensemble of transformers. *Neurocomputing*.

Omar Sharif, Eftekhar Hossain, and Mohammed Moshiul Hoque. 2021. NLP-CUET@DravidianLangTech-EACL2021: Offensive language detection from multilingual code-mixed text using transformers. In *Proceedings of the First Workshop on Speech and Language Technologies for Dravidian Languages*, pages 255–261, Kyiv. Association for Computational Linguistics.

Leslie N Smith. 2017. Cyclical learning rates for training neural networks. In *2017 IEEE winter conference on applications of computer vision (WACV)*, pages 464–472. IEEE.

Alane Suhr, Clara Vania, Nikita Nangia, Maarten Sap, Mark Yatskar, Samuel R. Bowman, and Yoav Artzi. 2021. Crowdsourcing beyond annotation: Case studies in benchmark data collection. In *Proceedings of the 2021 Conference on Empirical Methods in Natural Language Processing: Tutorial Abstracts*, pages 1–6, Punta Cana, Dominican Republic & Online. Association for Computational Linguistics.

Ashish Vaswani, Noam Shazeer, Niki Parmar, Jakob Uszkoreit, Llion Jones, Aidan N Gomez, Łukasz Kaiser, and Illia Polosukhin. 2017. Attention is all you need. In *Advances in neural information processing systems*, pages 5998–6008.

Bertie Vidgen and Leon Derczynski. 2021. Directions in abusive language training data, a systematic review: Garbage in, garbage out. *PLOS ONE*, 15(12):1–32.

Bertie Vidgen, Dong Nguyen, Helen Margetts, Patricia Rossini, and Rebekah Tromble. 2021. Introducing CAD: the contextual abuse dataset. In *Proceedings of the 2021 Conference of the North American Chapter of the Association for Computational Linguistics: Human Language Technologies*, pages 2289–2303, Online. Association for Computational Linguistics.

Sida I Wang and Christopher D Manning. 2012. Baselines and bigrams: Simple, good sentiment and topic classification. In *Proceedings of the 50th Annual Meeting of the Association for Computational Linguistics (Volume 2: Short Papers)*, pages 90–94.

Marcos Zampieri, Shervin Malmasi, Preslav Nakov, Sara Rosenthal, Noura Farra, and Ritesh Kumar. 2019. Predicting the type and target of offensive posts in social media. In *Proceedings of the 2019 Conference of the North American Chapter of the Association for Computational Linguistics: Human Language Technologies, Volume 1 (Long and Short Papers)*, pages 1415–1420, Minneapolis, Minnesota. Association for Computational Linguistics.

Xuhui Zhou, Maarten Sap, Swabha Swayamdipta, Yejin Choi, and Noah Smith. 2021. Challenges in automated debiasing for toxic language detection. In *Proceedings of the 16th Conference of the European Chapter of the Association for Computational Linguistics: Main Volume*, pages 3143–3155, Online. Association for Computational Linguistics.

Appendix

A Data Sources

Data samples were collected from public post/comment threads of Facebook and YouTube. We did not store the profile information of any users. The data collection procedure is consistent with the copyright and terms of service of these organizations [2]. Potential texts were culled from more than 200 Bengali YouTube channels and Facebook pages. The popularity and activity status of a few data sources are presented in table A.1.

B Annotator Demographics

Past studies (Suhr et al., 2021; Zhou et al., 2021) on benchmark dataset creation have emphasized knowing about the demographic, geographic, research and other related information of the annotators. Since aggression is a very subjective phenomenon, annotators perspective and experience play a crucial role in developing the dataset. Six students and an expert were involved in our dataset construction process. Annotators demographic information, research experience, the field of research, and personal experience of viewing online aggression are summarized in table B.1.

Some key characteristics of the annotators' pool are, (i) native Bengali speakers, (ii) have prior experience of annotation, (iii) not an active member of any political parties, (iv) not hold extreme view against religion, (v) viewed online aggression. Before requiting, the annotators' necessary ethical approval was taken, and they are substantially paid according to university regulations.

C Data Samples

The authors would like to state that the examples referred to in the figure C.1 presented as they were accumulated from the source. Authors do not use these examples to hurt individuals or promote aggressive language usage. The goal of this work is to mitigate the propagation of such language.

[2]https://www.facebook.com/help/1020633957973118, https://www.youtube.com/static?template=terms

Page/channel name	Type	Affiliation	No. of followers/ subscribers	Reactions per post (in avg.)	Frequency of posting)
Bidyanondo	FP	Non political org.	5M	10k	10 post/day
Prothom Alo	FP/YC	Newsgroup	14M	4.5k	180 post/day
Rafiath Mithila	FP	Artist	3.8M	15k	4 post/week
Mizanur Azhari	YC	Religious speaker	1.9M	50k	1 post/month
Jamuna tv	FP/YC	Media	12.9M	3.7k	80 post/day
Awami League	FP/YC	Political org.	890k	4.6k	15 post/day
Abu Toha Adnan	FP	Religious speaker	2M	18k	10 post/week
Salman BrownFish	YC/FP	Musician	3M	15k	7 post/month
Arif Azad	FP	Author	742k	87k	8 post/month
Somoynews tv	FP/YC	Media	8.1M	2K	120 post/day
Basher kella	FP	Political	45k	400	15 post/day
Roar Bangla	FP/YC	Media	50K	300	3 post/day
Shakib Al Hasan	FP	Public figure	15.3M	50k	15 post/month

Table A.1: Activity and popularity statistics of a few sources from where data were gathered. FP indicates a Facebook page, and YC denotes a YouTube channel. Reactions are counted in terms of likes, comments and shares.

	AN-1	AN-2	AN-3	AN-4	AN-5	AN-6	Expert
Research-status	Undergrad	RA	Undergrad	Graduate	RA	Graduate	Professor
Research area	NLP	NLP	NLP	NLP	NLP	NLP	NLP, Social computig, HCI
Experience (years)	1	1	0.5	2.5	1.5	3	21
Prior annotation experience	yes	yes	no	yes	yes	yes	yes
Gender	Male	Male	Female	Female	Male	Male	Male
Age	22	23	22	25	23	26	47
Religion	Islam	Hindu	Hindu	Islam	Islam	Islam	Islam
Viewed online aggression	yes	yes	yes	yes	yes	yes	yes
Targeted by online aggression	yes	no	no	yes	no	yes	yes

Table B.1: Summary of annotators information.

Text	Level-1	Level-2
আরে ভাই কিট পতংগের সাইজো বড়ো আছে হিন্দুধর্মের তুলনায় (Hey brother, the size of few insects are bigger than Hinduism)	AG	ReAG
মোল্লাদের ঘরের মেয়েদের এরকম ধরে যতদিন ধ**ন না করা হবে, তত দিন এরা শায়েস্তা হবেনা। (As long as the girls of the mullah's house are not r**d like this, they will not be punished)	AG	ReAG, VeAG, GeAG
ভোটার বিহীন অবৈধ সরকার ছাত্রলীগ দিয়ে দেশটাকে ধ**নের স্বর্গরাজ্যে পরিনত করেছে। (The illegitimate government without voters has turned the country into a paradise of r**e with Chhatra League.)	AG	PoAG, VeAG
মেয়েদের এত পড়ালেখা করে আর কি লাভ হুদাই টাকা নষ্ট (What is the benefit of educating girls so much. It is just a waste of money)	AG	GeAG
মহিলা রাজনীতিবিদদের সংসদ থেকে বের করা দেয়া উচিত। সবগুলো ছাগল দেশের টাকা নষ্ট করতেছে (Women politicians should be expelled from Parliament. All the goats are wasting the country's money)	AG	GeAG, PoAG
চাকমাদেরকে দেশ থেকে বের করে দেয়া হক। (The Chakmas should be expelled from the country)	AG	RaAG
হাজারো সালাম জানাই শিক্ষকদের, যাদের অবদানে এগিয়ে যাচ্ছে বাংলাদেশ (Thousands of salutations to the teachers, who are helping Bangladesh to move forward)	NoAG	-
সাকিব আল হাসান, বাংলাদেশের জান বাংলাদেশের প্রান। এগিয়ে যাও (Shakib Al Hasan, the soul of Bangladesh. Go ahead)	NoAG	-

Figure C.1: Few samples of M-BAD

How does fake news use a thumbnail? CLIP-based Multimodal Detection on the Unrepresentative News Image

Hyewon Choi
Soongsil University

Yejun Yoon
Soongsil University

Seunghyun Yoon
Adobe Research

Kunwoo Park *
Soongsil University

Abstract

This study investigates how fake news uses a thumbnail for a news article with a focus on whether a news article's thumbnail represents the news content correctly. A news article shared with an irrelevant thumbnail can mislead readers into having a wrong impression of the issue, especially in social media environments where users are less likely to click the link and consume the entire content. We propose to capture the degree of semantic incongruity in the multimodal relation by using the pretrained CLIP representation. From a source-level analysis, we found that fake news employs a more incongruous image to the main content than general news. Going further, we attempted to detect news articles with image-text incongruity. Evaluation experiments suggest that CLIP-based methods can successfully detect news articles in which the thumbnail is semantically irrelevant to news text. This study contributes to the research by providing a novel view on tackling online fake news and misinformation. Code and datasets are available at `https://github.com/ssu-humane/fake-news-thumbnail`.

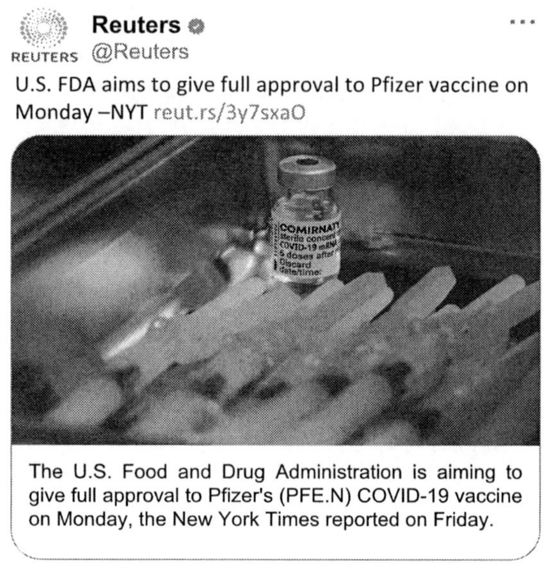

Figure 1: An example of a news article shared on Twitter. A visual summary of the article well represents the main content.

1 Introduction

We have been suffering from the infodemic as well as the coronavirus pandemic (Zarocostas, 2020). The proliferation of fake news during the pandemic has been a significant threat to the world by inducing hate crimes against East Asians, reinforcing the wrong beliefs of anti-vaxxers, etc. Fake news is defined as "fabricated information that mimics news media content in form but not in organizational process or intent" (Lazer et al., 2018). Motivated by the fact that unreliable sources generate most false articles, a line of research has attempted to understand the distinct characteristics of fake news sources. A notable study is Horne and Adali (2017), which focused on textual patterns of news articles and identified that overall title structure and the use of proper nouns in titles are significant markers that differentiate fake news from general news. Similarly, from consumption and spreading patterns on social media, Vosoughi et al. (2018) found that fake news spreads faster, deeper, and broader than general news. Other researchers showed that the reliability of news media could be predicted by various media-level features, including web traffic toward a news website (Baly et al., 2018).

In this study, we investigate the use of images in fake news articles; in particular, we focus on a thumbnail, an image displayed as a preview to a news article. When a news article is shared on social media, its title and thumbnail image are the only visible information before a user clicks the link. Since many readers skim news without carefully checking the content (Gabielkov et al., 2016), the visuals can mislead users into having a wrong

*Correspondence: `kunwoo.park@ssu.ac.kr`

Proceedings of the Workshop on Combating Online Hostile Posts in Regional Languages during Emergency Situations, pages 86 - 94
May 27, 2022

impression if the thumbnail does not represent the news content. Fake news sources are less likely to follow the journalistic standard but tend to employ undesirable techniques such as clickbait headlines (Chen et al., 2015). Therefore, we hypothesize that unreliable sources may use a less relevant image for the thumbnail to the news text to attract clicks and promote false beliefs.

To examine the hypothesis, we propose using CLIP (Radford et al., 2021), a deep multimodal representation that allows representing image and text in the same embedding space. Across three datasets, we measure image-text similarity over the CLIP embedding and confirm that the fake news media tend to use the semantically less relevant photograph in news content than trustworthy sources. Going further, we test CLIP's ability to detect the incongruity between news image and text. Multi-faceted evaluation experiments highlight that the CLIP-based methods can enable article-level detection on the unrepresentative thumbnail.

We summarize the contributions of this study three-fold.

1. We make a novel observation that fake news sources tend to use a less relevant news thumbnail than trustworthy media outlets.

2. We propose a new problem for detecting misinformed news articles using semantic incongruity between news text and thumbnail.

3. The paired dataset and manually annotated samples will be released for future usage.

2 Related Works

2.1 Multimodal representation

Researchers have explored methods that compute vector representations of multiple modalities (i.e., image and text) and align semantically similar content to the same embedding space. As examples of such attempts, building pretrained models trained with image-caption pairs shows potential as general backbone models of vision-and-language (VL) tasks (Lu et al., 2019; Chen et al., 2020). More recently, researchers collected large-scale image-caption data from the web and successfully trained models with a contrastive objective function. These models show robust performance in VL understanding tasks such as "image classification" and "image retrieval" even in the zero-shot setting (Radford et al., 2021; Jia et al., 2021; Kim et al., 2021).

As pretrained VL models can map semantically similar images and text descriptions into similar embedding spaces, they can be used to measure the quality of the image caption. Recent studies suggest a huge potential in building a better image-captioning metric using VL models (Lee et al., 2020, 2021; Hessel et al., 2021). Similarly, our study leverages the pretrained VL model to understand the relationship between news text and images.

2.2 Fake news detection

Fake news detection has been actively studied in data mining and computational linguistics (Shu et al., 2017). Technically, it was tackled as a classification problem; after collecting fact-checked claims on websites such as PolitiFact[1], researchers trained a classification model with a wide range of features on text patterns, source characteristics, audience reactions, etc. Ma et al. (2016) employed a recurrent neural network that captures patterns of contextual information of relevant posts over time. Ruchansky et al. (2017) introduced a model called CSI that incorporates the text of an article, the user response, and the source for the detection. Most recently, researchers developed a fake news detection framework that represents social contexts as a graph and learns through a graph neural network (Nguyen et al., 2020). This study does not aim to predict news veracity but to detect the case where the news thumbnail does not represent the main stories. While there have been a handful of studies tackling fake news detection using multimodal cues (Singhal et al., 2019; Qi et al., 2019; Giachanou et al., 2020; Khattar et al., 2019), to the best of our knowledge, no studies tackled the detection problem on incongruity between news text and image, nor investigated how fake news uses the thumbnail.

3 Media Difference on Semantic Similarity of News Text and Image

3.1 Problem and hypothesis

We aim at understanding media differences in the semantic relevance of the thumbnail picture to news text. Horne and Adali (2017) suggested that fake news exhibits text patterns that are qualitatively different. Similarly, we assume that fake news may exhibit a distinct pattern in the use of news photographs:

[1]https://www.politifact.com/

H. Fake news would use (semantically) a less relevant photograph to the news title for its thumbnail than general news.

We set the news title and thumbnail image, which is set as *meta_img* of the news HTML, as the target of analysis due to the following reasons. Journalism research suggests that a news title should provide a concise summary of the news article (Smith and Fowler Jr, 1982), and thus we consider the title as a proxy of the news article. Among images, we use the *meta_img* because it is automatically used as a preview when being shared on social media. That is, when a news article is shared, the thumbnail picture and news title become the first content shown to the users. Therefore, if a thumbnail does not represent the main story of a news article correctly, it could mislead readers into having a wrong impression of the target issue because social media users tend to consume news snippets without clicking the link (Gabielkov et al., 2016).

3.2 Method

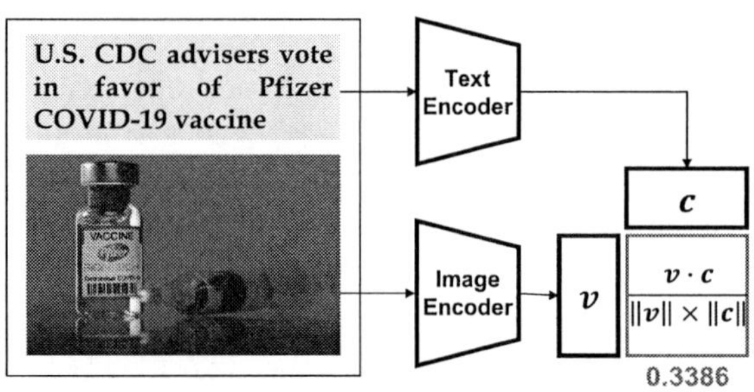

Figure 2: An illustration of CLIPScore

To test the hypothesis, we used CLIP that represents a pair of image and text into a multimodal space (Radford et al., 2021), which is the state-of-the-art model in multimodal representation learning. As shown in Figure 2, we computed visual CLIP embedding $\mathbf{v}$ and textual CLIP embedding $\mathbf{c}$ of news article. Then, we measured the cosine similarity for $\mathbf{v}$ and $\mathbf{c}$ to measure their semantic relevance, also known as CLIPScore (Hessel et al., 2021)[2]. We use the ViT-B/32 (Dosovitskiy et al., 2020) as backbone, and hence $\mathbf{c}, \mathbf{v} \in \mathbb{R}^{512}$.

Type	Whole	COVID	COVID-wo-faces
General	106,409	33,310	10,964
Fake	3,306	870	480
Total	109,715	34,180	11,444

Table 1: Dataset size

3.3 Data Collection

We collected news articles through the web links shared by official media accounts on social media, following a similar process proposed in a previous work (Park et al., 2021). Our data collection pipeline consists of the following steps.

Target media selection: To evaluate the main research hypothesis, we selected nine news outlets that run certified media accounts on Twitter as the target of analysis. Specifically, we focused on the five general news (FoxNews, New York Post, Reuters, The Guardian, Slate) and four fake news media (ActivitisPost, Judicial Watch, End Time Headlines, WorldNetDaily). The target list of fake news was selected from the media sources that were labeled as *red* news in a previous study (Grinberg et al., 2019), which is defined as "spreading falsehoods that clearly reflect a flawed editorial process." We selected the five general news from those labeled green in the same previous work. We confirmed the general media sources considered in this study are well balanced against the political bias rating[3].

Tweet collection: We collected tweets from January 2021 until the time of data collection (September 2021) using the Twint library[4]. We excluded tweets that do not contain URLs to their news articles.

News article collection: For each of the news URLs, we obtained the news title, body text, and URL for the thumbnail by using the newspaper3K library[5]. We stored the news data in JSON format and downloaded the images by the wget command. When the news data do not provide URLs for the thumbnail or we cannot download any images from the thumbnail URL, we did not include it in our data collection.

[2]The original implementation of CLIPScore applies a parametric ReLU to the cosine similarity. We used its canonical form without the ReLU function.

[3]`http://www.allsides.com`

[4]`https://github.com/twintproject/twint`

[5]`https://newspaper.readthedocs.io`

Figure 3: News examples with CLIPScore in each dataset. URLs of news articles are available in Appendix.

To see the robustness of the findings, we constructed two filtered versions of datasets for the analysis in addition to the original dataset (Whole). First, we limited the scope of the news topic to COVID-19 by selecting news articles containing at least one of the COVID-19 related keywords: coronavirus, corona, covid-19, corona virus, covid, covid19, sars-cov-2, pandemic, chinese virus, chinesevirus, and corona. The COVID-19 issue has been covered extensively during the period of CLIP training, and thus we assumed the CLIP embedding could understand the COVID-19 context better than random events. We call the COVID-19 filtered dataset COVID. Next, to minimize the number of false negatives (i.e., the model considers a relevant pair irrelevant), we further filtered out news articles in which the thumbnail picture contains faces from the COVID dataset (COVID-wo-faces. In a preliminary analysis, we found that CLIP is not good at matching a person's name in text and their appearance in an image, especially when they are not famous (e.g., the example in the bottom left of Figure 3 and Figure A1.)). We detected images with a face by the face detection model of the Google Cloud Vision[6]. Table 1 presents the size of three datasets that covers news articles from January to August 2021. We expect that the data leakage issue is minimal because our dataset period is less likely to overlap with the dataset used for training CLIP[7].

3.4 Results

Figure 3 presents the title-image pairs with the CLIPScore values. The three examples in the top row present the pairs with a high CLIPScore, which were sampled from the top-500 news articles in terms of CLIPScore. The bottom three examples were randomly selected from the bottom-500 examples in terms of CLIPScore. The high-score examples demonstrate the capability of CLIP in understanding a written text and the appearance of a visual object. On the other hand, the three examples at the bottom demonstrate two scenarios where a low CLIPScore can represent. First, the New York Post example from the whole dataset suggests that the CLIP encoder has difficulty recognizing a person's appearance in an image, a name in a text, or both. Second, the low-score examples for the COVID and COVID-wo-faces datasets represent the cases where a thumbnail does not represent the news text, suggesting the potential of CLIPScore

[6] https://tinyurl.com/ydfu2js3

[7] CLIP paper was released on Feb 26th, 2021, which does not explicitly mention the period of the training dataset.

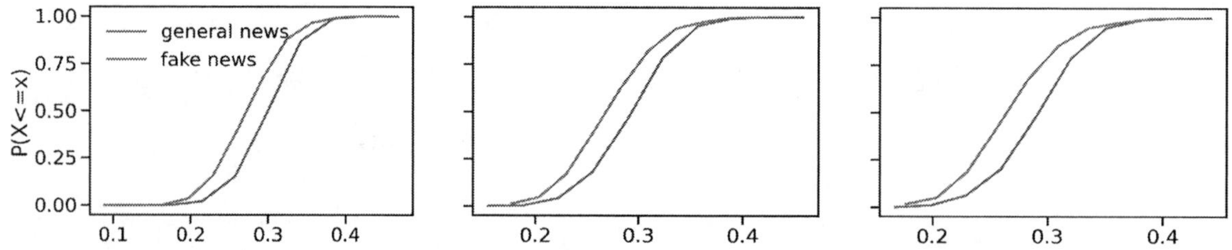

(a) Whole (0.596***) (b) COVID (0.545***) (c) COVID-wo-faces (0.594***)

Figure 4: CDFs of the CLIPScore measured for each dataset. Values within the parenthesis indicate Cohen's d corresponding to the difference of CLIPScore between general and fake news (***: $p<0.001$ by the t-test).

for capturing news articles with an unrepresentative thumbnail. Therefore, we used CLIPScore for understanding the media difference between fake news and trustworthy media in terms of semantic relevance between news title and thumbnail across the three datasets. The observations from the filtered datasets can function as a robustness check.

Figure 4 presents the difference of the semantic relevance of news title and thumbnail between fake and general news, measured by CLIPScore. We conducted the t-test to evaluate the statistical significance of a difference and calculated the Cohen's d for its effect size. The x-axis presents the CLIPScore threshold, and the y-axis presents the probability that the CLIPScore takes a value less than or equal to the threshold from the distribution. Results indicate that fake news tends to have a lower CLIPScore than general news with a statistical significance across the three datasets. The corresponding effect size is 0.596, 0.545, and 0.594 for the Whole, COVID, and COVID-wo-faces dataset, respectively. The values are considered medium effect sizes, which suggests that fake news tends to use a thumbnail picture that is semantically less similar to the news title than general news and therefore supports the main hypothesis in §3.1.

4 Detection of News Articles with the Incongruous Image

4.1 Motivation

As we observed in the previous section, Fake news media tend to use a photograph that is semantically less relevant to the news text than general news. Motivated by the observation, we turned to a detection problem aiming at identifying news articles with the incongruous thumbnail among articles shared by fake news outlets. We focused on the scope of detection of fake news media because the potential negative impact of image-text incongruity can be worse when used to promote false claims. Also, previous research suggested visuals can give a more significant impression to readers than textual signals (Seo, 2020).

Formally, we define the problem as a classification task using image-text multimodal data: given a pair of news text T and image I, we aim at predicting the binary incongruity label L on whether I is semantically (in-)congruent with T.

4.2 Data generation

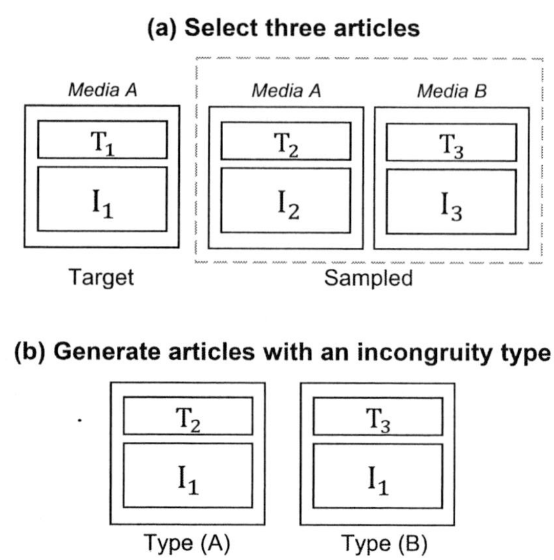

Figure 5: An illustration of data generation process (T: news title, I: thumbnail image).

A significant challenge in implementing a classification model for the target task is the lack of a dataset. While we have more than 20k image-text pairs, they are unlabeled, and it is costly to annotate the incongruity label for all the pairs manually. Therefore, inspired by a previous study (Yoon et al., 2019), we utilized an alternative method that generates a pair of I and H with the incongruity label

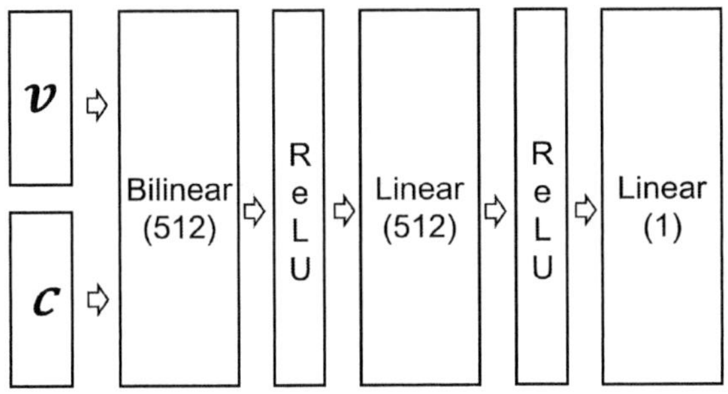

Figure 6: CLIP-classifier's model architecture. The value within parenthesis indicates the output dimension size.

L automatically. The data generation method is language-agnostic, such that it can be easily extended to any other language as long as one can construct a pool of trustworthy news articles.

Figure 5 demonstrates the data generation process. At first, among the news articles generated by trustworthy news sources in the COVID-wofaces dataset, we selected the top 75% of the image-text pairs in terms of CLIPScore to be congruent samples. As a result, we obtained 8223 target samples. We manually inspected the bottom-100 samples and confirmed that the image represents the news content well. To be used for generating train/validation/test datasets in the next step, we divided the 8223 pairs into three pools: 6575, 824, and 824, respectively.

The next step is to generate news articles with the incongruity between news title and thumbnail. As shown in Figure 5(a), for each pair in the congruent dataset, we randomly sampled two different pairs, one from the same media and another from one of the other outlets. We called the two pairs *sampled*. Then, as in Figure 5(b), we automatically generated samples with the incongruity by linking the image of the target article (I_1) to the title of the sampled articles (T_2, T_3). That is, the class ratio is 2:1 in the dataset. We applied the generation process to each pool separately, and therefore there are no overlapped articles between one dataset to another.

In total, we obtained 8223 congruent and 16446 incongruent pairs, and there are 19725, 2472, and 2472 samples for train/validation/test, respectively.

4.3 Experimental Results

We used a machine equipped with the AMD Ryzen Threadripper Pro 3975WX CPU and two Nvidia RTX A6000 GPUs for the experiments. We evaluated three different methods for detecting image-text incongruity among fake news articles.

Model	Validation		Test	
	ACC.	AUROC	ACC.	AUROC
ViLT (zero-shot)	0.646	0.667	0.601	0.624
CLIPScore (zero-shot)	0.942	0.985	0.934	0.984
CLIP-classifier	0.920	0.977	0.927	0.975

Table 2: Evaluation on the generated set.

- ViLT (zero-shot): As a baseline model, we employed a recent vision-and-language pretrained model, ViLT (Kim et al., 2021), which was fine-tuned on the MS COCO dataset. Using the cosine similarity between image and text vectors, we implemented a simple threshold-based classifier; If a similarity value is above the threshold, the model predicts the text well represents the image. Otherwise, a pair is considered unmatched. We obtained the decision threshold by a class-wise unweighted average for the similarity scores measured on all samples in the validation set. The obtained threshold was also used for test set inference.

- CLIPScore (zero-shot): Using the pretrained CLIP model, we computed the CLIPScore for each news title and thumbnail pair for implementing a threshold-based classifier. The decision threshold was obtained following the same procedure used for ViLT (zero-shot).

- CLIP-classifier: Figure 6 shows the neural architecture of the proposed model. CLIP-classifier takes as input $\boldsymbol{c}$ (text embedding) and $\boldsymbol{v}$ (visual embedding) from CLIP's text and visual encoder, respectively, and classifies the pair as 'congruent' (well-matched) or 'incongruent' (not-well-matched). The model was trained to minimize the binary cross-entropy loss by the AdamW optimizer (at a learning rate of 0.001) with a batch size of 128. We did not update the CLIP backbone during training. We used gradient clipping with a threshold of 1.0 and early stopping.

Table 2 presents the evaluation results of the three models. The two CLIP-based models outperformed ViLT (zero-shot) with a large margin. These observations suggest that the CLIP pretrained model is more generalizable than the ViLT model, and hence it is more suitable for the detec-

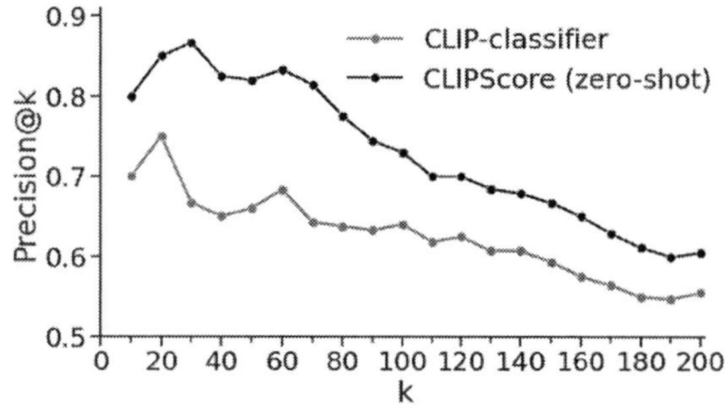

Figure 7: Manual evaluation results on the top-k fake news articles by CLIPScore and CLIP-classifier's predictions score

tion of fake news articles that use an unrepresentative thumbnail.

To test the ability of CLIP in real-world detection, we conducted additional experiments with human annotations. We supposed a situation where it is required to detect fake news articles using the incongruous thumbnail. Hence, we inferred prediction scores for the fake news samples in the COVID-wo-faces dataset by CLIPScore and CLIP-classifier, respectively. Then, we manually inspected the top-200 examples of each model in terms of the prediction score to test whether the models correctly predict the samples of an unrepresentative thumbnail. We considered the incongruous label as the positive label; Hence, a higher prediction score indicates a model predicts a given pair having the incongruity between news title and thumbnail picture with higher confidence. For consistency, we used $(1 - similarity)$ for the prediction score of CLIPScore.

Figure 7 shows the top-k precision of each model's prediction on the fake news articles. The x-axis represents the number of evaluated articles after being sorted by a model's prediction score. The y-axis shows the precision of the top-k articles evaluated by humans. Two authors participated in the manual annotation process and obtained a complete inter-annotator agreement after several iterations. They examined a total of 259 news-thumbnail pairs on whether the image represents the news content. We release the paired dataset with manual annotation for broader usage on the github repository.

Results show that CLIPScore outperformed CLIP-classifier, especially for the highly-ranked examples. The model achieved a precision of 0.8 for k=10, 0.85 for k=20, and 0.87 for k=30; its performance gap against CLIP-classifier is around 0.1. The gap decreased as more examples were evaluated; the precision difference is 0.05 for k=200. The observation highlights the representation power of the CLIP backbone and implies that the two CLIP-based methods could be incorporated for more effective detection in practice.

5 Limitation and Future Direction

This study bears several limitations. First, the findings were observed from the dataset of nine news media. Even though they are well-balanced against political bias and trustworthiness, the findings could not represent general patterns and thus should be carefully interpreted. Future studies could examine the hypothesis using more extensive data. Second, since this study employs CLIP as a backbone, our results are subject to unknown biases which CLIP might learn from training. Future studies could adopt pretraining tasks to mitigate the issues. Third, we focused on news titles as a proxy of news content. The method could be invalid for some cases where the news title is incongruent with the main text (Yoon et al., 2019). Future studies could develop a method that exploits body text as a reference, which contains more fruitful information yet is more challenging to be analyzed.

6 Conclusion

This paper examined the usage of news thumbnails and asked whether fake news sources exhibit distinct patterns. By applying CLIP to the pair of news title and image, we identified the difference between fake news and trustworthy media sources in the image-text similarity: Fake news tends to use a less similar thumbnail picture to the news text than general news. Next, we tackled the article-level detection problem that targets fake news articles in which the thumbnail picture does not represent the news content. To the end, we generated a paired dataset of 24,669 image-text pairs, each image of which is semantically (in-)congruent to the text. Evaluation experiments showed that CLIP-based models could detect news articles with an unrepresentative thumbnail with high accuracy. These observations highlight the potential of CLIP for identifying these misinformed articles in the real world. To the best of our knowledge, this is one of the initial attempts to understand fake news characteristics in the use of thumbnail and focus on its semantic representativeness to news content. We hope our methodology and dataset can not only make an impact on the ongoing efforts to curtail fake news dissemination, but also contribute to broader research communities on vision and language.

Acknowledgements

H. Choi and Y. Yoon equally contributed to this work. This work was supported by the Basic Science Research Program through the National Research Foundation of Korea (NRF) funded by the Ministry of Science and ICT (No. NRF-2021R1F1A1062691).

References

Ramy Baly, Georgi Karadzhov, Dimitar Alexandrov, James Glass, and Preslav Nakov. 2018. Predicting factuality of reporting and bias of news media sources. In *Proceedings of the 2018 Conference on Empirical Methods in Natural Language Processing*, pages 3528–3539, Brussels, Belgium. Association for Computational Linguistics.

Yen-Chun Chen, Linjie Li, Licheng Yu, Ahmed El Kholy, Faisal Ahmed, Zhe Gan, Yu Cheng, and Jingjing Liu. 2020. Uniter: Universal image-text representation learning. In *ECCV*.

Yimin Chen, Niall J. Conroy, and Victoria L. Rubin. 2015. Misleading online content: Recognizing clickbait as "false news". In *Proceedings of the 2015 ACM on Workshop on Multimodal Deception Detection*, WMDD '15, page 15–19, New York, NY, USA. Association for Computing Machinery.

Alexey Dosovitskiy, Lucas Beyer, Alexander Kolesnikov, Dirk Weissenborn, Xiaohua Zhai, Thomas Unterthiner, Mostafa Dehghani, Matthias Minderer, Georg Heigold, Sylvain Gelly, Jakob Uszkoreit, and Neil Houlsby. 2020. An image is worth 16x16 words: Transformers for image recognition at scale. *CoRR*, abs/2010.11929.

Maksym Gabielkov, Arthi Ramachandran, Augustin Chaintreau, and Arnaud Legout. 2016. Social clicks: What and who gets read on twitter? In *Proceedings of the 2016 ACM SIGMETRICS International Conference on Measurement and Modeling of Computer Science*, SIGMETRICS '16, page 179–192, New York, NY, USA. Association for Computing Machinery.

Anastasia Giachanou, Guobiao Zhang, and Paolo Rosso. 2020. Multimodal multi-image fake news detection. In *2020 IEEE 7th International Conference on Data Science and Advanced Analytics (DSAA)*, pages 647–654.

Nir Grinberg, Kenneth Joseph, Lisa Friedland, Briony Swire-Thompson, and David Lazer. 2019. Fake news on twitter during the 2016 u.s. presidential election. *Science*, 363(6425):374–378.

Jack Hessel, Ari Holtzman, Maxwell Forbes, Ronan Le Bras, and Yejin Choi. 2021. CLIPScore: A reference-free evaluation metric for image captioning. In *Proceedings of the 2021 Conference on Empirical Methods in Natural Language Processing*, pages 7514–7528.

Benjamin Horne and Sibel Adali. 2017. This just in: Fake news packs a lot in title, uses simpler, repetitive content in text body, more similar to satire than real news. In *Proceedings of the International AAAI Conference on Web and Social Media*, volume 11.

Chao Jia, Yinfei Yang, Ye Xia, Yi-Ting Chen, Zarana Parekh, Hieu Pham, Quoc Le, Yun-Hsuan Sung, Zhen Li, and Tom Duerig. 2021. Scaling up visual and vision-language representation learning with noisy text supervision. In *International Conference on Machine Learning*, pages 4904–4916. PMLR.

Dhruv Khattar, Jaipal Singh Goud, Manish Gupta, and Vasudeva Varma. 2019. Mvae: Multimodal variational autoencoder for fake news detection. In *The World Wide Web Conference*, WWW '19, page 2915–2921, New York, NY, USA. Association for Computing Machinery.

Wonjae Kim, Bokyung Son, and Ildoo Kim. 2021. Vilt: Vision-and-language transformer without convolution or region supervision. In *International Conference on Machine Learning*, pages 5583–5594. PMLR.

David M. J. Lazer, Matthew A. Baum, Yochai Benkler, Adam J. Berinsky, Kelly M. Greenhill, Filippo Menczer, Miriam J. Metzger, Brendan Nyhan, Gordon Pennycook, David Rothschild, Michael Schudson, Steven A. Sloman, Cass R. Sunstein, Emily A. Thorson, Duncan J. Watts, and Jonathan L. Zittrain. 2018. The science of fake news. *Science*, 359(6380):1094–1096.

Hwanhee Lee, Seunghyun Yoon, Franck Dernoncourt, Trung Bui, and Kyomin Jung. 2021. UMIC: An unreferenced metric for image captioning via contrastive learning. In *Proceedings of the 59th Annual Meeting of the Association for Computational Linguistics and the 11th International Joint Conference on Natural Language Processing (Volume 2: Short Papers)*, pages 220–226.

Hwanhee Lee, Seunghyun Yoon, Franck Dernoncourt, Doo Soon Kim, Trung Bui, and Kyomin Jung. 2020. Vilbertscore: Evaluating image caption using vision-and-language bert. In *Proceedings of the First Workshop on Evaluation and Comparison of NLP Systems*, pages 34–39.

Jiasen Lu, Dhruv Batra, Devi Parikh, and Stefan Lee. 2019. Vilbert: Pretraining task-agnostic visiolinguistic representations for vision-and-language tasks. *Advances in neural information processing systems*, 32.

Jing Ma, Wei Gao, Prasenjit Mitra, Sejeong Kwon, Bernard J. Jansen, Kam-Fai Wong, and Meeyoung Cha. 2016. Detecting rumors from microblogs with recurrent neural networks. In *Proceedings of the Twenty-Fifth International Joint Conference on Artificial Intelligence*, IJCAI'16, page 3818–3824. AAAI Press.

Van-Hoang Nguyen, Kazunari Sugiyama, Preslav Nakov, and Min-Yen Kan. 2020. Fang: Leveraging social context for fake news detection using graph representation. In *Proceedings of the 29th ACM international conference on information & knowledge management*, pages 1165–1174.

Kunwoo Park, Haewoon Kwak, Jisun An, and Sanjay Chawla. 2021. How-to present news on social media: A causal analysis of editing news headlines for boosting user engagement. In *Proceedings of the International AAAI Conference on Web and Social Media*, volume 15, pages 491–502.

Peng Qi, Juan Cao, Tianyun Yang, Junbo Guo, and Jintao Li. 2019. Exploiting multi-domain visual information for fake news detection. In *2019 IEEE International Conference on Data Mining (ICDM)*, pages 518–527.

Alec Radford, Jong Wook Kim, Chris Hallacy, Aditya Ramesh, Gabriel Goh, Sandhini Agarwal, Girish Sastry, Amanda Askell, Pamela Mishkin, Jack Clark, et al. 2021. Learning transferable visual models from natural language supervision. *arXiv preprint arXiv:2103.00020.*

Natali Ruchansky, Sungyong Seo, and Yan Liu. 2017. Csi: A hybrid deep model for fake news detection. In *Proceedings of the 2017 ACM on Conference on Information and Knowledge Management*, CIKM '17, page 797–806, New York, NY, USA. Association for Computing Machinery.

Kiwon Seo. 2020. Meta-analysis on visual persuasion–does adding images to texts influence persuasion. *Athens Journal of Mass Media and Communications*, 6(3):177–190.

Kai Shu, Amy Sliva, Suhang Wang, Jiliang Tang, and Huan Liu. 2017. Fake news detection on social media: A data mining perspective. *SIGKDD Explor. Newsl.*, 19(1):22–36.

Shivangi Singhal, Rajiv Ratn Shah, Tanmoy Chakraborty, Ponnurangam Kumaraguru, and Shin'ichi Satoh. 2019. Spotfake: A multi-modal framework for fake news detection. In *2019 IEEE Fifth International Conference on Multimedia Big Data (BigMM)*, pages 39–47.

Edward J Smith and Gilbert L Fowler Jr. 1982. How comprehensible are newspaper headlines?

Soroush Vosoughi, Deb Roy, and Sinan Aral. 2018. The spread of true and false news online. *Science*, 359(6380):1146–1151.

Seunghyun Yoon, Kunwoo Park, Joongbo Shin, Hongjun Lim, Seungpil Won, Meeyoung Cha, and Kyomin Jung. 2019. Detecting incongruity between news headline and body text via a deep hierarchical encoder. In *Proceedings of the AAAI conference on artificial intelligence*, volume 33, pages 791–800.

John Zarocostas. 2020. How to fight an infodemic. *The lancet*, 395(10225):676.

A Appendix

Figure A1: An example of news article that CLIP has difficulty at matching a person's name and face (CLIP-Score: 0.04694, URL: https://tinyurl.com/y4y89b3x).

	CLIPScore	Source	URL
Whole	High	Foxnews	https://tinyurl.com/ydrc32kl
	Low	New York Post	https://tinyurl.com/y7794djr
COVID	High	The Guardian	https://tinyurl.com/y8r7o2b7
	Low	World Net Daily	https://tinyurl.com/yalznxnn
COVID-wo-faces	High	Reuters	https://tinyurl.com/ydozsybd
	Low	Activist Post	https://tinyurl.com/ycjkbell

Table A1: URLs for news articles in Figure 3

Detecting False Claims in Low-Resource Regions: A Case Study of Caribbean Islands

Jason S. Lucas **Limeng Cui** **Thai Le** **Dongwon Lee**

The Pennsylvania State University, PA, USA
{jsl5710,lzc334,thaile,dongwon}@psu.edu

Abstract

The COVID-19 pandemic has created severe threats to global health control. In particular, misinformation circulated on social media and news outlets has undermined public trust in government and health agencies. This problem is further exacerbated in developing countries or low-resource regions where the news may not be equipped with abundant English fact-checking information. This poses a question: *"are existing computational solutions toward misinformation also effective in low-resource regions?"* In this paper, to answer this question, we make the first attempt to detect COVID-19 misinformation in English, Spanish, and Haitian French populated in the Caribbean region, using the fact-checked claims in US-English. We started by collecting a dataset of real & false claims in the Caribbean region. Then we trained several classification and language models on COVID-19 from high-resource language regions and transferred this knowledge to the Caribbean claim dataset. The experimental results show the limitations of current false claim detection in low-resource regions and encourage further research toward the detection of multi-lingual false claims in long tail.

1 Introduction

In this work, we refer to *false claim* as assertions that are not supported by facts and are made with the objective of misleading or deceiving the public (Molina et al., 2021). Social media platforms enable people to independently publish and share media content without scrutiny filters for credibility and integrity[1]. Therefore, inaccurate, false, malicious, and propagandistic content have become abundant in social media. Furthermore, when false claims travel across regions and often get translated/modified, it becomes increasingly difficult for machine learning (ML) models to detect such false claims. Online surveillance (i.e., false claim detectors) systems are often primarily pre-trained on high-resource languages (e.g., English, Chinese). Despite significant progress in ML models, however, building and maintaining ML models in low-resource languages (e.g., Tagalog, Haitian Creole) are still challenging due to its scarce data or language lexicon and translation barriers which are indigenous to low-resource language settings.

This poses a natural question: "**how effective are computational ML solutions developed in high-resource regions to detect false claims circulating in low-resource regions?**" In this paper, to answer this question, we propose the first thorough case study on the detection of false claims in the Caribbean Islands.

Fact-checking initiatives are scarce and inept in low-resource settings, especially for the Caribbean Islands due to the cultural and linguistically diverse nature of their languages. The Caribbean region is a developing, heterogeneous, interconnected archipelago that is vulnerable to false claims campaigns. It consists of 35 states and territories bordering the Gulf of Mexico and Caribbean Sea[2]. The Caribbean has six official languages: Spanish, English, French, and Dutch, as well as two indigenous Creoles (Haitian Creole and Papiamento)[3]. Our data curation initiative shows that this region lacks essential technological resources and infrastructure to combat false claim propagation. Few fact-checking organizations exist, and they have limited data covering the Caribbean. Major news outlets such as Loop News make significant efforts to debunk false claims. These initiatives are essential but inadequate to effectively respond to prevailing false claims during crises.

In particular, we studied two research questions:

[1] https://www.who.int/news-room/feature-stories/detail/immunizing-the-public-against-misinformation

[2] https://studyincaribbean.com/about-caribbean.html

[3] https://www.caribbeanandco.com/caribbean-languages/

Proceedings of the Workshop on Combating Online Hostile Posts in Regional Languages during Emergency Situations, pages 95 - 102
May 27, 2022 ©2022 Association for Computational Linguistics

RQ1: How do ML models trained in high-resource languages perform with current Caribbean false claims?

RQ2: Are more sophisticated ML techniques (e.g., Transfer Learning), useful to detect false claims in the Caribbean?

Note that the focus of our investigation is on the COVID-19 related false claims in the Caribbean islands. ML models trained in high-resource languages are not easily transferable to low-resource languages. One of the main challenges comes from data scarcity (i.e., lack of labeled training data in low-resource languages). This issue is further exacerbated by the application of false claims detection that suffers from imbalance (i.e., where the number of labeled false claims is significantly smaller than that of labeled true claims). Therefore, to thoroughly study false claims in the Caribbean Islands, more sophisticated ML techniques that address indigenous nuances need to be tested.

2 Related Work

Since the onset of the COVID-19 pandemic, misinformation in different languages has been circulating on social media. The COVID-19 misinformation datasets can be roughly divided into two categories: monolingual and multilingual. CoAID (Cui and Lee, 2020), ReCOVery (Zhou et al., 2020), CMU-MisCOV19 (Memon and Carley, 2020), CHECKED (Yang et al., 2021) and COSTRAINT task dataset (Patwa et al., 2020) are monolingual datasets in high-resource languages (English or Chinese). CoAID is a diverse COVID-19 misinformation dataset, including 5,216 news about COVID-19, and ground truth labels. Multilingual datasets contain news pieces in multiple languages. MM-COVID (Li et al., 2020) contains false & real news content in 6 different languages. FakeCovid (Shahi and Nandini, 2020) has 5,182 COVID-19 fact-checking news pieces in 40 languages.

With the urge to combat the infodemic in developing countries or immigrant communities speaking low-resource languages, researchers have been studying how to transfer the pre-trained models on high-resource domains to low resource domains. Du et al. (2021) proposed a cross-lingual false claims detector called "CrossFake", which is trained based on a high-resource language (English) COVID-19 news corpus and used to predict news credibility in a low-resource language (Chinese). Bang et al. (2021) proposed two model generalization methods on COVID-19 fake news for more robust fake news detection in different COVID-19 misinformation datasets. In this paper, we chose the false claim detection in the Caribbean region as a showcase. It is a challenging problem due to the multiculturalism and multilingualism of Caribbean people. We studied how to leverage the pre-trained models from high-resource regions (CoAID) to detect misinformation in a low-resource region (Caribbean false claim data).

3 Main Proposal: Datasets and Research Questions

3.1 Caribbean Claims Dataset

This investigation utilized CoAID, a high-resources language COVID-19 false claims dataset written in English and curated from the United States (Cui and Lee, 2020). CoAID corpus comprises of 260,037 claims and news articles (Cui and Lee, 2020). This study assessed CoAID's pre-trained baseline models ability to accurately detect false claims in Caribbean dataset, given indigenous data challenges such as scarcity and language barrier.

Fact-checking institutions are trustworthy sources for determining the veracity of claims (Shu et al., 2019). They use rigorous methods to investigate the veracity and correctness of assertions, including references and URLs where false claims originate (Shu et al., 2019). Unfortunately, the Caribbean territory lacks these critical technological resources, notably fact-checking institutions with adequate regional data to combat the spread and growth of false claims. Instead, majority of fact-checking is primarily performed by respected Caribbean news outlets such as *Loop News* that do not consistently adhere to stringent fact-checking procedures. As a result, Caribbean fact-checked false claims are primarily assertions rarely linked to original content or the origin of such claims. This is the reason why we study Caribbean false claims detection in this work (Molina et al., 2021).

We manually crawled the accessible fact-checking and news organization websites given the aforementioned status quo. Then, we extract only original assertions, or alternatively extract the annotated claims when the original assertions were inaccessible. See Table 1 for all web sources that are crawled. We further inspect the Caribbean web

Table 1: Web sources and news claim articles curated from each source

Institution	Source Name	# Articles
News Outlet	Loop	188
News Outlet	Diario Libre	35
News Outlet	Aljazeera	25
News Outlet	St. Lucas Times	7
News Outlet	GBN	3
News Outlet	St. Vincent Times	3
News Outlet	Barbados Today	2
News Outlet	Mikey LiVE	1
Fact-checker	Poynter	9

Table 2: The language composition of the curated Caribbean dataset.

Language	Qty.	%
English	171	63%
Spanish	66	24%
French	36	7%

sources and solicited data from 9 institutions' websites detailed in Table 1. The final dataset totaled 273 articles published mostly between 2019 and 2022. All data collected are COVID-19 claims except for two Dominican Republic vaccine-related health claims published in 2010. The corpus consists of 121 annotated news and 152 original news claims. The dataset covers 3 of 6 official languages spoken in the Caribbean: English, Spanish and French (Table 2). The labels are comprised of 54% real claims and 46% false claims (Table 4). See Table 4 for the character length distribution of the two labels. The contents of our Caribbean dataset contains language cues that help ML model distinguish between false and real claims (Cui et al., 2020).

3.2 RQ1: Baseline Model Performance on Caribbean False Claims

To establish a baseline, we used pre-trained models trained on a large amount of English moderated COVID-19 data. Since CoAID contains a large amount of English news claims in the United States (Cui and Lee, 2020), the baseline models were trained on CoAID. We sectionized **RQ1** experiment into three sub tasks to ascertain empirical explainability. Each task uses different test sets to answer **RQ1**.

Task I Get the baseline performance using the CoAID dataset . Test set is CoAID dataset.

Task II Assess CoAID models' ability to predict Caribbean English false claims. Test set is Caribbean English claims.

Task III Assess the baseline model with another English Caribbean claims translated from Spanish and French. Test set is a translated to English Caribbean claims dataset .

3.3 RQ2: Applying Transfer Learning

This experiment adopted a self-supervised BERT-based transformer model, pre-trained on a large corpus of monolingual data. We encode the news using BERT. We adopt the binary cross-entropy loss function in the training. We fine-tuned the BERT model using the CoAID dataset and used it to conduct **RQ2** experiments.

Our hypothesis is that the answer to **RQ1** will not be sufficient to solve the task of detecting false claims accurately in Caribbean languages. Therefore, we propose a more sophisticated method to improve model's performance. Specifically, we studied the performance of transfer learning using a pre-trained BERT model. We break **RQ2** experiment in two tasks to answer this question and maintain empirical consistency with **RQ1** experiments.

Task IV Assess fine-tuned BERT model's ability to predict Caribbean English false claims. Test set is Caribbean English claims.

Task V Assess the fine-tuned BERT model with another English Caribbean claims translated from Spanish and French. Test set is a translated to English Caribbean claims dataset .

Table 3: Caribbean dataset composition of false and real news by **RQs** tasks respectively

RQS Tasks	Claims	False	Real	Total
RQ1: T2 & RQ2: T4	Original-En	95	76	171
RQ1: T3 & RQ2: T5	Translated-En	52	50	102

4 Empirical Evaluation

4.1 Set-Up

This research has three main test sets.

Table 4: Dataset statistics

Corpus	Size	Min_{char}	$\text{Mean}_{\text{char}}$	Max_{char}
Real claims	126	67	1187	3141
false claims	147	26	183	969

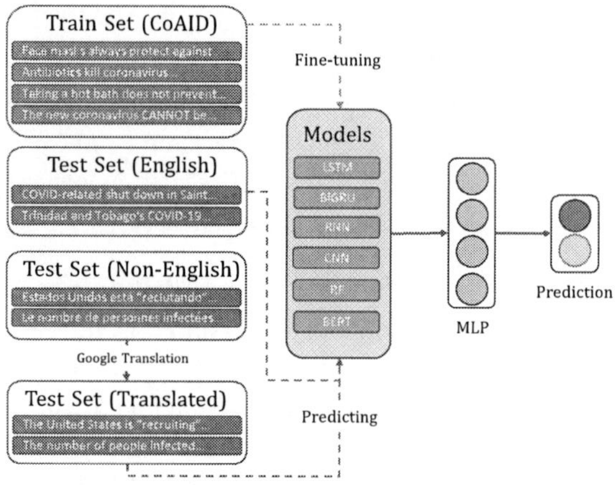

Figure 1: The framework overview of the false claim detector. For **RQ1**, we train the models on CoAID dataset and test on English Caribbean dataset and Translated English Caribbean dataset. For **RQ2**, we fine-tune the BERT model with CoAID dataset, and English Caribbean dataset and Translated English Caribbean dataset.

1. CoAID Test Set: this is only used for **RQ1**.
2. Original Caribbean English Set: this is used for **RQ1**: Task II and **RQ2**: Task IV (Table 3).
3. Translated-English Caribbean Set: this is used for **RQ2**: Task III and **RQ2**: Task V (Table 3).

Given the unique challenges with Caribbean false claims data, this research selected five baseline models:

- Long short-term memory (LSTM)
- Bidirectional Gated Recurrent Unit (BiGRU) (Bahdanau et al., 2015)
- Recurrent Neural Network (RNN)
- Convolutional Neural Network (CNN)
- Random Forest (RF)

The framework overview is shown in Figure 1. For the first task in **RQ1**, we first encode the news using GloVe (Pennington et al., 2014), a language pre-training model, and fit the embeddings into the models. The Glove wordembedding is used for all the baseline models except for Random Forest, which encodes the text with TF-IDF.

The baseline models were evaluated using F1, Kappa and Precision-Recall Area Under the Curve (PR AUC) scores from the models' output:

1. **Area Under the Precision-Recall Curve** (PR-AUC):

$$\text{PR-AUC} = \sum_{k=1}^{n} \text{Prec}(k)\Delta\text{Rec}(k),$$

where k is the k-th precision and recall operating point $(\text{Prec}(k), \text{Rec}(k))$.

2. **F1 Score**: $\text{F1 Score} = 2 \cdot (\text{Prec} \cdot \text{Rec})/(\text{Prec} + \text{Rec})$, where Prec is precision and Rec is recall.

3. **Cohen's Kappa**: $\kappa = (p_o - p_e)/(1 - p_e)$, where p_o is the observed agreement (identical to accuracy), and p_e is the expected agreement, which is probabilities of randomly seeing each category.

One of our primary interests is the precision-recall of the positive class, which is the positive false claim classification in our assessment of the models' performance.

We implement all models with Keras. The train and test sets use the 75:25 ratio, respectively. For all models, we use RMSProp (Hinton et al., 2012) with a mini-batch of 50 and the training epoch is 30. In order to have a fair comparison, we set the hidden dimension as 100 for all models. For the pre-trained BERT model, we use a BERT base model[4] (uncased) pre-trained on a large corpus of English data. All methods are trained on an Ubuntu 20.04 and Nvidia Tesla K80 GPU.

4.2 Results

First, to establish the research baseline performance, we pre-trained machine learning models on CoAID claims in English and tested them on English Caribbean false claims. Table 5 details the performance of the baseline models. LSTM model demonstrated high accuracy with F1 and Kappa evaluation matrices; however, CNN has the highest PR AUC predictive accuracy.

Next, Task II was performed using a total of 171 claims consisting of 95 false and 76 real Caribbean news claims detailed in table 3. Task I results are shown in table 6. Compared to Task I baseline output, Task II shows a general decline with all models' performance. Task II evaluation matrix scores are within a lower range compared to Task I. Task I output shows F1: 0.34 - 0.60, Kappa: 0.33 - 0.57 and PR AUC: 0.61 - 0.76. Task II matrix

[4] https://huggingface.co/bert-base-uncased

scores show: F1: 0. 33 - 0.54, Kappa: -0.64 - 0.02 and PR AUC: 0.51 - 0.56. LSTM outperformed all models with F1 while RNN having the highest Kappa and PR AUC scores.

The Task III assesses CoAID models' ability to classify Caribbean false claims translated from Spanish/French to English using Google Translate API. As shown in table 3, a total of 102 claims were used; 52 were false and 50 were real Caribbean news. Task III results, as shown in table 7, show an overall decrease in all models' predictive power in comparison to the baseline output in Task I. Task III evaluation matrix scores are within a lower ranges compared to Task I. Task I output shows F1: 0.34 - 0.60, Kappa: 0.33 - 0.57 and PR AUC: 0.61 - 0.76. Task III matrix scores shows: F1: 0. 30 - 0.53, Kappa: -0.52 - 0.02 and PR AUC: 0.50 - 0.55. BiGRU outperformed all models with F1 scores whereas RNN has the highest Kappa and PR AUC scores. Overall, all models showed a drop in performance when classifying translated Caribbean news claims in English.

Task IV encompasses running English Caribbean news claims through the refined BERT model and assessing its performance. The result from this experiment shows that transfer-learning with BERT out-performed Task II for **RQ1** models which used the same dataset detailed in table 3. The BERT model's F1 score is 0.55, whereas Task II for **RQ1** top F1 score is 0.54. Also, BERT's PR AUC score is 0.59, whereas Task II for **RQ1** top PR AUC is 0.56. However, BERT Kappa score of -0.16 was less than Task II for **RQ1** score, 0.02. Transfer learning technique using BERT achieved better predictive performance.

Finally, in the Task V, we assessed the pre-trained, fine-tuned BERT model's ability to accurately predict Caribbean false claims translated from French/Spanish to English. The results from this experiment indicate that BERT transfer-learning out-performs Task III for **RQ1** models which basically used the same dataset detailed in table 3. The BERT model's F1 score is 0.55, whereas Task III for **RQ1** top F1 score is 0.52. Also, BERT's PR AUC score is 0.57, whereas Task III for **RQ1** top PR AUC is 0.55. However, BERT Kappa score of -0.17 was less than Task III for **RQ1** score, 0.02.

Table 5: Comparison on Task I for **RQ1**. The false claims classification performance with standard deviation across five runs. The final prediction denotes the average of each evaluation matrix's score from all runs. The results in this table show that LSTM has the best F1 & Kappa scores, while CNN has the highest PR AUC score.

Model	F1	Kappa	PR AUC
LSTM	$\mathbf{0.5991}_{0.060}$	$\mathbf{0.5721}_{0.062}$	$0.6923_{0.032}$
BiGRU	$0.5708_{0.062}$	$0.5457_{0.062}$	$0.6792_{0.026}$
RNN	$0.4147_{0.188}$	$0.3950_{0.186}$	$0.6651_{0.074}$
CNN	$0.5326_{0.181}$	$0.510_{0.178}$	$\mathbf{0.7565}_{0.097}$
RF	$0.3439_{0.121}$	$0.3261_{0.118}$	$0.6152_{0.085}$

Table 6: Comparison on **RQ1** Task II. The false claims classification performance with standard deviation across five runs. The final prediction denotes the average of each evaluation matrix's score from all runs. This experiment shows an overall performance declined observed compared to Task I baseline models output in table 5.

Model	F1	Kappa	PR AUC
LSTM	$\mathbf{0.5405}_{0.059}$	$-0.0704_{0.099}$	$0.5361_{0.042}$
BiGRU	$0.5020_{0.056}$	$-0.3164_{0.139}$	$0.4632_{0.049}$
RNN	$0.2013_{0.120}$	$\mathbf{0.0213}_{0.027}$	$\mathbf{0.5603}_{0.040}$
CNN	$0.3574_{0.134}$	$-0.1864_{0.200}$	$0.5151_{0.045}$
RF	$0.3316_{0.012}$	$-0.6427_{0.015}$	$0.5121_{0.008}$

5 Discussion

5.1 RQ1 Experiments

RQ1: **Task I**. We established our baseline performance. It is clear from Task I results that CoAID baseline models are resilient with classifying claims despite imbalance dataset with majority real claims. The CNN PR AUC score was approximately 76% accurate in predicting the minority false claims regardless of imbalanced binary classification in the dataset. This suggest that CoAID high-resource language models perform fairly well at predicting news claims curated from the US high-resource language settings.

RQ1: **Task II**. assessed CoAID models' ability to accurately detect Caribbean news claims originally written in English. When classifying Caribbean news claims in English, we observed an overall performance decline in all models. Thus, this outcome suggests that pre-trained high-resource detection models perform poorly on low-resource language context data written in En-

Table 7: Comparison on Task III for **RQ1**. The false claims classification performance with standard deviation across five runs. The final prediction denotes the average of each evaluation matrix's score from all runs. This experiment shows an overall performance declined observed compared to Task I baseline models output in table 6.

Model	F1	Kappa	PR AUC
LSTM	0.4649$_{0.168}$	-0.0735$_{0.100}$	0.4990$_{0.089}$
BiGRU	**0.5268**$_{0.049}$	-0.1809$_{0.166}$	0.4954$_{0.018}$
RNN	0.2963$_{0.175}$	**0.0226**$_{0.114}$	**0.5543**$_{0.037}$
CNN	0.4884$_{0.097}$	-0.0830$_{0.175}$	0.5164$_{0.091}$
RF	0.3923$_{0.009}$	-0.5196$_{0.008}$	0.5384$_{0.007}$

Table 8: Comparison on Task IV & V for **RQ2**. The false claims classification performance with standard deviation across five runs. The final prediction denotes the average of each evaluation matrix's score from all runs. A performance increase was observed in these experiments compared to Task II & III models output in table 6 and table 7 respectfully.

Task	F1	Kappa	PR AUC
Bert $_{IV}$	0.5476$_{0.018}$	-0.1578$_{0.306}$	0.5852$_{0.113}$
Bert $_{V}$	0.5485$_{0.047}$	-0.1656$_{0.039}$	0.5695$_{0.117}$

glish.

RQ1: **Task III**. assessed CoAID models' ability to accurately detect Caribbean news claims translated to English. When claims translated to English, pre-trained high-resource detection models under-perform on low-resource language context data. These results suggest a language translation loss. We propose the term language translation loss to encapsulate the phenomena that occur when a model's predictive power decreases due to translation nuances. Examples are politically loaded COVID-19 false claims propaganda and slang hidden in datasets that weaken signals impacting ML models' predictive power.

RQ1 Summary. **RQ1** results show a steady decline in all models' performance when introduced to Caribbean news claims that are originally written or translated to English (see Fig 3 & 2). These findings are clear indicators that high-resource language ML models are substandard with detecting low-resource language false claims such as the Caribbean region news claims data. These findings validated the research hypothesis: high-resource language models are not appropriate for detecting COVID-19 false claims in diverse, low-resources language settings.

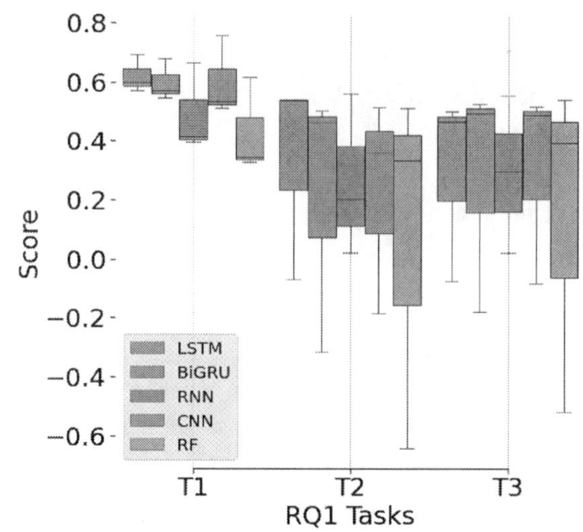

Figure 2: Overview of **RQ1** ML models' performance from Tasks I to III. The box plot shows that decline in ML models' performance on Caribbean data

5.2 RQ2 Experiments

The above results prompted the need for more robust, novel, and clever techniques to best address the nuances and false claims phenomena specific to the Caribbean. Thus, we experiment with transfer learning methodology to garner insight on Caribbean false claims detection challenges.

RQ2: **Task IV & V** assessed transfer learning technique on Caribbean false claims detection. Task IV results indicate that the transfer learning technique using BERT achieved better predictive performance than English pre-trained high-resource language models. Similarly, Task V data demonstrate that the transfer learning technique achieves better model performance. Given indigenous Caribbean data challenges, these findings indicate that advance ML techniques have better learning mechanisms to address low-resource language setting detection (see Fig 4 & 5).

RQ2 Summary: results give clear indication that sophisticated, refined ML approaches achieve better performance. Transfer learning is shown to optimize performance with addressing Caribbean data scarcity issues. The linguistic similarity between CoAID and Caribbean false claims leveraged the model's performance through transfer learning.

6 Research Implication

News outlet websites, Factcheckcaribbean.com and Poynter.com are most reputable organizations to

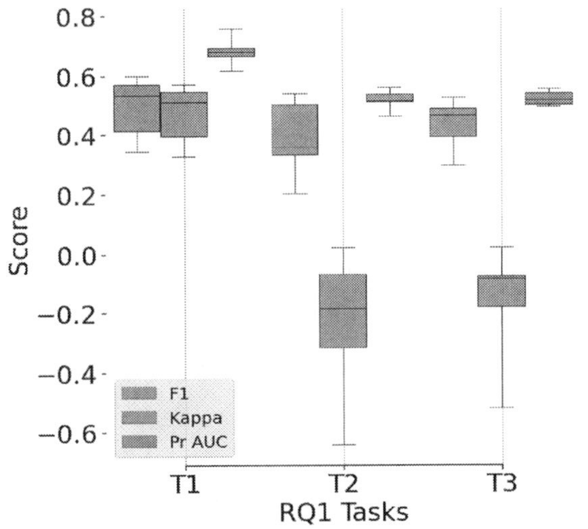

Figure 3: Overview of **RQ1** Models Evaluation Matrices from Tasks I to III. This box plot is shows a decline in performance using F1, Kappa and PR AUC.

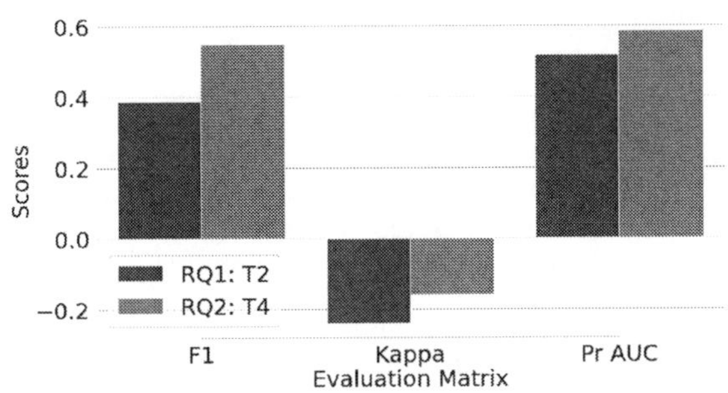

Figure 4: Overview of **RQ1** ML models' performance matrices scores compared to **RQ2** scores. This bar chat compares the performance of CoAID **RQ1**: Task II models performance with **RQ2**: Task IV fine-tuned Bert transformer model. This graph shows that transfer learning achieves better performance.

curate Caribbean false claims data. These institutions have limited data covering only a few islands. Loop news has the largest coverage and quantity of Fact-checked news claims compared to other sources. Although news outlets have more data, fact-checking institutions have better quality data. News outlet organizations do their best to verify and debunk false claims. In the Caribbean region there is need for more rigorous processes for false claims fact checking (Seo et al., 2022). This initiatives can be establish by non-government organization (NGOs) such as the Pan American Health Organization (PAHO) and Caribbean Public Health Agency.

This research did not address data imbalances in Caribbean data, which can be addressed by fu-

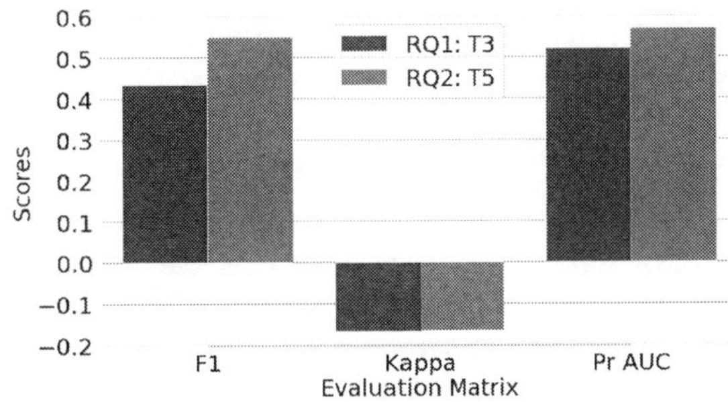

Figure 5: Overview of **RQ1** performance compared to **RQ2**. This bar chat compares the performance of CoAID **RQ1**: Task III models with **RQ2**: Task V fine-tuned Bert transformer model. This graph shows that transfer learning via Bert achieves better performance.

ture work using state-of-the-art techniques. Future studies can focus in developing or utilizing interesting AI techniques such as meta-transfer learning, data augmentation techniques and Multilingual Bert transformer model to address false claims propagation in the Caribbean low-resource setting.

Context is imperative when considering computational solutions to address low-resource language setting false claims phenomena. In the Caribbean region context, numerous barriers implicate false claims detection when using high-resources language ML models. These barriers include: language, data scarcity, and rare full-coverage fact-checking institutions. Such barriers are not researched and thus poorly understood. This suggest the need for more exploratory studies to have in depth understanding of the false claims phenomena in the Caribbean region.

7 Conclusion

High-resource detection models have low accuracy with classifying Caribbean false claims data. Region-specific data challenges have shown to reduce the performance of high-resource ML models. This encourages the use of sophisticated ML techniques and AI methodologies to capture signals that current models are unable to recognize.

Our experiment with transfer learning has shown improvements with ML models' performance. The findings in this research support our hypothesis: high-resource language model performs poorly on low-resource language data. Future studies need to focus efforts on improving false claims detection in the Caribbean. A major challenge is that every island has its unique Creole, which complicates ML models trained in formal settings. Since the

Jamaican languages are a combination of several languages, even the best language translator are ineffective in accurately translating the language to English. This poses another difficulty to the problem of false claims detection.

False claims are the greatest threat to public health in the Caribbean and globally. As we saw with COVID19, if we do not address false claims, epidemic/pandemic diseases will spread exponentially (Brainard and Hunter, 2020).

Acknowledgements

This research was supported in part by NSF awards #1820609, 915801, and #2114824.

References

Dzmitry Bahdanau, Kyunghyun Cho, and Yoshua Bengio. 2015. Neural machine translation by jointly learning to align and translate. In *3rd International Conference on Learning Representations, ICLR 2015, San Diego, CA, USA, May 7-9, 2015, Conference Track Proceedings*.

Yejin Bang, Etsuko Ishii, Samuel Cahyawijaya, Ziwei Ji, and Pascale Fung. 2021. Model generalization on covid-19 fake news detection. In *International Workshop on Combating Online Hostile Posts in Regional Languages during Emergency Situation*, pages 128–140. Springer.

Julii Brainard and Paul R Hunter. 2020. Misinformation making a disease outbreak worse: outcomes compared for influenza, monkeypox, and norovirus. *Simulation*, 96(4):365–374.

Limeng Cui and Dongwon Lee. 2020. Coaid: Covid-19 healthcare misinformation dataset. *arXiv preprint arXiv:2006.00885*.

Limeng Cui, Haeseung Seo, Maryam Tabar, Fenglong Ma, Suhang Wang, and Dongwon Lee. 2020. Deterrent: Knowledge guided graph attention network for detecting healthcare misinformation. In *Proceedings of the 26th ACM SIGKDD international conference on knowledge discovery & data mining*, pages 492–502.

Jiangshu Du, Yingtong Dou, Congying Xia, Limeng Cui, Jing Ma, and S Yu Philip. 2021. Cross-lingual covid-19 fake news detection. In *2021 International Conference on Data Mining Workshops (ICDMW)*, pages 859–862. IEEE.

Geoffrey Hinton, Nitish Srivastava, and Kevin Swersky. 2012. Neural networks for machine learning lecture 6a overview of mini-batch gradient descent. 14:8.

Yichuan Li, Bohan Jiang, Kai Shu, and Huan Liu. 2020. Mm-covid: A multilingual and multimodal data repository for combating covid-19 disinformation. *arXiv preprint arXiv:2011.04088*.

Shahan Ali Memon and Kathleen M Carley. 2020. Characterizing covid-19 misinformation communities using a novel twitter dataset. *arXiv preprint arXiv:2008.00791*.

Maria D Molina, S Shyam Sundar, Thai Le, and Dongwon Lee. 2021. "fake news" is not simply false information: A concept explication and taxonomy of online content. *American behavioral scientist*, 65(2):180–212.

Parth Patwa, Shivam Sharma, Srinivas PYKL, Vineeth Guptha, Gitanjali Kumari, Md Shad Akhtar, Asif Ekbal, Amitava Das, and Tanmoy Chakraborty. 2020. Fighting an infodemic: Covid-19 fake news dataset.

Jeffrey Pennington, Richard Socher, and Christopher D Manning. 2014. Glove: Global vectors for word representation. In *Proceedings of the 2014 conference on empirical methods in natural language processing (EMNLP)*, pages 1532–1543.

Haeseung Seo, Aiping Xiong, Sian Lee, and Dongwon Lee. 2022. If you see a reliable source, say something: Effects of correction comments on covid-19 misinformation. In *Proceedings of the AAAI Conference on Web and Social Media*.

Gautam Kishore Shahi and Durgesh Nandini. 2020. Fakecovid–a multilingual cross-domain fact check news dataset for covid-19. *arXiv preprint arXiv:2006.11343*.

Kai Shu, Limeng Cui, Suhang Wang, Dongwon Lee, and Huan Liu. 2019. defend: Explainable fake news detection. In *Proceedings of the 25th ACM SIGKDD international conference on knowledge discovery & data mining*, pages 395–405.

Chen Yang, Xinyi Zhou, and Reza Zafarani. 2021. Checked: Chinese covid-19 fake news dataset. *Social Network Analysis and Mining*, 11(1):1–8.

Xinyi Zhou, Apurva Mulay, Emilio Ferrara, and Reza Zafarani. 2020. Recovery: A multimodal repository for covid-19 news credibility research. In *Proceedings of the 29th ACM international conference on information & knowledge management*, pages 3205–3212.

Author Index

Association for Computational Linguistics
209 N. Eighth Street
Stroudsburg, Pennsylvania 18360

ISBN 978-1-7138-6731-9

CURRAN ASSOCIATES INC.
proceedings.com